MW00563321

Disappearing architecture

from real to virtual to quantum

with contributions by

Michael Beigl
Aaron Betsky
Ole Bouman
Neil Brown
Ignacio Cirac
Andrew Daley
Dennis Del Favero
David Deutsch
Elizabeth Diller
Winka Dubbeldam
Georg Flachbart
Monika Fleischmann
Torsten Fröhlich
Dagan Gilat
Sulan Kolatan
Rolf Kruse
William J. Mac Donald
Holger Marten
William J. Mitchell
Kas Oosterhuis
Hani Rashid
Ivan Redi
Andrea Schröttner
Ricardo Scofidio
Jeffrey Shaw
Wolfgang Strauss
Stuart A. Veech
Tom Verebes
Peter Weibel
Peter Zoller

Edited by Georg Flachbart and Peter Weibel

Birkhäuser – Publishers for Architecture
Basel · Boston · Berlin

Disappearing Architecture _From Real to Virtual to Quantum

Editors
Georg Flachbart and Peter Weibel

Visual Concept and Design
mind(21)factory for Knowledge Engineering and Knowledge Design
Stuttgart_Frankfurt/M_Berlin
Georg Flachbart
Thomas Nagel

Lithography
COMYK | Roland Merz
Karlsruhe

Production
ZKM | Publications
Ulrike Havemann
Jens Lutz
Miriam Stürner

Cover Visual
Winka Dubbeldam | Archi-Tectonics, NYC
"From HardWare to SoftForm"

Illustration p. 2
Julie Rousset | xplicit bln
"I am many"

Special Thanks
xplicit ffm
ÖkoMedia Stuttgart
Silke Müller

A CIP catalogue record for this book is available from the Library of Congress,
Washington D.C., USA

Bibliographic information published by Die Deutsche Bibliothek
Die Deutsche Bibliothek lists this publication in the Deutsche Nationalbibliografie;
Detailed bibliographic data is available in the Internet at http://dnb.ddb.de.

© 2005 Birkhäuser – Publishers for Architecture, P. O. Box 133, CH-4010 Basel,
Switzerland
Part of Springer Science and Business Media
Printed on acid-free paper produced from chlorine-free pulp. TCF ∞

Printed in Germany
ISBN-10: 3-7643-7275-3
ISBN-13: 978-3-7643-7275-0

9 8 7 6 5 4 3 2 1

"If you please – draw me a sheep!"
said the little Prince, thinking not
about a real sheep, but a virtual one.
For a virtual sheep requires very
little space and can live a long time.

contents

preface

"Civilization advances by extending the number of important operations which we can perform without thinking about them."

This quote by the famous mathematician and philosopher Alfred North Whitehead implies that a threshold moment in evolution can be surpassed only once humans have been able to automate increasingly complex tasks. This quote is also the motto of IBM's new perspective on the state of information technology: *the Grand Challenge* (cf. Dagan Gilat in this volume).

IBM believes that we are at this very threshold right now in computing. We believe that we are at this very threshold right now in thinking, too – in thinking the postmechanical paradigm "Net." We live in the Age of the Global Net, whether or not we are inclined to accept it. Living in the Global Net means living in dynamic open spaces. There is a permanent draught. If we don't perpetually keep on the move, it can get pretty cold. That's why living in the Global Net calls for permanent activity – interactivity. A net only makes sense if there are many nets simultaneously. At its heart, a net is an ambivalent entity. In a net, a) everything is intertwined – 1; b) a net is empty – 0. In a word, a net is a mixed-reality environment, dominated by *liquid logic*; a place which "is nowhere in particular but everywhere at once"; a space which "is fundamentally and pro-

foundly antispatial" [1]. In the ultimate limit, there will be no other choice but to go to quantum parallelism in which 1 and 0 are literally present at once.

If we do not harness and automate the liquid logic of quantum parallelism, running 1 and 0 at once, we will, in the long run, be incapable of taming the exponentially increasing complexity of the Global Net and thus of surpassing the next threshold moment in evolution. That way we will be incapable of keeping up with computing in the future, notably with next-generation quantum computing, based just upon 1 and 0 at once, which will increase computational power by astronomical amounts. There is a menace, then, that our thinking will be sucked into the black hole of networked complexity, while computing will not. So the basic question we face today is the same that was raised by Félix Guattari about a decade ago: "How to produce, tap, enrich, and permanently reinvent our subjectivity in order to make it compatible with the Universe of changing values?" [2] – or with the Multiverse, as we will say in this volume (cf. David Deutsch in this volume).

We believe that a new kind of architecture – *heterarchitecture* –, conceived as a hybrid, mixed-reality environment, could help accelerate the process of our automating liquid logic in much the same way as IBM's vision of autonomic computing could help manage the increasing system complexity of high performance information technology application environments, which will be largely self-managing, self-diagnostic and transparent to the user.

The contributions to this volume share a common assumption in that each is an attempt to stretch our awareness of this problem as well as to outline an approach both in designing and constructing a new kind of authentic architecture of the digital era and in organizing the architectural practice as well. Of course, it takes much more than a new kind of architecture to solve the problem. However, architecture has always been a multi-layered discipline, playing a catalytic role within society: architecture as representation. This is why we, non-architects, have decided to discuss the interplay between society and technology on the playing field of contemporary architecture. To be sure, it will be a home game for architects to be playing *Disappearing Architecture* with us, and probably easy enough for them to win. But in any case, playing this game can help extend "the number of important operations which we can perform without thinking about them."

The book *Disappearing Architecture: From Real to Virtual to Quantum,* based on the principle of shared research interests, has its origins in the international conference *IT WORKS OR IT NETWORKS – Development of Real and Virtual Space in the Age of the Global Net* held at the Slovak University of Technology in Bratislava, Slovakia, in September 2003. The conference, which was developed and hosted by mind(21)-factory for Knowledge Engineering and Knowledge Design Stuttgart, Frankfurt/M, Berlin in cooperation with SPECTRA Center of Excellence at the Faculty of Architecture, STU Bratislava, was made possible through initial organizational efforts by Maros Finka and Nada Hraskova, both of them members of the Faculty of Architecture STU Bratislava, and Georg Flachbart, mind(21)factory Stuttgart.

On this occasion, we would like to extend our special thanks to all conference speakers for coming to Bratislava to share their knowledge; and to the Institute for Visual Media at ZKM Center for Art and Media in Karlsruhe, Germany, for presenting their much-acclaimed interactive multimedia artwork *Web of Life*, created by Michael

Gleich and Jeffrey Shaw, as an integral part of the conference.

Special thanks go also to all the contributors to this volume, notably to all "newcomers" who did not attend the conference, for their positive reactions to our invitation to cooperate in making this book happen; and to David Deutsch for suggesting the subtitle of the book.

Thanks also to xplicit ffm for actively supporting the design process. Lastly, we would like to thank the publisher, Birkhäuser – Publishers for Architecture, and Ulrich Schmidt, chief editor in architecture and design, and Ulrike Ruh, editor, for believing in the idea of this book.

And now, let's start playing *Disappearing Architecture* – a home game for architects and an away game for us.

July 2005
Georg Flachbart and Peter Weibel

References

[1] William J. Mitchell, "City of Bits: Space, Place, and the Infobahn," MIT Press, Cambridge, Mass., 1995, p. 8.

[2] Félix Guattari, "Chaosmosis: An Ethical-Aesthetic Paradigm," Indiana University Press, Bloomington, 1995, p. 124.

Democracy Unrealized, even in the so-called liberal states, was the diagnosis made by the organizers of the art show Documenta 11. The question is now: Is democracy realizable at all? At least for us, naïve monsters, referring to Prometheus, the answer is quite simple: yes, by a further increment in the liberating dimension of technology, not ideology; or, in other words, by conceiving architecture as a quantum object, in which real and virtual space are coherently superposed, the impact of materiality could exponentially be reduced and investment of capital minimized. Architecture as an enabling platform – for all.

Georg Flachbart is director of mind(21)factory for Knowledge Engineering and Knowledge Design Stuttgart, Frankfurt/M, Berlin, founded in 1999. He studied philosophy, psychology and formal logic at Charles University in Prague, where he obtained his PhD degree in 1974. He worked as a scientific assistant in the Department of Philosophy of Science at the Institute of Philosophy and Sociology of the Slovak Academy of Sciences in Bratislava from 1974-80. Currently, he is a writer, director and producer in audiovisual media and the performing arts, but his chief occupation is action philosophy. Flachbart has won many top media awards at international festivals in Chicago, New York, Hamburg.

GEORG FLACHBART:

Disappearing architecture_ from Real to virtual to quantum

DISAPPEARING ARCHITECTURE _
FROM REAL TO VIRTUAL TO QUANTUM

In February 2003 I was in Graz, Austria, to see the exhibition *Latent Utopias – Experiments within Contemporary Architecture*, curated by the famous architect Zaha Hadid and her studio director Patrik Schumacher. In the preface to the exhibition catalogue the curators made the following ambivalent diagnosis:

"Every time needs its utopia(s). A society that no longer reflects its development is uncanny, a monstrosity. However, utopian speculation is rather dubious today. In recent years the very notion of progress and the ambition to project a future has itself come to be regarded as monstrous. Utopian thinking seems naïve, dangerous hubris" [1].

This statement automatically provokes two questions: a) How to live without utopia(s) and not be a monster? and b) How to talk utopia(s) and not be a monster? Well, there is an easy answer to that one. No matter what we decide we will in both cases be monsters. So given this no-win situation, I would say let's take up the provocation of Latent Utopias and, for a while, keep our eye on utopian thinking and try to project a future, risking of course being regarded as naïve, dangerous, and monstrous.

Utopia(s) against Utopia

The 2002 art show Documenta 11 in Kassel, Germany, consisted of five Platforms. Platform 1 was a series of conferences and lectures held in Vienna in the spring and in Berlin in the fall of 2001. It was called *Democracy Unrealized*. According to the Documenta organizers there were few more significant topics than the fate and future of democracy, but despite this there was no place on earth yet where

the notion of democracy had already been fully realized – not even in the so-called liberal states. "If democracy is thus quite unrealized in our contemporary world, is it realizable?" – asked *expressis verbis* Immanuell Wallerstein, one of the contributors to Documenta Platform 1 [2]. Indeed, a challenging question; let's attempt to answer it.

In their 1972 benchmark work entitled *Anti-Oedipus. Capitalism and Schizophrenia*, Gilles Deleuze and Félix Guattari fully attest the liberating impact of capitalism. Capitalism – not unlike schizophrenia – defines itself by a process of decoding and deterritorializing all traditional codes and territories of power, and it unleashes unprecedented social dynamics. The only problem is, Deleuze and Guattari argue, referring to Karl Marx, that this process of decoding and deterritorializing does not go far enough, that capitalism is not, so to speak, *schizo* enough to keep pace with its own dynamics [3]. To retain control over what goes on, capitalism sets itself immanent limits, generates new codes, new re-territorializations, new divans, and, in so doing, castrates itself in a double-sense:
a) it becomes anti-productive: codes turn up only where saturated bodies reign, sitting comfortably on divans as "instances of anti-production" par excellence, and
b) it becomes anti-democratic: it excludes – entirely against its own original interests – the majority of others from direct access to institutional power games. Thus, by setting the old democratic principles of "liberty and equality for all" aside, capitalism generates, instead of competing adversaries, new enemies, a new antagonism [4].

So the question today is still the same as it was in the 19th century: Is there a possibility of accelerating the liberating process of decoding and deterritorializing, which capitalism unleashed, without falling again and again back into the archaism of generating codes, axiomatics, reterritorializiations, identities, divans as anti-productive and anti-democratic instances par excellence? A question that Karl Marx and Friedrich Nietzsche were first to raise for us, a long time ago. For Marx, by the way, the solution was communism, for Nietzsche schizophrenia – a state of permanent frenzy in nothingness (no-place, nonlocation).

What a "robust democratic life" today needs – says Chantal Mouffe, another contributor to Documenta Platform 1 – is "the possibility for antagonism to be transformed into 'agonism'. By which I mean that in democratic societies, while conflict cannot be and should not be eradicated, neither should it take the form of a struggle between enemies (antagonism), but rather between adversaries (agonism)." So what we urgently need in order to realize democracy – she concludes – is "a vibrant agonistic public sphere, thanks to which democracy can be kept alive and deepened" [5]. This conclusion, however, automatically raises a very pragmatic question: How can such a "vibrant agonistic public sphere" be created with the least investment of capital we can afford so that access to worldwide knowledge and, *eo ipso*, institutional power games might be granted to all?

At least for us, naïve monsters, referring to Prometheus, the answer might be once again quite simple: by a further increment in the liberating dimension of technology, not ideology. In other words, by designing and constructing a new kind of architecture – *heterarchitecture* –, in which real space (1, OFF-line) and virtual space (0, ON-line) are coherently superposed, thus obeying the rules of quantum mechanics (1 and 0, OFF and ON at once) rather than classical physics, the impact of materiality

(including computer hardware) could exponentially be reduced and investment of capital minimized. Architecture as a quantum object.

Democracy Realized

We think of the following ON/OFF scenario: You enter a space and switch on, instead of the light, a data flow, which fills the space in a sec with a "world" – yours or somebody else's. And you are suddenly in the Louvre, at a bazaar in Cairo, on board a spaceship travelling to Mars, in a research lab, or simply at home – *chez vous*. A utopia? Absolutely not! For all you need is data – plus super-fast data transfer, plus super-fast computing power, plus the right architecture. And all is already in place – apart from the right architecture.

Of course, visions of spaces like that are not new. Cyberpunk fiction is full of them. What we are talking about here are large-scale "instruments of displacement" – mixed reality environments of the post-mechanical paradigm 'Net', where "the virtual is seamlessly embedded in the physical" [6]. We must imagine these environments as an omnipresent super-computer of the *beyond-the-desktop-era* embedded in the world, a computer that ... does not exist, at least not as a single piece. What does exist is: a) an interconnected information technology infrastructure for open, distributed and heterogeneous application environments (grid, ubiquitous, autonomic computing), based on quantum information processing, exchange and storage, increasing computational power and data transfer by astronomical amounts, inconceivable by means of current binary computing that only knows either-or, i.e., either 1 or 0. By implementing this infrastructure, powerful distributed knowledge spaces, which will be largely self-managing, self-

13

diagnostic and transparent to the user, could be created, enabling higher-order acting by the individual as well as multi-institutional virtual organizations in an unprecedented way.

What does exist as the next level is: b) an architecture which integrates this interconnected IT infrastructure in a way that enables one to conceive buildings as quantum objects, i.e., objects able to be literally in two states at once – ON and OFF, 1 and 0, real and virtual. It is an architecture against architecture [7] – at least of the traditional kind, which knows only either-or; either 1 or 0, either inside or outside, either enclosing or excluding. It is an invisible architecture that makes numerous parallel virtual worlds visible. It is an upside-down architecture. Architecture as a pure infrastructure. Architecture as an enabling platform – for all.

William J. Mitchell, one of the pioneers of the digital era and contributor to this book, offers a lucid diagnosis of this shift in thinking architecture: "A world governed less and less by boundaries and more and more by connections requires us to reimagine and reconstruct our environment and to reconsider the ethical foundations of design, engineering, and planning practice" [8].

The present volume was conceived as a further attempt at both reimagining and reconstructing our environment as well as reconsidering architectural practice. An attractive mix of well-known, lesser known and unknown architects, artists, authors and scientists – all experts in mixed-reality topics – were invited to share their knowledge and present their work in contributing an article to this book. A quick glimpse at the table of contents will tell you more than any short (to name only a few...), and unfair, enumeration focused solely on a few celebrated names amongst.

Our key intention was to present the first still very modest steps – in the form of project designs as well as realized projects – on the way towards an heterarchitecture of the future, an architecture that does not prescribe any particular kinds of spatial experience but enables them all.

At its heart, it is an architecture of the AND which also functions as an AND. A genuine interface between the real *and* the virtual – a dynamic open space, an enabling platform. A place of "permanent frenzy in nothingness," a place of "production désirante sans cesse" or, in simpler terms, a place of "ceaseless innovation and change," which today is, by the way, prerequisite no. 1 for sustainable economic growth. No stasis, no divans. "A place" – as Elizabeth Grosz put it in a nutshell – "related to other places but with no place of its own" [9]. In short, an architectural schizo, a *real* utopia – a no-place (*outopos*). For only no-place is the good place: *eutopos* – happy, fortunate, good place. (Thomas More's neologism "utopia" is the result of two different fusions from Greek roots: *outopos* and *eutopos* [10].) It is also *the* place where quantum properties begin to emerge in our (macro)world on its way from the Either-Or- to the And-Society.

The challenge for architects today is to make use of these properties in order to conceive buildings as *good no-places* (quantum objects), helping liberate the schizo (source of ceaseless innovation and change) in each of us from psychical constraints (identities) in much the same way as high-performance information technology does with physical constraints.

"As humans", argues Kas Oosterhuis in this volume, "we must learn to relate to the dynamics of super-fast real-time computational processes. We must build the computational tools for collaborative design and engineering in order to meet the rich expectations created by looking at the world from one or two levels up. ... it leads in the same manner to a major paradigm shift in the way we connect to buildings as running processes. ... This new kind of building is not only designed through computation, it is a computation" [11].

"For this new spatial effect", says Ole Bouman at the end of this book, "physical space is no longer strictly necessary, although duplication has its attractions. The great leap consists of uncoupling spatial perception and architectural structure. Now that really is 'lite' architecture" [12].

And this is, by the way, what the little Prince already knew a long time ago. Do you remember how much he was delighted when the pilot drew, instead of a sheep, an empty box with three holes?

Conclusion

By conceiving architecture as a quantum object that can literally be in two states at once (real and virtual, 1 and 0, OFF and ON), numerous "vibrant agonistic public spheres"– good no-places – could be created, providing people of all ages with the capabilities and skills necessary for competing ways of life in the Age of the Global Net – an age of difference, ambivalence and extreme openness. Thanks to that, the liberating process of decoding and deterritorializing based on the old democratic principles of liberty and equality for all, which capitalism unleashed with its disruptive energy of ceaseless innovation and change, could be accelerated. So what we obviously need to achieve *Democracy Realized* is simply a) more capitalism – capitalism against capitalism, and b) less architecture – architecture against architecture.

Welcome to the realm of *quantum schizo*, where the medium is the architecture and myself means many selves – at least two: 1 and 0 [13].

References

[1] Zaha Hadid, Patrik Schumacher (eds.), "Latent Utopias – Experiments within Contemporary Architecture," Springer Verlag, Vienna 2002, p. 7.

[2] Okwui Enwezor, Carlos Basualdo, Ute Meta Bauer, Susanne Ghez, Sarat Maharaj, Mark Nash, Octavio Zaya (eds.), "Democracy Unrealized," Hatje Cantz, Ostfildern 2002, p. 107.

[3] See Gille Deleuze, Félix Guattari, "L'Anti-Œdipe. Capitalisme et Schizophrénie," Les Editions de Minuit, Paris 1972, pp. 41–43, 292–295, p. 306.

[4] See in this context also Slavoj Zizek, "The Prospects of Radical Politics Today," in Okwui Enwezor, Carlos Basualdo, Ute Meta Bauer, Susanne Ghez, Sarat Maharaj, Mark Nash, Octavio Zaya (eds.), "Democracy Unrealized," Hatje Cantz, Ostfildern 2002, pp. 79–80.

[5] Chantal Mouffe, "For an Agonistic Public Sphere," in ibid., p. 90.

[6] William J. Mitchell in this volume, p. 20.

[7] This notion was used in the catalogue "Film+Arc 2," edited by Charlotte Pöchacker, Graz 1995.

[8] William J. Mitchell, "Me++ : The Cyborg Self and the Networked City," MIT Press, Cambridge/Mass. 2003, jacket.

[9] See Elizabeth Grosz, "Architecture from the Outside. Essays on Virtual and Real Space," MIT Press, Cambridge/Mass. 2001, p. 91 ff.

[10] Ibid., p. 135.

[11] Kas Oosterhuis in this volume, pp. 103, 105, 106, 109.

[12] Ole Bouman in this volume, p. 262.

[13] "Does the logic of network existence entail radical schizophrenia – ...?," William J. Mitchell, "City of Bits: Space, Place, and the Infobahn," MIT Press, Cambridge, Mass. 1995, pp. 14–15.

the
infra
struc
ture

Information Technology Infrastructure for Open, Distributed and Heterogeneous Application Environments

The digital revolution of the late 20th century is over. What has remained is a pervasive, global system. One part of this system is a mostly invisible digital telecommunication infrastructure that efficiently connects just about every inhabited place on the face of the earth to every other. Its complement is an enormous and growing collection of electronic instruments of displacement distributed throughout the human habitat – instruments of spatial displacement through remote connection, and of temporal displacement through recording and replay. These instruments link the new global infrastructure to particular places and human activities. They embed the virtual in the physical, and weave it seamlessly into daily urban life.

William J. Mitchell is Professor of Architecture and Media Arts and Sciences, Head of the Media Arts and Sciences Program, and former Dean of the School of Architecture and Planning at MIT. He previously taught at UCLA, Cambridge and Harvard universities. His publications include City of Bits (1995), E-topia (1999), and Me ++ : The Cyborg Self and the Networked City (2003). He is a Fellow of the Royal Australian Institute of Architects and Fellow of the American Academy of Arts and Sciences.

william
J. mitchell
:
after the
Revolution _
instruments
of
Displacement

AFTER THE REVOLUTION _
INSTRUMENTS OF DISPLACEMENT

Introduction

It took just 20 years for the personal computer to go from glamorous, newly invented avatar of the future to drab, quotidian
commodity that anonymous corporations
produce and distribute by the millions at
the lowest possible price points. IBM's
recent sale of its personal computer division to a Chinese outfit that most Ameri-
cans and Europeans had never heard of is
a sure sign that the digital revolution of
the late 20th century is over. Media ma-
nia is no more. But as the tumult and the
shouting of the journalists and the flacks
dies, the captains and the kings of industry depart the hallowed ground of Silicon
Valley (retiring to their McMansions to
dream of breaking into bio or nano), the
legendary labs close their doors one by
one, and the Internet bubble of the wan-
ing millennium fades into history like the
tulip frenzy and the great gold rushes,
we can begin to understand the immense,
irreversible, multifaceted change that all
this has brought to our cities. It is a moment, I suppose, like that shrewdly seized
by Siegfried Giedion when he looked back
to write about the transformation of buildings and urban space by the industrial
revolution. From the vantage point of the
1940s, he could reduce what had been an
immensely complex and messy process to
the heroically simplified, epic-scale narratives of technology triumphant in *Space,
Time and Architecture* and *Mechanization
Takes Command.*

A postindustrial Giedion would begin the
story of the digital revolution with the
invention of the bit and the pioneering
days of computer science and technology
in the 1940s and 1950s, then move brisk-
ly to packet switching and computer networking in the 1960s, the growth of the

microprocessor industry during the 1970s
leading to the personal computers of the
1980s, the development of the World Wide
Web and search engines in the 1990s, and
finally the addition of mobile, wireless
connectivity in the 2000s. There are some
remaining rough edges and bugs in what
has emerged, but it now adds up to a pervasive, global system.

Instruments of Displacement

One part of this system, as every commen-
tator will tell you, is a mostly invisible
digital telecommunication infrastructure
that efficiently connects just about every
inhabited place on the face of the earth
to every other. Its complement is an enormous and growing collection of electronic
instruments of displacement distributed
throughout the human habitat – instruments of spatial displacement through
remote connection, and of temporal displacement through recording and replay.
These instruments link the new global
infrastructure to particular places and
human activities. They embed the virtual
in the physical, and weave it seamlessly
into daily urban life. The smallest and now
most numerous of them are the ones that
fit in your pocket – mobile telephones,
Blackberries, iPods, digital cameras and
video cameras, video game players, GPS
guidance systems, and other more specialized little boxes of electronics. Since pocket real estate is limited, and the miniaturization of electronics shows little sign of
slowing down, boxes that were initially
separate keep fusing to form new combinations.

Thus telephones have merged with digital
cameras and Web browsers, and are now
acquiring audio and video recording and
replay capability. Heading down different
evolutionary pathways towards approximately the same destination, personal digital assistants are acquiring wireless con-

nectivity and audio, and MP3 players are being adapted to store pictures as well as tunes. Furthermore, with the imperialism that we have come to expect from the digital, these finger-friendly boxes have inexorably been virtualizing and taking over the functions of former occupants of pocket space – notebooks, address books, diaries, wallets, identity cards, and key chains. Eventually, there will be extremely versatile pocket devices that sense and replay in multiple modes, store and process enormous quantities of information, and connect wirelessly to global networks. They will allow you to summon the distant and the past to the palm of your hand.

Being in Anywhere at Any Time

Miniaturized instruments of displacement become extensions of the mobile body. They can be used in sedentary mode, while walking or running, or even (at some peril) while driving. They scramble familiar spatial categories by extending the range of activities that an individual can engage in anywhere, at any time, and they enable new forms of social coordination and control by providing continuous accessibility, tracking, and verification of identity. You can spontaneously arrange an assignation on your mobile telephone, and take a picture when you get there, but you will also leave traces in cyberspace as you do so.

At the next step up in scale, there are instruments that you can carry in your briefcase or backpack, and that engage furniture by temporarily occupying a desktop, tabletop, laptop, or aircraft tray table. These, too, have sucked surrounding functions into screen space – first those of old-fashioned desktop items, which immediately reappeared as virtual documents, folders, trashcans, clocks, calendars, and other now-familiar graphical user interface icons. Over time, book-sized versions of these devices have displaced their

bulkier, less mobile predecessors. They have multiplied on-screen icons in the process of repeatedly conquering new functional frontiers and ruthlessly exterminating the indigenous artifacts that had held sway before. This has radically changed our everyday material culture, and overlaid the (mostly) ancient, sedentary activities of the reader, writer, viewer, listener, scholar, librarian, file clerk, and accountant onto architectural settings that had not previously encompassed them. A café table becomes a place for a student to write a term paper, and an aircraft seat a place for a sales-person to edit a Power-Point presentation. Simultaneously, demand for specialized sites of information work, such as office cubicles, library carrels, and computer clusters seems to be diminishing.

At the next scale up again, instruments of displacement become part of the architecture. Built-in instruments can trace their ancestry to the framed picture on the one hand, and to early television sets and personal computers on the other. As solid-state displays have supplanted cathode ray tubes, fat boxes have shrunk to slim slabs that can either be propped up on pedestals (like canvases on easels) or hung on walls to provide programmable signage, news and entertainment, and advertising. Still larger display surfaces now slip their frames to spread across entire walls, as on the facades fronting Times Square, or ceilings, as on the canopy covering Fremont Street in Las Vegas. Here they take over the decorative and iconographic functions of architecture, prompting Robert Venturi to enthuse, in a recent essay: "*Viva* the facade as computer screen! *Viva* facades not reflecting light but emanating light – the building as a digital sparkling source of information, not as an abstract glowing source of light! . . . *Viva* iconography – not carved in stone for eternity but digitally chang-

ing for *now*, so that the inherently dangerous fascist propaganda, for instance, can
be temporarily, not eternally, proclaimed!"
[1]

Homo Electronicus

At the largest scale, instruments of displacement occupy the subject's entire sensory
field to create an immersive experience.
Movie theaters introduced this strategy,
with their darkened spaces, huge screens,
and stereophonic sound. The pioneers of
computer graphics quickly figured out
that they could get an even more powerful effect, in a smaller space and with
less material and energy, by moving the
components as close as possible to the
relevant organs – position-sensitive displays right up against eyeballs, speakers
clamped on the ears, a microphone at the
mouth, and gesture-sensing force-feed-
back devices in the hands – so that a virtual environment completely masked the
subject's physical surroundings.

Immersive virtual reality and augmented
reality systems were all the rage for a
while, like flared pants or *Wired* magazine, and inspired a whole subgenre of
cyberpunk fiction, but they turn out to
have fairly limited, specialized uses in
simulation and entertainment. Where the
tiny screen and low-output speaker of a
pocket device introduces a fragment of
digital display into a predominantly material *mise-en-scene*, an immersive system
defines the other end of the spectrum of
possibilities – allowing the digital to dominate, and making it a shocking surprise
to stub your toe on something solid.

These electronically driven and interconnected instruments of displacement, in
their varied forms, have become essential,
unremarkable parts of our everyday surroundings. Their ubiquitous presence, producing a profound transformation of sub-

jectivity, is the lasting legacy of the digital revolution. Like the instruments of
paper-based reading, writing, and text
storage and distribution before them,
they have shifted us a step further away
from the Edenic condition of living entirely in the here and now, and allow *homo
electronicus* endless shifts of attention and
engagement throughout the reaches of
space and time.

Fusion Space

These various forms of overlays of the
digital on the real are increasingly producing fusion space – architectural space
in which electronic instruments of spatial
and temporal displacement enable new
and socially valuable combinations of
people or activities. Here are some examples.

These days, the seminar rooms at MIT
fuse the hitherto distinct activities of
group discussion and Web surfing. The
students bring their wireless laptop computers to class. Whenever I introduce a
topic, somebody Googles it – and then
interjects any relevant discoveries back
into the conversation. This radically changes the social and intellectual dynamic
in the space. It produces a very high level
of intellectual engagement, generates
a thrilling, high-speed, vividly grounded
discourse, and shifts the role of the teacher. I can no longer rely on my superior
command of the subject matter to maintain my classroom authority!

In university dormitories, isolated working under intense academic pressure
turns out to be a triggering factor for
student depression, binge drinking, and
even suicide. Networking dormitory rooms
for personal computers can exacerbate
this. But creating fusions of study space
and social space – lounges with wireless
connectivity, and quiet corners to work

as well as areas for socializing – reduces isolation and increases opportunities for peer-group support.

In research libraries, the former functions of the carrel and the telephone box are fusing. You can frequently find young researchers with their laptops open, surounded by books and journals, talking on their mobile phones. If you eavesdrop, you find that they are not just blabbing, but are getting guidance from their supervisors or coordinating with distant collaborators. Then, when they find interesting pages of text or images, they simply snap pictures with their camera phones. Librarians disapproved of all this at first, much as classical chefs looked askance when they first encountered the new wave of fusion cuisine. Then they started to see it as an important new intellectual practice – and to demand space designed to accommodate it.

Walk around a building that accommdates a high tech company and you will probably find that a surprising number of the private offices are locked and dark. But look, by contrast, at the electronically supported work going on in airplane seats, high-speed train seats, airline lounges, cafés, hotel rooms, and even park benches. Much of the activity has shifted from classically conceived, single-purpose, assigned space to fusion space.

Imagine an apartment that is jammed with sensors everywhere, and that processes the resulting data stream to recognize the current activities of the occupants. (Kent Larson, at the MIT Media Laboratory, has recently constructed just such a dwelling – known as PlaceLab.) It knows when you are making a cup of tea, or folding the laundry. Now imagine that, based on what it observes of your behavior patterns over time, it offers carefully calculated, well-grounded advice on diet, exer-

cise, taking the opportunity to go out for a walk, taking your medication, and other things that will keep you healthy. It fuses the private apartment and the elderly-care nursing home. If you are an ageing baby-boomer, it might enable you to live independently in your community for many more years.

Finally, imagine a school bus that uses its GPS location system to retrieve and present information about the areas that it is passing through. It fuses the geography, history, ecology, and civics classrooms with transportation and the public space of the city.

Conclusion

The digital revolution – now receding into history – has produced extraordinary new architectural challenges. But these turn out, to the surprise of many, to be defined in very basic, human terms. The most crucial post-revolutionary task facing architects is not the engineering of buildings to accommodate networks and computers; that isn't so hard. Nor is it the exploration of the formal and cultural possibilities of immersive virtual reality – which can be fascinating but, as we have seen, only engages the limit case of a spectrum of possibilities. The challenge, instead, is to start thinking like creative fusion chefs – to create spaces that satisfy important human needs in effective new ways, and that surprise and delight us through digitally enabled combinations of the unexpected.

References

[1] Robert Venturi, Denise Scott Brown, "Architecture as Signs and Systems," Cambridge, The Belknap Press of Harvard University Press, 2004, p. 94-99.

Convergent evolution, both in biology and in human thought, gives rise to similar designs even where there has been no causal contact between the systems concerned. By considering the parallel universes of quantum physics, we understand that all evolution, and all conscious design, are really convergent evolution. This gives us a broad perspective on the physical nature of knowledge creation – especially if we look into the future, when quantum computation will allow entirely new modes of harnessing nature.

David Deutsch is a founding member of the Centre for Quantum Computation at the Clarendon Laboratory, Oxford University, where he is currently a Visiting Professor of Physics. His papers on quantum computation laid the foundations for that field, breaking new ground in the theory of computation as well as physics, and won him such awards as the Dirac Medal of the Institute of Physics, and a Distinguished Fellow-ship of the British Computer Society. His work has triggered an explosion of research worldwide into quantum computation, which is yielding both deep philosophical in-sights and practical technology. He is an authority on the theory of parallel universes, and is the author of the highly acclaimed book "The Fabric of Reality."

David Deutsch:

The architecture of the multiverse

THE ARCHITECTURE OF THE MULTIVERSE

Convergent Evolution

Architects often pride themselves on the uniqueness of a design. Yet it is common for buildings that have been designed independently, nevertheless to resemble each other, visually or structurally. Usually this is because some of the ideas have been intentionally borrowed, or because shared traditions have been followed. But sometimes it is not: sometimes, the similar features have no common origin. A clear example of this is that there are ancient pyramids both in Egypt and in South America, yet, as far as we know, the cultures that built them never communicated and were not even contemporaneous. Some people whose sense of wonder has overwhelmed their critical faculties have taken this congruence of design as evidence that either there was some contact between those distant cultures after all, or there was a common cause: fanciful theories have been proposed about extraterrestrial visitors having brought the knowledge of pyramid-building to Earth.

Certainly whenever similar patterns are found in separate places, the concurrence cries out for explanation. But *communication* and *common origin* are only two of the possible explanations. Another would be the laws of physics: many galaxies have a similar spiral appearance, not because of any common origin but because the laws of physics that govern the luminosity and motion of their stars are the same. Thus their similarity is a manifestation of the regularity of the world, the universality of its laws. But this essay is about a further possibility, which is the existence, in different places, of *problem-solving* processes that share a common problem. In biology this is called *convergent evolution*. A shark and a dolphin look similar in many ways because their common shape is the solution to the problem of how to swim fast in the sea. There are many other examples of pairs of organisms that look and behave alike, yet have no common ancestor sharing those similarities. What caused the similarity between the ancient Egyptian pyramids and the Mayan and Aztec ones is also convergent evolution, in this case due to human creative and critical thought.

Biological Evolution and Conscious Thought

The difference between problem solving and mere obedience to the laws of physics is that problem solving involves a *design* – such as a DNA sequence or a blueprint or an idea in a human mind; there is no design for a galaxy. Whenever a problem-solving entity faces a problem, this constrains the possible ways in which it can survive the challenge, and there are better designs and worse designs for prospering under the constraint. The surviving designs will tend to converge on the better ones. In the case of biological adaptations the problem-solving process is evolution, and in the case of human artifacts it is thinking. These two are the only problem-solving processes that are known to exist, and although they have many differences, they, too, are remarkably alike. Both involve the variation (mutation or conjecture) of designs, alternating with selection (natural selection, or criticism and testing). The better designs are retained and the worse ones abandoned.

If there are civilisations on other planets, then some of them may face similar problems to ours. If they have rocks at their disposal, and if they need to find ways of coming to terms with death, or glorifying their leaders or their ancestors or their gods, then they may pass through a pyramid-building stage just as some people

26

on Earth did, in which case their pyramids may well look rather like ours. If they then progress past the pyramid era into the skyscraper era, then the chances are high that their skyscrapers will look more like ours than their ancestors' pyramids looked like those of our ancestors. Why? Because a skyscraper is the endresult of vastly more extensive problem-solving than a pyramid. It embodies more knowledge, and therefore will tend to be more similar to other solutions of the same problems. The further we and these hypothetical extraterrestrials proceed down the avenue of ever-increasing knowledge or adaptation, the more their designs and ours will look the same. If they build microchips, they will be even more like ours than their skyscrapers, and so on.

By converging on designs that solve a problem better, separate problem-solving processes also converge as a side effect. Conversely, whenever two causally unrelated designs strongly converge, we can be sure that problems are being solved: knowledge is being created. However, there are many organisms on Earth – humans are a good example – that incorporate design elements that do not resemble those of any unrelated organism. For instance, the functionality of the human brain has no analog in any unrelated species. The distinctive adaptations of such species have been created by evolution, but as far as we can observe, they do not exhibit *convergent* evolution.

Moreover, my speculations above about extraterrestrial technology may not correspond to any fact: suppose there are no extraterrestrials anywhere in the universe. In that case, we on Earth would be the only source in the universe of microchips or skyscrapers or pyramids. So it looks, on the face of it, as though most evolution is not convergent evolution: that most ideas have only one original source.

The Multiverse

But this may be a parochial misconception, for some physicists, myself included, have become convinced that certain subatomic phenomena can only be explained if the universe that we see around us – with all its matter and energy and people and stars and galaxies – is not the only one that exists. Physical reality must be a much larger structure, often called the *multiverse*, in which there are many such universes, some very like ours, some very different, though all with the same laws of physics. (Many physicists propose an even larger multiverse, across which even the laws of physics vary – but for present purposes we can ignore those.) In some universes, there are counterparts of you, some of whom have led identical lives so far and are physically identical to you. Some of them differ from you in some respects, yet are still similar enough to be called "the same person" as you, just as different instances of you at different *times* are rightly called the same person.

We call the universes that strongly affect ours, at a given instant, "the past" (of that instant), and we call the universes that we strongly affect, "the future." The remaining universes (which are the overwhelming majority) are often called "parallel" universes because, at the level of the accuracy of human senses, they seem unaffected by each other's presence (the analogy being with parallel lines, which never touch along their whole, infinite length). But in fact they are not strictly "parallel": Firstly, they do affect each other – these effects, known as *quantum interference effects*, are described by quantum theory, which is arguably the deepest theory known to science. And secondly, they are continually branching out: whenever an event has random outcome – such as a lottery – *all* of the possible outcomes actually happen, in different universes. However, according to the laws of quantum physics, none of these effects permits the transfer of information – in particular, *designs* – from one universe to another. Therefore, it is not after all true that only one instance of the invention of microchips has ever happened in reality. There are countless universes very similar to ours, down to microscopic details, and in many of those, microchips have been invented independently of ours. This is convergent evolution across the multiverse.

Knowledge in the Multiverse

Consider a pyramid, or a microchip, or any entity that embodies knowledge. Then consider a nearby universe in the multiverse that is infinitesimally different from ours. In most such universes, *the form of the knowledge-laden object will be the same or similar*. In fact, this persistence of form is in the very nature of knowledge, for in all the universes in which that same problem is being solved, worse solutions are being discarded in favor of better ones, and that is why the universes are becoming alike. Although the frills and inessentials of such objects will differ from universe to universe, there is a core of the design – the core that embodies the knowledge – that is alike, and becomes ever more so over time. In the multiverse, therefore, *all* evolution or knowledge creation takes the form of convergent evolution.

Now cast your imaginary gaze a little farther away in the multiverse, to a planet Earth that has had a different history: that famous asteroid that exterminated the dinosaurs never struck; evolution has resulted in intelligent dinosaurs instead of intelligent apes; the moment at which pyramids are about to be constructed has happened. Those intelligent dinosaurs face some of the same problems as humans once did, and so, even though their bodies

are unlike ours, their pyramids, in many cases, look like ours. Some of them are of different sizes, in different locations and so on (just as they are in different human-inhabited universes), but many of the designs are the same, even in such distant and alien worlds. And when the descendants of those dinosaurs come to build microchips, there will be very little trace of the dinosaur left in them, just as there is little of the ape in ours: they will be alike.

Thus, the design of any object that has been created by problem-solving is similar across a wider range of universes than any other type of object, except for those (such as atoms) whose shape is directly mandated by the laws of physics. Whenever we look at a physical object, be it a pyramid or a rocky outcrop, what we are seeing is just one small facet of a much larger object whose structure extends into the multiverse. But from a multiverse perspective, there is a striking difference between the pyramid and the rocky outcrop. For the outcrop has been formed by random accidents of geology and weather, and therefore has very different shapes in different universes. But in those universes in which it, or some other outcrop, is quarried and shaped by thinking beings into a pyramid, the shape will be constant over many more universes. Similarly, structures such as galaxies, which have no evolved design, differ greatly in their detail from one universe to another (though their gross appearance is similar because they obey the same laws of physics). In contrast, objects that embody knowledge, such as pyramids and microchips, share a detailed design across wide, branching swathes of universes. It follows that knowledge-containing entities are "bigger" and "sharper" in the multiverse than any other structures. They form huge, branching chains, by far the largest coherent structures in the multiverse.

Quantum Computation

A new technology known as *quantum information technology* is currently being developed, which puts the hidden multiplicity of quantum systems to various good uses in communication systems.

One of the most intriguing applications, which has recently moved from the laboratory and into the commercial market, is *quantum cryptography*. While conventional cryptog-raphy disguises information by putting it through a mathematical transformation which, in the absence of a secret key, would require unacceptably large resour-ces to invert, quantum cryptography uses the laws of physics to make communications absolutely secure, even against all possible future technology. It works, in effect, by hiding the information in other universes; and the key is not a code but a physical object (typically, a photon, or particle of light), without which that information is absolutely inaccessible.

Though these are humble beginnings, this is nothing less than an entirely new way of harnessing nature to human purposes – by sharing the burden with our counterparts in other universes. One day in the future, perhaps decades or more hence, this technology will be taken to its logical conclusion: *universal quantum computation*. In a universal quantum computer, enormous numbers of instances of the computer in different universes will collaborate on a computational task. Even quite a small quantum computer will be capable of sharing certain tasks among more universes than there are atoms in the whole of our visible universe. Despite not being able to send each other information, they will be able, according to the laws of quantum physics, to affect each other's computations in such a way that they all end up with the result of the collaborative parallel computation. (Not all parallel computations are allowed, only those that do not allow signals to be sent between universes.)

Contrary to what some commentators have suggested, there is no reason to believe that the human brain is already a quantum computer: a brain is much too hot, a neuron much too large and crude, to sustain quantum computational processes. Nor is there any reason to believe that a futuristic artificial intelligence, running on a quantum computer, will be able to do what we currently call "thinking" any better than a nonquantum computer with the same speed and memory capacity. However, one day, when fully multiversal artificial-intelligence computer programs are living and thinking inside quantum computers, they will in addition be capable of entirely new modes of thought that have no analog in anything that is possible today. I am not talking about anything psychedelic here. Because of the limitations on inter-universe communication, such entities would be able to infer, but not to perceive, the presence of their other-universe counterparts. So their novel experiences would be intellectual ones, such as being able to prove certain mathematical results without passing through the intractably large number of steps that would be required to state the proof.

From the perspective of quantum computation, what we know today as computation, thought and evolution are all analogous to pyramid-building: the computations in different universes are merely stacked one on top of the other to make a tall, but simply layered, multiversal structure. With quantum computers, we shall created non-trivial structures across vast numbers of universes, and so attain true multiversal engineering and multiversal architecture.

special reports

the next-Generation computing

IBM's vision of autonomic computing embraces the development of intelligent, open systems capable of running with minimal human intervention, adapting to varying circumstances in accordance with business policies and objectives, and preparing their resources to most efficiently handle the workloads we put upon them. These autonomic computing systems will: manage complexity, "know" themselves, continuously tune themselves, adapt to unpredictable conditions, prevent and recover from failures, provide a safe environment.

Dagan Gilat is a manager in the Active Technologies Department of the IBM Research Lab in Haifa, Israel. He is responsible for the development of ARAD (Active Real-time Automated Decision Making) and ADI (Active Dependency Integration) technologies and for the IBM e-business Management Project (e-BMS) and Autonomic Computing activities. He studied at the Technion – Israel Institute of Technology, where he received a PhD in Information Systems and M.Sc in Operations Research, and where he has lectured in Internet technologies since 1998.

Dagan Gilat:

autonomic computing — Building self-managing computing systems

AUTONOMIC COMPUTING _BUILDING
SELF-MANAGING COMPUTING SYSTEMS

Introducing Autonomic Computing

"Civilization advances by extending the
number of important operations which
we can perform without thinking about
them." _ Alfred North Whitehead

This quote made by the preeminent mathematician Alfred North Whitehead holds
both the lock and the key to the next era
of computing. It implies a threshold moment surpassed only after humans have
been able to automate increasingly complex tasks in order to achieve forward
momentum. IBM believes that we are at
just such a threshold right now in computing. The millions of businesses, bil-
lions of humans that compose them, and
trillions of devices that they will depend
upon all require the services of the IT
industry to keep them running. And it's
not just a matter of numbers. It's the
complexity of these systems and the way
they work together that is creating a
shortage of skilled IT workers to manage
all of the systems. It's a problem that's
not going away, but will grow exponentially, just as our dependence on technology has.

In short, we can't keep computing as we
have for years. Autonomic computing systems have the ability to manage themselves and dynamically adapt to change
in accordance with business policies and
objectives. Self-managing systems can
perform management activities based on
situations they observe or sense in the IT
environment. Rather than IT professionals
initiating management activities, the system observes something about itself and
acts accordingly. This allows the IT professional to focus on high-value tasks while
the technology manages the more mundane operations.

Why Autonomic Computing?

Why is autonomic computing important
today? The cost of technology continues
to decrease yet overall IT costs do not.
With the expense challenges that many
companies face, IT managers are looking
for ways to improve the return on investment of IT by reducing total cost of own-
ership, improving quality of service, accelerating time to value and managing IT
complexity. E-business is a reality, and
outages are proving to be expensive and
embarrassing. Adding to this complexity
is the proliferation of heterogeneous ven-
dor and technology environments, which
require the components of a given solution to be integrated and customized
into unique customer business processes.
The increased need to distribute data,
applications and system resources across
geographic and business boundaries further contributes to the complexity of the
IT infrastructure. The additional complexity keeps the costs of managing (deploying, tuning, fixing, securing) the IT infrastructure high.

Introduction of Self-management

Systems with self-managing components
reduce the cost of owning and operating
computer systems. IT infrastructure components take on the following characteristics: self configuring, self-healing, self-
optimizing and self-protecting.

Self-configuring

With the ability to dynamically configure
itself on the fly, an IT environment can
adapt immediately – and with minimal
human intervention – to the deployment
of new components or changes in the IT
environment. Dynamic adaptation helps
verify continuous strength and productivity of an e-business infrastructure –
often the single determining factor between business growth and chaos.

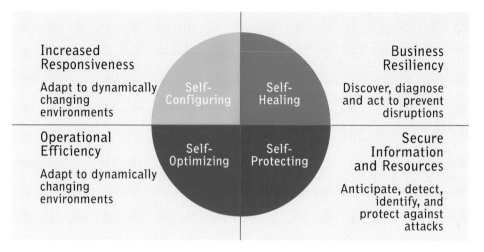

Fig. 1: Autonomic Computing – 4 Themes

Self-healing

Self-healing IT environments can detect improper operations (either proactively through predictions or otherwise) and then initiate corrective action without disrupting system applications. Corrective action could mean that a product alters its own state or influences changes in other elements of the environment. Day-to-day operations do not falter or fail because of events at the component level. The IT environment as a whole becomes more resilient as changes are made to reduce or help eliminate the business impact of failing components.

Self-optimizing

Self-optimization refers to the ability of the IT environment to efficiently maximize resource allocation and utilization to meet end users' needs with minimal human intervention. In the near term self-optimization primarily addresses the complexity of managing system performance. In the long term self-optimizing components may learn from experience and automatically and proactively tune themselves in the context of an overall business objective. Self-optimization verifies optimum Quality of Service for both system users and their customers.

Self-protecting

The goal of self-protecting environments is to provide the right information to the right users at the right time through actions that grant access based on the users' role and pre-established policies. A self-protecting IT environment can detect hostile or intrusive behavior as it occurs and take autonomous actions to make itself less vulnerable to unauthorized access and use, viruses, denial-of-service attacks and general failures.

The self-protecting capability allows businesses to consistently enforce security and privacy policies, reduce overall security administration costs and ultimately increase employee productivity and custo-mer satisfaction. Self protection is also about recognizing and dealing with overload conditions that could jeopardize the integrity of the system.

Collectively these intuitive and collaborative characteristics can enable enterprises to operate efficiently with fewer human resources, helping decrease costs and enhancing a company's ability to react to change.

An Evolution, not a Revolution

Delivering system-wide autonomic environments is an evolutionary process enabled by technology, but it is ultimately implemented by each enterprise through the adoption of these technologies and supporting processes. The path to autonomic computing can be thought of in five levels, shown in Fig. 2. These levels, defined below, start at basic and continue through managed, predictive, adaptive and finally autonomic.

1. Basic level—a starting point of IT environments. Each infrastructure element is managed independently by IT professionals who set it up, monitor it and eventually replace it.

2. Managed level—systems management technologies can be used to collect information from disparate systems onto fewer consoles, reducing the time it takes for the administrator to collect and synthesize information as the IT environment becomes more complex.

3. Predictive level—new technologies are introduced to provide correlation among several infrastructure elements. These elements can begin to recognize patterns, predict the optimal configuration and provide advice on what course of action the administrator should take.

4. Adaptive level—as these technologies improve and as people become more comfortable with the advice and predictive

power of these systems, we can progress to the adaptive level, where the systems themselves can automatically take the right actions based on the information that is available to them and the knowledge of what is happening in the system.

5. Autonomic level—the IT infrastructure operation is governed by business policies and objectives. Users interact with the autonomic technology to monitor the business processes, alter the objectives, or both.

Autonomic Computing Architecture Concepts

A standard set of functions and interactions govern the management of the IT system and its resources, including client, server, database manager or Web application server. This is represented by a control loop (shown in the diagram in Fig. 3) that acts as a manager of the resource through monitoring, analysis and taking action based on a set of policies.

These control loops, or managers, can communicate with each other in a peer-to-peer context and with higher-level managers. For example, a database system needs to work with the server, storage subsystem, storage management software, the Web server and other system elements to achieve a self-managing IT environment. The pyramid in Fig. 4 represents the hierarchy in which autonomic computing technologies will operate. The bottom layer of the pyramid consists of

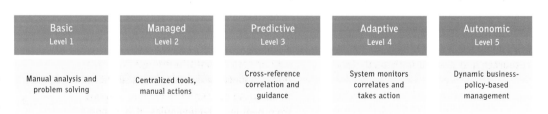

Fig. 2: Autonomic computing levels

Basic Level 1	Managed Level 2	Predictive Level 3	Adaptive Level 4	Autonomic Level 5
Manual analysis and problem solving	Centralized tools, manual actions	Cross-reference correlation and guidance	System monitors correlates and takes action	Dynamic business-policy-based management

the resource elements of an enterprise – networks, servers, storage devices, applications, middleware and personal computers. Autonomic computing begins in the resource element layer, by enhancing individual components to configure, optimize, heal and protect themselves.

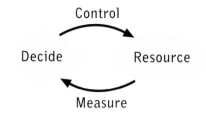

Fig. 3: Autonomic computing – Control loop

Moving up the pyramid, resource elements are grouped into composite resources, which begin to communicate with each other to create self-managing systems. This can be represented by a pool of servers that work together to dynamically adjust workload and configuration to meet certain performance and availability thresholds. It can also be represented by a combination of heterogeneous devices (databases, Web servers and storage subsystems) that work together to achieve performance and availability targets.

At the highest layer of the pyramid composite resources are tied to business solutions, such as a customer-care system or an electronic auction system. True autonomic activity occurs at this level. The solution layer requires autonomic solutions to comprehend the optimal state of business processes – based on policies, schedules, service levels and so on – and drive the consequences of process optimization back down to the composite resources and even to individual elements.

Autonomic Computing Requires Open Standards

Many IT infrastructures have components supplied by different vendors. For multi-vendor components to participate in autonomic systems, there needs to be a set of standards for the managed elements' sensors and effectors and for the knowledge to be shared between autonomic managers that describe the interaction between the elements of an IT system. Some existing and emerging standards relevant to autonomic computing include:

¬ Distributed Management Taskforce
¬ Common Information Model
¬ Internet Engineering Taskforce (Policy, Simple Network Management Protocol)
¬ Organization for the Advancement of Structured Information Standards (OASIS)
¬ Java™ Management Extensions
¬ Storage Networking Industry Association
¬ Open-grid systems architecture
¬ Web Services Security

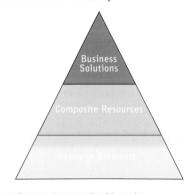

Fig. 4: Autonomic computing hierarchy

How Will Self-management Change the Business of IT?

Small and large IT organizations perform similar sets of tasks to manage their systems. Because self-managing is about shifting the burden of managing systems from people to technologies, it is important to understand how self-managing capabilities impact the business of IT. The business of IT can be viewed as a collection of best practices and processes. For example, IT Infrastructure Library (ITIL) – shown in Fig. 6 – is a set of best practices and processes that IT organizations can use to deliver IT services to end users in a controlled, disciplined way. The ITIL service-management disciplines provide a framework that enables IT and end users to define their required levels of service performance (depicted in the diagram in Fig. 1. ITIL leverages processes and tools to help realize high gains in efficiency – more than would be realized by improving either of those two entities alone.

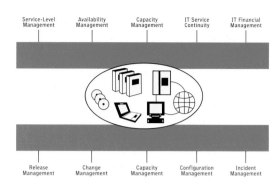

Fig. 6: IT Infrastructure Library (ITIL)

Implementing Autonomic Computing

Shifting the burden of managing systems to self-managing technologies does not happen overnight and cannot be solely accomplished by acquiring new products. Skills within the organization need to adapt, and processes need to change to create new benchmarks of success. As companies progress through the five levels of autonomic computing (Fig. 7), the processes, tools and benchmarks become increasingly sophisticated, and the skills requirement becomes more closely aligned with the business.

The **basic level** represents the starting point for many IT organizations. If IT organizations are formally measured, they are typically evaluated on the time required to finish major tasks and fix major problems. The IT organization is viewed as a cost center, with variable labor costs preferred over an investment in centrally coordinated systems management tools and processes.

In the **managed level** IT organizations are measured on the availability of their managed resources, their time to close trouble

tickets in their problem management system and their time to complete formally tracked work requests. To improve on these measurements, IT organizations document their processes and continually improve them through manual feedback loops and adoption of best practices. IT organizations gain efficiency through consolidation of management tools to a set of strategic platforms and through a hierarchical problem management triage organization.

In the **predictive level** IT organizations are measured on the availability and performance of their business systems and their return on investment. To improve, IT organizations measure, manage and analyze transaction performance. The critical nature of the IT organization's role in business success is understood. Predictive tools are used to project future IT performance, and many tools make recommendations to improve future performance.

In the **adaptive level** IT resources are automatically provisioned and tuned to optimize transaction performance. Business policies, business priorities and service-level agreements guide the autonomic infrastructure behavior. IT organizations are measured on comprehensive business system response times (transaction performance), the degree of efficiency of the IT infrastructure and their ability to adapt to shifting workloads.

In the **autonomic level** IT organizations are measured on their ability to make the business successful. To improve business measurements they understand the financial metrics associated with e-business activities and supporting IT activities. Advanced modeling techniques are used to optimize e-business performance and quickly deploy newly optimized e-business solutions.

evolutionary shift in the way IT systems are managed will free the IT staff from detailed mundane tasks and allow them to focus on managing business processes. It can be accomplished through a combination of process changes, skills evolution, new technologies, architecture and open industry standards.

IBM has named its vision for the future of computing "autonomic computing." This new paradigm shifts the fundamental definition of the technology age from one

Basic Level 1	Managed Level 2	Predictive Level 3	Adaptive Level 4	Autonomic Level 5
Process informal, reactive, manual	Process Documented, improved over time, leverage of industry best practices, manual process to review IT performance	Process Proactive, shorter approval cycle	Process Automation of many resource management best practices and transaction management best practices, driven by service-level agreements	Process All IT service management and IT resource management best practices are automated
Tools Local, platform and product-specific	Tools Consolated resource management consoles, problem management system, automated software install, intrusion detection, load balancing	Tools Role-based conscies with analysis and recommendations, product configuration advisors; realtime view of current and future IT performance; automation of some repetitive tasks; common knowledge base of inventory and dependency management	Tools Policy management tools drive dynamic change based on resource-specific policies	Tools Costing financial analysis tool, business and IT modelling tools, tradeoff analysis; automation of some e-business management roles
Skills Platform-specific, geographically dispensed with technology	Skills Multiple platform skills, multiple management tool skills	Skills Cross-plattform system knowledge, IT workload management skills, some business-process knowledge	Skills Service objectives and delivery per resource, analysis of impact on business objectives	Skills e-business cost and benefit analysis, performance modelling, advanced use of financial tools for IT context
Benchmarks Time to fix problems and finish tasks	Benchmarks System availability, time to close trouble tickets and work requests	Benchmarks Business system availability, service-level agreement attainment, customer satisfaction	Benchmarks Business system response time, service-level agreement attainment, customer satisfaction, IT contribution to business success	Benchmarks Business success, competitiveness of service-level agreement metrics, business responsiveness

Fig. 7: Service Support

Conclusion

Companies want and need to reduce their IT costs, simplify management of their IT resources, realize a fast return on their IT investment and provide high levels of availability, performance, security and asset utilization. Autonomic computing addresses these issues, and it is not just about new technology. This fundamental

of computing to one defined by data. Access to data from multiple, distributed sources, in addition to traditional centralized storage devices, will allow users to transparently access information when and where they need it. At the same time, this new view of computing will necessitate changing the industry's focus on processing speed and storage to one of developing distributed networks that are largely self-managing, self-diagnostic, and transparent to the user. This new computer paradigm means the design and implementation of computer systems, software, storage and support must exhibit these basic fundamentals from a user perspective:

¬ **Flexible.** The system will be able to sift data via a platform- and device-agnostic approach.

¬ **Accessible.** The nature of the autonomic system is that it is always on.

¬ **Transparent.** The system will perform its tasks and adapt to a user's needs without dragging the user into the intricacies of its workings.

The pursuit of autonomic computing gives us a unique opportunity to define the next era of computing. Since their conception, computers have failed to live up to expectations nearly as often as they have exceeded them. Autonomic computing provides an opportunity to recalibrate the higher purpose of computers from one of convenience to a tool that allows us to exploit previously unnavigable challenges.

Progressively autonomic computers will enable the tools to analyze complex problems. For instance, machines with cellular architecture, such as Blue Gene, will enable the study of phenomena occurring in fractions of a second at an atomic scale. Greater access to more computing power through grid computing combined with the implementation of open standards will enable researchers to more easily collaborate on complex problems for the global good. Autonomic computing will be able to better harness existing processing power to run complex mathematics for functions such as weather simulations and other scenarios that inform public systems and infrastructure.

The *Grand Challenge* of autonomic computing gives us a new horizon to reach for.

This new paradigm shifts the fundamental definition of the technology age from one of computing to one defined by data. Access to data from multiple, distributed sources, in addition to traditional centralized storage devices, will allow users to transparently access information when and where they need it. At the same time, this new view of computing will necessitate changing the industry's focus on processing speed and storage to one of developing distributed networks that are largely self-managing, self-diagnostic, and transparent to the user.

A Grid is a worldwide communication infrastructure that allows seamless transparent access to instruments, data and computing power on demand. The currently growing number and size of Grid projects with significant industrial contributions all over the world indicates that we are not too far from changing the World Wide Web into a World Wide Grid. This paper outlines the vision of Grid computing, explains the technologies under development, and illustrates some of the current Grid projects. One of them, the LHC Computing Grid Project is discussed in more detail.

Holger Marten studied physics and holds a PhD in astrophysics from the University of Kiel, Germany. He gained ten years of experience in physics applications development on high performance computers and worked for two years in the user support for numerical code development and optimization. He is the Managing Director of the Grid Computing Center Karlsruhe (GridKa), Institute for Scientific Computing at the Research Center Karlsruhe, Germany.

Holger Marten:

Grid computing – Basis of multi-institutional virtual organizations

GRID COMPUTING _BASIS OF
MULTI-INSTITUTIONAL VIRTUAL
ORGANIZATIONS

Introduction

The rapid evolution of science and technology during the last centuries significantly changed not only our everyday life
but also our scientific working methods.
Observations of nature probably exist since the beginning of mankind. However,
inventions of scientific instruments like
the microscope or the optical telescope
in the 17th century and their further
developments led to revolutionary and
ever increasing insights into biology,
medicine, astronomy, and so on. Today
we are able to resolve atomic structures
with scanning tunnel microscopes, look
into a patient with computer tomographs,
or send huge telescopes into outer space
to make sky surveys in many different
wavelength ranges.

The parallel development of imaging techniques significantly helped to analyze,
store and disseminate these observations.
One of the most famous examples of the
past is the photograph made by Wilhelm
Conrad Röntgen in 1895 showing an x-ray
image of the hand of his wife. With the
development of CCD chips in the second
half of the 20th century it became possible to take digital images and directly
store them in bits and bytes on appropriate media. Today, thousands of digital
images per day are sent down to earth by
meteorological satellites, and everybody
can easily fill whole DVDs with films from
the last summer's holidays.

The evolution of mathematics as a description language led to another new quality
in science between the 17th and the 19th
centuries. Analytical solutions of mathematical models not only described existing
observations and experiments, but even
stimulated new ones by predicting their
results. With the development of informatics in the 20th century, these "analytical
sciences" largely evolved into "computational sciences." Huge sets of equations
(the mathematical model) are discretized,
validated with partial (e.g. analytical)
solutions or with measurement results,
and finally used for further predictions,
because respective experiments are too
time consuming, too expensive or even
not (yet) possible at all. Fine examples
from our everyday life are weather fore-
casts evaluated on huge supercomputers.
Today, the terms "computational" or
"informatics" accompany almost every
scientific branch: computational physics,
chemistry, mathematics, astrophysics,
bio informatics, medical informatics, etc.

The construction and operation of many
scientific facilities evolved into multidisciplinary and multi-national projects,
constituting huge collaborations with partners from all over the world. Enormous
data rates are produced; we are currently
talking about hundreds of TeraBytes or
even PetaBytes per year, and projects like
the Human Genome Project or the Sloan
Digital Sky Survey have already entered
the next generation "data exploration
sciences" by organizing their data in huge
data bases and publishing them on the
Web. Huge computing facilities and new
sophisticated data mining services are
necessary to digest these immense quantities of information or to prove our theories by simulations.

The vision of scientists is to combine all
these resources into the Grid – a common
worldwide infrastructure that allows seamless transparent access to instruments,
data and computing power on demand.

The Vision

The Grid is a hardware and software infrastructure which provides qualitatively new functionalities to end users on the basis of conventional networking technologies. Resources like computing power, data, software products, instruments, sensors etc. are offered in the form of services that are accessible at any place in the world. Without doubt, the single technological components (software packages, supercomputers, telescopes, etc.) will continue to be developed and maintained by independent entities. And it is also very likely that the basic data structures of the single components will continue to be heterogeneous and that the whole environment will change dynamically – one cannot be sure that the computer one is using today will be available tomorrow. However, the user shouldn't care! The Grid itself should manage the resources and offer all services in a user-friendly, secure and reliable way, thus hiding the enormous complexity of the underlying platforms where the services are actually executed. By analogy with the electrical power grid (that's where the name "Grid" comes from), the Grid should provide computing power and data "from a plug in the wall." We don't care where our electrical power is produced and we also shouldn't in the case of data and computing power. This vision of the Grid is impressively described by Ian Foster and Carl Kesselman in their book *The Grid – Blueprint for a New Computing Infrastructure* [1].

The following example should outline the possible benefits of the Grid in more detail. Suppose that a team of surgeons is preparing a bypass operation. The traditional method to decide about the bypass location is based on a computer tomography of the patients arteries, taking into account the patients general health, experiences from similar interventions in the

past, latest medical findings, opinions of other expert teams, etc. The success of this method shows up a few weeks or months after the operation.

The Grid vision of this scenario might look as follows (Fig. 1): A computer tomography is done at the patients local hospital. The surgeons mark their first guess of the bypass location on the resulting 3D digital images and place an order via the Grid with Fluid Dynamics Inc. in Canada to simulate the bloodflow of the region surrounding the bypass. At Fluid Dynamics, the worldwide leading specialist in software development for bloodflow simulations, the geometry of the arteries is automatically converted into an optimized numerical mesh for simulations. Together

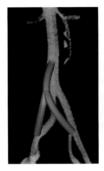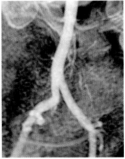

Fig. 1: Biomedical Grid application from EU project CrossGrid. Two arterial structures from scans with proposed bypasses (top left, top right), and a view of the arterial structure in an immersive 3D environment (bottom). Application development by the University of Amsterdam.

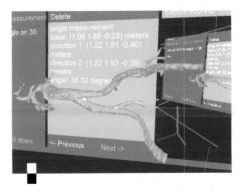

with their newest simulation code and these geometry parameters, Fluid Dynamics places a Grid order to perform a complete simulation set for six different heartbeat frequencies and to return a movie of the simulation results within five minutes. The Grid selects four different supercomputing centers which together just offer enough free capacity. Two minutes later, the simulation results arrive at Visualisation Corp. in Switzerland and are converted to a 3D movie of simulated blood pressures and flow velocities of the whole bypass region. Having received the movies, the surgical team decides to repeat the whole process for a slightly larger bypass diameter because the simulations indicate that neighboring arteries might become too much loaded at more than 140 heartbeats per minute.

In this example, the Grid brought together completely different expert services and provided computing power on demand. The hospital would neither have the money nor the expertise to buy and maintain a supercomputer, and the surgeons would not have started this analysis if the whole process chain took weeks, especially in order not to endanger the patient.

There do exist many other situations that benefit from Grid computing power on demand: The automatic analysis software of a wheather satellite just identified a hurricane over the Pacific, initiates a Grid simulation to forecast its speed and direction, and sends out warnings to the possibly affected regions. At the same time, a small bio company designed a new active substance against a virus and wishes to simulate its impact in combination with a few thousand other substances. Elsewhere, a river starts to swell due to heavy rainfall, and a crisis support team submits a Grid order for flood simulations with actual measurements of the 20 nearest weather stations (Fig.2).

Obviously, the Grid gives benefits wherever large computing power is needed on demand but cannot be installed permanently for economic reasons, or whenever huge distributed data sets are to be analyzed or correlated. The terms "Computing Grids" and "Data Grids" are found in the literature for these "compute intensive" or "data intensive" extremes.

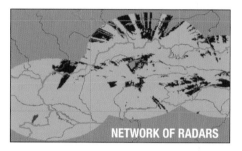

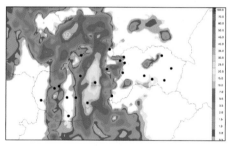

Fig. 2: Grid application for flood forecasting and crisis support from EU project CrossGrid. The process chain contains rainfall monitoring by a network of weather radars (top), weather forecasting (above) and flood simulation (bottom, here: Váh River, Slovakia). Application development by the Institute of Informatics of the Slovak Academy of Sciences.

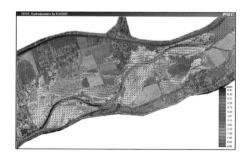

Bricks and Stones

An imperative condition for the success of the Grid is the existence of high-speed networks with a guaranteed quality of service. In Europe, Géant [2] provides a pan-European research network connecting national research and education networks with up to 10 Gbit/s. Several nodal points connect Géant with Japan and the United States. TeraGrid [3] is an effort to build and deploy the world's largest and fastest distributed infrastructure at this time for open science research. Five supercomputer centers will be connected through a network that will operate at 40 Gbit/s. TeraGrid will include a computing and storage capacity equivalent to 10,000-15,000 modern PCs, high resolution visualization environments, and toolkits for Grid computing.

Grid security and trust relations are other interesting subjects of current research. A Grid user (e.g. a company) must be sure that his sent or received data are neither accessible by someone else nor corrupted. This can be done, for example, by data encoding, however at the expense of additional computing time. Likewise, a system administrator needs a guarantee that a user is really the person he seems to be (authentication) and is authorized to use his machine. Authentication of users and Grid jobs is currently done by certificates, kinds of digital keys, which are signed by well-known and accepted certificate authorities. Several such certificate authorities have been built within Grid projects during the last years.

Concerning authorization, every Grid user must be a registered member of one or more virtual organizations (VOs). An administrator may or may not accept a VO on his system, or may restrict the access rights of user groups or single members of a VO. The complexity of the physical and data infrastructure should be hidden to the user by a virtualization software layer, which is called "Grid middleware". What remains is a user interface similar to the desktop of an operating system which allows one to access the Grid from a local workstation or a mobile device.

One of the most frequently used middleware packages is the Globus Toolkit [4]. It allows one to prove the identity of the user, carry out a task, keep an account of the Grid resources, locate data in a distributed environment, and organize data streams. The Globus Project was established in 1995 by the U.S. Argonne National Laboratory, at the University of Southern California and the University of Chicago. On September 1, 2003, the University of Edinburgh and the Swedish Royal Institute of Technology joined the Globus Project and the project transformed itself into the Globus Alliance.

Communication does not work if we are able to speak but use different languages. Likewise, global virtualized Grid computing would not become successful without a definition of standards. The Global Grid Forum, GGF [5], acts as a standardization body in Grid computing, similar to the Internet Engineering Task Force (IETF). It was founded as a merger of the US Grid Forum with the European Grid Forum EGrid and the Asia-Pacific Grid Forum community. The GGF organization and two to three yearly working meetings are sponsored by numerous partners from industry and science. Dozens if not even hundreds of scientific and industrial projects all over the world contribute to the implementation and further development of these standards. In Europe, 24 Grid projects are promoted within the 5th Framework Program of the European Commission with a total funding of 58 million euros. Two of these projects should be mentioned here:

a) The European DataGrid Project, EDG [6], aims to develop, implement and exploit a large-scale data and CPU-oriented computational Grid to enable next generation scientific exploration, which requires intensive computation and analysis of shared large-scale databases across widely distributed scientific communities. The "scientific communities" (their applications) in this case come from high-energy physics, bio-informatics and earth observation sciences. EDG uses the Globus Toolkit as a basis for further middleware development.

b) The European project CrossGrid [7] aims at providing a Grid framework for development and execution of parallel and interactive applications. CrossGrid builds middleware on top of Globus and EDG. The American Particle Physics Data Grid [8] is similar to EDG. Here the applications are coming from high-energy physics and astrophysics. Interestingly, many other Grid initiatives are driven by high-energy or particle physicists as well, because of their enormous data storage requirments. Examples are the US Grid Physics Network [9], the UK project GridPP [10], or the LHC Computing Grid Project which is outlined in more detail in the next section. Of course, the above list of current Grid projects is by far incomplete, but it should be noted that the standardization and collaboration effort among all of them is extremely large.

The LHC Computing Grid Project

The Large Hadron Collider, LHC [11], is a ring accelerator of 27 km circumference which is currently constructed at the European Particle Physics Laboratory CERN in Geneva. LHC will host four huge detectors (also referred to as "LHC experiments") to analyse the structure of matter from fragments of particle collisions from 2007 onwards. The estimated data volume generated by this gigantic machine is 8 PetaBytes (8 Million GigaBytes) per year, complemented by another 4-6 PetaBytes of simulation data. Analyzing this will require the equivalent of 70,000 of today's fastest PC processors. The goal of the LHC Computing Grid Project (LCG [12]) is to meet these unprecedented computing needs by deploying a worldwide computational Grid service, integrating the resources of scientific computing centers spread across Europe, America and Asia into a global virtual computing organisation. About 5,000 scientists are expected to evaluate the data of the forthcoming LHC.

The computing model that is to cope with this massive data flood is shown in Fig. 3. Data and computing resources are distributed over a few hundred Grid installations of different complexity and size. Each of the levels (Tiers) take over respective functionalities. Raw data of the experiments will be stored and pre-processed at CERN (Tier-0), large regional centers store re-constructed data and simulate particle collisions with Monte Carlo methods (Tier-1), filtered data streams go to national (Tier-2) and local (Tier-3) computing centers, and selected datasets are finally stored and processed at the working places of the scientists (Tier-4). The data, instruments and computing resources of each of the four LHC experiments, ALICE, ATLAS, CMS and LHCb, build the virtual organizations, and their members get transparent access via the LCG Grid middleware, which is indicated by the cloud in Fig. 3.

At the request of and in close collaboration with the German particle and nuclear physics communities, Forschungszentrum Karlsruhe has taken up the task of developing, installing and operating the Grid Computing Center Karlsruhe, GridKa. Besides CERN, RAL, IN2P3 and others,

GridKa will be one of the eight to ten Tier-1 Centers within the network [13, 14]. The official inauguration of GridKa took place at the end of October 2002, and today GridKa already hosts 1070 Linux processors, 220 TeraBytes of usable disk space and 370 TeraBytes of tape storage. Part of these resources are made availabe to already running high-energy physics experiments: BaBar at SLAC, CDF and D0 at FermiLab and Compass at CERN will generate a data volume of about 1/10 of LHC during the next years, and they are thus optimal cadidates to test and validate the scaling of the hard- and software infrastructure.

In 2007, at the startup of LHC, GridKa will host about 4000 processors, 1500 TeraBytes online and 3800 TeraBytes tape storage, and co-operate via a few dozen Gigabit connections with hundreds of other Grid installations worldwide. However, many detailed questions, which are the subject of current research, have to be answered before then:
How to organize the access to 12 Peta-Bytes of worldwide distributed data per year? How well do the necessary network, processor, disk and tape technologies scale? How to "hide" the complex Grid infrastructures from the user who only wishes to have an analysis of a selected dataset stored "somewhere in the world?" How to administer and charge the global activities of a few thousand users? And, last but not least, how to organize and guarantee seamless user support over many different time zones? LCG aims at providing answers to these and further questions.

At this writing, the first prototype service, LCG-1, is being deployed. It provides the LHC physicists with a basic set of Grid tools built from middleware components of the European DataGrid project and the Virtual Data Toolkit, which on the other

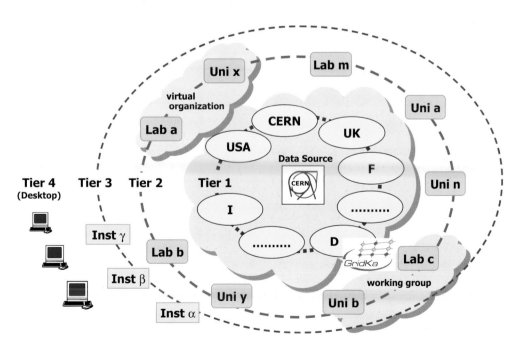

Fig. 3: Computing model of the LHC Computing Grid (LCG) Project. Computing centers of different complexity and size (Tier) form a collaborative virtual computing environment.

hand is the product of several US Grid research projects [15]. A part of these activities will be taken up by the project Enabling Grids and E-science in Europe, EGEE [16], which was launched in April 2004 within the 6th Framework Program of the European Commission. 70 institutions from 27 European countries will form a multi-science Grid to provide a prototype solution for other demanding applications in science and industry.

In April 2005, scientific grid computing achieved a new record: eight major computing centers, among them GridKa, managed to sustain an average continuous data flow of 600 MegaBytes per second for ten days. The total volume of data transmitted between CERN, Geneva, and seven sites in the US and Europe, amounting to 500 TeraBytes or half a PetaByte, would take about 250 years to download using a typical 512-kb/s household broadband connection. This was a key step on the way to managing the torrents of data anticipated from the LHC when it starts operating in 2007, producing more than 1500 MegaBytes of data every second for over a decade. It will be the most data-intensive physics instrument on the planet.

Conclusion

There is a striking resemblence between the Grid and the World Wide Web. Originally developed by Tim Berners-Lee at the European Particle Physics Laboratory CERN as a medium for scientific knowledge and data exchange, the opening of the Web to companies and the general public led to completely new communication and business models. The HyperText Transfer Protokoll (HTTP) as a communication standard for the Web was officially released by CERN in a press conference in 1993, and the Web had a few hundred scientific users at that time. Today, only

12 years later (!) about 950 million people have access to approximately five billion Web pages. The currently growing number and size of Grid projects with significant industrial contributions all over the world indicates that we are not too far from changing the World Wide Web (WWW) into a World Wide Grid (WWG).

References

[1] I. Foster, C. Kesselman, "The Grid – Blueprint for a New Computing Infrastructure," Morgan Kaufmann Publ. 1999.

[2] Géant – The pan-European Research Network, http://www.dante.net.

[3] TeraGrid – A Network of Supercomputer Centers, http://www.teragrid.org.

[4] Globus – The Globus Alliance and the Globus Toolkit, http://www.globus.org.

[5] GGF – The Global Grid Forum, http://www.gridforum.org.

[6] EDG – The European DataGrid Project, http://www.eu-datagrid.org.

[7] CrossGrid – The European CrossGrid Project, http://www.eu-crossgrid.org.

[8] PPDG – The Particle Physics Data Grid, http://www.ppdg.net/.

[9] GriPhyN – Grid Physics Network, http://www.griphyn.org/.

[10] GridPP – The Grid for UK Particle Physics, http://www.gridpp.ac.uk.

[11] LHC – The Large Hadron Collider at CERN, http://www.cern.ch/lhc.

[12] LCG – The LHC Computing Grid Project, http://www.cern.ch/lcg.

[13] P. Braun-Munzinger, et al., "Requirements for a Regional Data and Computing Center in Germany (RDCCG)," http://www.gridka.de/LHCComputing-1july01.pdf.

[14] H. Marten, et al., "A Grid Computing Center at Foschungszentrum Karlsruhe," http ://www.gridka.de/RDCCG-answer-v8.pdf.

[15] VDT – The Virtual Data Toolkit, http://www.lsc-group.phys.uwm.edu/vdt/.

[16] EGEE – Enabling Grids and E-Science in Europe, http://www.eu-egee.org.

One cannot be sure that the computer one is using today will be available tomorrow. However, the user shouldn't care! The Grid itself should manage the resources and offer all services in a user-friendly, secure and reliable way, thus hiding the enormous complexity of the underlying platforms where the services are actually executed. We don't care where our electrical power is produced, and we also shouldn't in the case of data and computing power.

Today's computers are easily identified by a human: Their explicit interface makes them noticeable no matter what designs are in favor. Embedded Ubiquitous computers, on the other hand, will not be noticeable to the user. This paper will give a short overview of embedded Ubicomp computer systems issues in regard to two important and required capabilities, i.e., sensing the environment and independently processing information. Implementing these two functions results in computers that not only sense the environment but in essence also develop a sense of the environment they are in.

Michael Beigl obtained both his MSc and PhD degrees in computing at the University of Karlsruhe. His PhD thesis about ubiquitous computing environments received the FZI prize for the best thesis of the year 2000. Beigl joined the University's Telecooperation Office (TecO), a computer science unit conducting collaborative projects in applied telematics, in 1995 as the technical head of the group's ubiquitous computing effort. He is now senior researcher and manager of the TecO.

michael Beigl:

ubiquitous computing — computation embedded in the world

UBIQUITOUS COMPUTING _
COMPUTATION EMBEDDED IN THE
WORLD

Introduction

Ubiquitous Computing (Ubicomp) is a term
first coined by Mark Weiser [1] more than
a decade ago. In his vision, computers are
no longer isolated objects sitting on the
desk, but surround us everywhere: walls
could be electronic boards and displays;
books could be electronic information
stores and cameras act as digital picture
libraries. Some of this vision has already
come true with wall-sized Smart Boards
that support writing, editing and captur-
ing of electronic text, while PDAs can be
used for diaries, e-books and note-taking,
where some of them are also integrated
with digital cameras. While such computers largely follow the PC paradigm, where
one computer is dedicated to one user at
one point in time, new types of computer
systems are arising in Ubicomp that are
invisibly embedded into our everyday environment. Such computers will change the
way we make use of computing: Rather
than *explicitly* being the "user" of a computer a human will *implicitly* profit from
services running between computers hidden in mundane objects or the enviroment
without even taking notice of them [2].

Today's computers are easily identified
by a human: Their explicit interface makes
them noticeable no matter what designs
are in favor. Embedded Ubiquitous computers on the other hand will not be noticeable to the user. Don Norman calls such
computers invisible computers because
they are no longer perceived as computers
[3], particularly not in the sense that we
perceive them today. According to Weiser,
there are basically two classes of *invisible
computers*, those that are literally vanishing into mundane objects by being integrated into those objects, and those that

are only mentally invisible, meaning not
recognized as a computer by the human.

Mostly without taking notice, we are already surrounded by a large number of
such devices. Modern mobile phones contain much more computer electronics
than telephony parts, a process that will
continue until software radio will enable
us to remove all traditional analog electronics. This process is not only a matter
of substituting current technology with
newer ones that improve quality of the
product or lower its cost. Rather, due to
the communication and autonomic computing capabilities of such computer systems, it also leads to an explosion of possibilities through the subsequent connection of functionality between devices.

This is even more the case with novel
upcoming electronic artifacts. While we
might expect existing electronic devices
to be transformed to small computers,
the same intuitive conclusion is not reached with regards to non-electric devices.
Nevertheless, early research prototypes
show that it is also feasible and constructive to embed computing technology into
nearly every object. An early example of
such an embedded device is the Media-
Cup [4], a cup with hidden electronic
inside the rubber base (Fig. 1). This cup
requires no superfluous knowledge from
the human – except the knowledge of
how to use a cup – and no explicit interaction with the computer hidden inside.
Instead the computer in the base "observes" the human and the status of the cup
and interprets this information as "input"
to the system. Researchers call this way
of interaction implicit interaction to make
it clear that such computers do not explicitly require users to provide input to the
computer system. The added value of this
technology comes from the collaboration
of cups together and with other computer
systems in the environment. Devices like

the coffee machine can profit from knowing the habits of coffee consumption beforehand, electronic meeting room doorplates recognize meetings and change the display accordingly, etc. Because there is no extra effort or learning phase required from the user, and because these computers are unobtrusive, small and cheap, they will soon be widespread in our environment. Potentially any everyday object and the environment will be equipped with a computer, leading to scenarios with hundreds of computer systems inside every room.

Fig. 1: MediaCup

Apart from this quantitative difference, there will also be a qualitative distinction between embedded Ubicomp environments and today's computer systems. "Applications" will be provided by computers through ad hoc collaboration between these devices rather than by following fixed instructions. This requires computers – especially those embedded in mobile objects – to spontaneously communicate with other computers and to adapt to new environments without human interference. This paper will give a short overview of embedded Ubicomp computer systems issues in the following sections.

Embedding into the Fabric of Our Lives

Embedded computers have been around us now for years: Embedded into processing equipment, embedded in mundane objects or the fabric of buildings, they control the conveyer in a factory, individually manipulate the temperature of each of the trays of modern freezers, or trigger the airbag in a car. Today such computers provide a well-defined set of functionalities in a well-defined setting. Future computers will be ubiquitously embedded into the fabric of our everyday life and therefore will work often in previously unknown environments. Their functionality will need to adapt to the conditions in the current environment.

There are three factors that accelerate the development towards computer systems embedded into everyday objects and environments: decreased price, decreased size and increased smartness. The latter factor refers to the fact that such computing systems are able to work autonomously and independent of any user administration, configuration and explicit user input. These computers will therefore not be perceived as computer systems anymore. Instead they will be perceived by their primary function, namely, the cup, the refrigerator or the oven.

A world with such computing systems works towards one of the very early visions of Ubicomp: Calm Computing [5]. This concept emphasizes that computers should be more like everyday objects that are often used intentionally, without explicitly taking notice of them. In a similar manner to everyday objects, computers should also be able to seamlessly change between foreground and background attention of the user and hence to be used on demand. This requires embedded computers to react on such behavior in context of usage and situation, which is made possible through a new kind of functionality of such devices: perceiving the environment and context.

Perceiving Environment and Context

The aforementioned new type of embedded computers possesses two important capabilities that are required and radical new approaches in computing: sensing the environment and independently processing information. Implementing these two functions result in computers that not only *sense the environment* but in essence also *develop a sense of the environment* they are in. Sensing allows small devices to perceive the situation of the surrounding environment or the state of an object. Information can be used by the system in the same way that manual input is used by computers today: to trigger functions and applications or as direct input to these applications. For example, instead of data-entry of product information in a supermarket by typing or scanning at the checkout, the cash computer can scan the identification of products in a trolley without any explicit human interaction.

However, sensed information from the physical world can provide the basis for even more sophisticated evaluation of the surrounding environment. This is carried out by processing a multitude of sensor values and interpreting them as the *situational context* of the environment around the computer. Derived context information can be used either for improving the functionality of existing applications or to implement applications solely based on context information. The process to detect this context or situation from the environment is called *context or situation recognition*. Context recognition uses physical data delivered from sensors and concludes context and situation information specified at a high level.

Fig. 2: DigiClip Prototype with embedded sensor and computing system

Other prototypes like the DigiClip appliance (Fig. 2) allow one to detect misuse of objects – e.g. documents – or wrong storage conditions and can warn the user or personnel [6]. The Digi-Clip system consists of a sensor system electronic embedded into a paper clip and can recognize certain contextual situations. The system can be configured to warn users via a speaker or to warn personnel via wireless communication when a violation of handling rules is detected.

To enhance detection quality, an embedded Ubicomp device uses a variety of sensors. Fig. 3 shows Smart-Its, an example of an embedded device with a multitude of sensors built in. In Smart-Its, light sensors are used to detect illumination conditions, 3D-acceleration sensors to detect fine-grained movements, temperature and humidity sensors to indicate room conditions, and a microphone to interpret audio and noise in the environment. The use of multiple sensors allows these small computers to evaluate situations based on several physical parameters. The use of multiple sources is therefore often needed to detect different situations. For example, to detect situations like "in a car" acceleration, movements and vibration are primary indicators, while audio or light sensors may be used as secondary inputs for situation verification. The situation "in a meeting" relies more on audio, while data from light sensors may raise the confidence of the detection. An increase in the number of used sensors often leads to a lower detection error rate, although the overall error rate for detecting complex situations still remains a major subject of research with situation detection systems.

Networked Embedded Computing

Interconnecting such small, embedded systems allows the collaborative employment of capabilities between different devices in one environment. By working together computer systems can solve problems better or even provide services not practicable otherwise. While simple systems only communicate their sensor values, more powerful systems may use a high-level communication language with known syntax and semantics, which may be extended. Using such sophisticated communication principles overcomes previous technical restrictions and allows a progression from central approaches to truly distributed systems. For example, a house control system needs various input information to regulate temperature, airflow and lights that come from a distributed set of sensing nodes. Simple systems just communicate sensor data to a central computer which in turn sends commands to actuators like sun blinds or heating. More sophisticated systems will decide on room conditions ad hoc, by collaboratively including preference settings from a "personal preference device" worn/carried by humans in the room.

Spontaneous collaboration can also increase the reliability of a system. In an industrial environment more sensors are added to ensure reliable measurements. With today's technology this requires

changes in the application or configuration and often the use of special, proprietary hardware. In a Ubicomp setting any sensor that is supplementary can be used – given that it can prove its operational dependability and reliability of information for the task to be carried out.

Spontaneous ad hoc communication leads to several demands for these new types of networks. First, computers must have a common understanding of format and meaning (ontology) of exchanged information. Rather than using the AI approach and trying to define a complete ontology many Ubicomp systems use a bottom-up process. Communication primitives are defined for embedded Ubicomp systems in one scenario and new primitives are added when new types of systems and scenarios arise. In this case, all devices are not equipped to understand all communication but each device is capable of interpreting and processing identified segments and formats of the communication. To be independent of the used communication primitives some of the embedded Ubicomp systems communicate abstract information. For example, in the

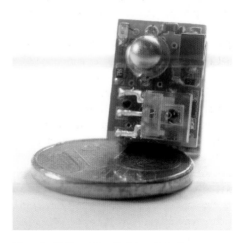

Fig. 3: TecO's Smart-Its with integrated micro-controller, sensors (here light, movement), communication and battery

MediaCup setting (Fig. 1), cups do not communicate their measured sensor information but detected situations such as "cup is filled up," "someone is drinking," or "someone is walking with the cup." Using more abstract descriptions lets the MediaCups communicate with each other and with other devices in the environment, such as coffee machines, door-plates or computer watches, regardless of which MediaCup hardware version is used.

An important technical requirement for communication in Ubicomp comes from the ad hoc and real-time nature of communication. An example for such ad hoc and time-critical communication is user interaction using a wearable device (Fig. 3). Here a user's movements are supervised and – in cases where he is located in front of a screen – interpreted as input.

Typically, networks used in embedded Ubicomp devices are able to provide a configuration-free networking that can instantly communicate to any device in an unknown environment, often in a matter of milliseconds. To save energy and cost they provide rather low bandwidth typically in the range between 10 kbit/s to 400 kbit/s. This bandwidth can be considered fast enough for transferring non-multimedia data as they are commonly used in such embedded computer networks. Existing networks as we know them will not disappear but will build a "backbone" for these new types of networks and will therefore be connected to the embedded computer systems described. Existing services will be able to access information from embedded computers and profit from their information. Consequently, embedded computers take benefit from using resources as information databases or high-speed backend connections.

Technical Platforms

There are currently several technical platforms available that all follow a similar concept. As an overview, the platforms consist of a generic, but simple to extend hardware platform and support for writing software for these platforms. Examples of such platforms are Berkeley Motes [7] and Smart-Its [8] (Fig. 1), to name only two out of a dozen. These platforms, each consisting of hardware and software components, can be seen as the enabling technology for context-aware Ubiquitous Computing applications.

A major task of such devices is the processing of context and communication. To provide these tasks, they contain, in addition to the usual processor and memory, special circuits for connecting to various types of sensors and communication units, and include special features for real-time reaction and energy saving. Embedded Ubicomp computers are intended not to run stand-alone but to be embedded into everyday objects or the environment. To make the computer "disappear" into objects, embedded Ubicomp platforms have to be small in size and of low power consumption, to facilitate integration in a large range of devices and a long runtime (the order of years) respectively. Systems available today are only a few square millimeters in size, with the tiniest ones available being the Mots (6.25 cm^2) and Smart-Its Particle (1 cm^2).

Although for some application areas with less demand on resources, power consumption is low enough to ensure runtimes of a year or more, many applications still incur high-power consumption, especially with high usage of sensors and communication. Upcoming new technology is heading for more integration and less energy consumption, which will lead

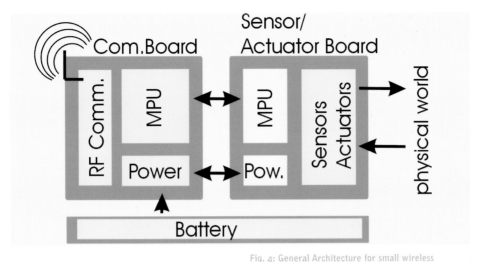

Fig. 4: General Architecture for small wireless embedded devices

to embedded Ubicomp systems in the next few years that are able to operate without battery change over the lifetime of an everyday object.

All the above-mentioned systems follow a similar approach to generate and use information sensed throughout the environment – the context. Physical parameters are detected from the environment with the aid of sensors and additional analog circuitry integrated into these devices. The integrated computing subsystem then processes these physical parameters in order to produce context information. In many applications, detected contexts are then communicated among peers in the environment mostly using Radio Frequency (RF) communication. Context communication has two aspects that this paper investigates. The hardware as enabling technology to produce and communicate context and the software – especially for networking – that enables devices to communicate context among peers.

Small, embedded devices, as introduced above, are often used to retrieve and distribute context information among peers in the environment. They basically contain three central functions:

1. Detecting Context. Devices have to be able to detect physical parameters from the physical world. They therefore need various sensors to detect the physical environment. Sensing physical parameters is best done directly at the place where the effect emerges or where the impact is of interest. This requires the devices to be wireless and consequently to communicate wirelessly. Such wireless and battery driven devices are often embedded in difficult-to-access places. Enhanced robustness and extreme low power consumption enables a runtime of several years, with minimal administration, configuration and maintenance.

2. Computing Context. After detecting basic physical parameters, such devices are required to compute context out of this information. The environment these devices operate in can be manifold and changes rapidly. Devices may therefore not rely on external services but have to be able to compute the context themselves. This requires minimal computing power and memory resources.

3. Communicating Context. The devices have to be able to communicate this information to peers in the environment.

As one of the requirements for such systems is wireless usage, protocols supporting wireless communication are mandatory.

To provide a flexible enabling solution, almost all device architectures of such small, embedded wireless sensor devices are split into two hardware parts: one for supporting sensors and the other for core processing and communications (Fig. 2). The division of the system into two parts allows separation of the two major concerns of such systems: *Perception of Context and Distribution of Context.* This separation is motivated by the main usage of such devices. To detect different types of context, different types of sensors and actuators to interface with the physical world are required. Using specialized sensors enables higher performance in context detection and also appropriate hardware configuration for each of the applications. To separate the concerns of detection from the distribution, a separate board for the sensing allows for independent development of both the detection and the communication/computation tasks.

Conclusion

Today there are only a few prototype applications in existence showing the full potential of embedded Ubicomp systems, including spontaneous communication, autonomous processing and sensing the environment, but more and more enabling systems are being built, providing the basis for such development. Initial efforts are now being made to integrate the technology into business-relevant applications such as supply-chain management, supervision of logistics or factory settings and office settings where a return of investment can be expected.

References

[1] M. Weiser, "The Computer of the 21st Century," Scientific American 265, 3, September 1991, pp. 66-75.

[2] A. Schmidt, "Implicit Human Computer Interaction Through Context," Personal Technologies, Vol 4(2), June 2000.

[3] D. Norman, "The Invisible Computer," MIT Press, 1998.

[4] M. Beigl, H. Gellersen, A. Schmidt, "MediaCups: Experience with Design and Use of Computer-Augmented Everyday Objects," Computer Networks, Special Issue on Pervasive Computing, Elsevier, Vol. 35, No. 4, March 2001, Elsevier, p. 401-409.

[5] Mark Weiser and John Seely Brown, "The Coming Age of Calm Technology," Xerox Parc, 1996.

[6] A. Schmidt, A. Takaluoma and J. Mäntyjärvi, "Context-Aware Telephony over WAP," Personal Technologies 4(4), December 2000.

[7] K. S. J. Pister, J. M. Kahn, B. E. Boser, "Smart Dust: Wireless Networks of Millimeter-scale Sensor Nodes," University of California, USA 1998.

[8] M. Beigl, H. Gellersen. "Smart-Its: An Embedded Platform for Smart Objects," Smart Objects Conference (sOc) 2003, Grenoble, France.

New types of computer systems are arising in Ubiquitous Computing (Ubicomp) that are invisibly embedded into our everyday environment. Such computers will change the way we make use of computing: Rather than explicitly being the "user" of a computer a human will implicitly profit from services running between computers hidden in mundane objects or the environment without even taking notice of them.

Interest in the use of systems obeying the laws of quantum mechanics to perform computing tasks has been rapidly expanding over the past two decades. Such Quantum Computers would make the implementation of new algorithms possible, performing certain tasks much more efficiently than a classical computer. In this article we give an introduction to the field of quantum computing, and discuss the current state of the art in the development of quantum hardware, especially with respect to trapped ions and neutral atoms.

Andrew Daley is a PhD student working in the research group of Peter Zoller in the Institute for Theoretical Physics at the University of Innsbruck and in the Institute for Quantum Optics and Quantum Information of the Austrian Academy of Sciences in Innsbruck, Austria. He graduated from the University of Auckland, New Zealand, in 2002 with the degree of Master of Science with First Class Honors in Physics, and his current work involves the application of atoms in optical lattices to quantum computing.

Ignacio Cirac is Director of the Theory Division at the Max Planck Institute for Quantum Optics, Germany, and Honorary Professor at the Technical University of Munich, Germany. His research interests include quantum optics, atomic physics and quantum information, in particular implementation of quantum information processing with quantum optical systems.

Peter Zoller is a professor in the University of Innsbruck's Institute for Theoretical Physics and at the Institute for Quantum Optics and Quantum Information of the Austrian Academy of Sciences in Innsbruck. His research interests include quantum optics, atomic physics and quantum information, in particular implementation of quantum information processing with quantum optical systems.

Andrew Daley, Ignacio Cirac, Peter Zoller:

The Development of Quantum Hardware for Quantum Computing

THE DEVELOPMENT OF QUANTUM HARDWARE FOR QUANTUM COMPUTING

Introduction

The development of technology and our understanding of the physical world are necessarily deeply intertwined. New understanding in physics leads to the development of new technology, which in turn provides both new tools for studying the physical world, and new challenges for physicists wishing to improve on this technology. In this sense, the impact over the last century of quantum mechanics – the physics of microscopic particles and systems – has been extreme. In the last two decades alone the explosion of technology based on lasers and semiconductor electronics has been staggering, and these devices are now not only central to our daily lives (in the form of computers, entertainment systems, and medical and industrial equipment), but are also important tools in all branches of physics.

One product of this, the development of information technology, stands as one of the crowning intellectual achievements of the last century. However, the development of this technology now brings us back to quantum mechanics as we wonder how the current rate of development in computer equipment is to be either maintained or surpassed in the future. Since the mid 1960s, Moore's law [1] has accurately described the growth in the number of transistors present on manufactured chips, with this number doubling approximately every couple of years. As the number of transistors grows, the size of each transistor decreases, which contributes to an increasing processing speed. But as the size shrinks, these devices come closer to a regime where their quantum mechanical nature may play a more significant role in their function. This will create significant technical challenges

for classical computing, and provides a clear ultimate limit to the development of computer technology in the classical sense: A transistor cannot be made smaller than the atoms out of which it is constructed. More importantly though, it provides a challenge: Could the quantum mechanical properties of microscopic systems be used directly to create a new, more powerful computing technology?

This question has interested rapidly growing numbers of physicists over the last 20 years, and it is already well known that a "quantum computer" could make use of the special properties of quantum mechanics to perform certain tasks much more efficiently than its existing classical counterparts [2]. And while how best to go about building the required quantum hardware still remains the hottest topic in this field, the growing collection of theoretical proposals and proof of principle experimental demonstrations give us a great deal of hope for the future of this technology.

The potential benefits are great. Quantum computers would provide the opportunity for technology to advance past the restrictions of Moore's Law, for computer science to deal with problems previously considered to be too complex for classical computers to solve, and for physicists to gain further insights into quantum mechanics and its manifestation in nature.

In this article we give a brief introduction to quantum mechanics and quantum computing, and describe how it is that quantum computers could improve upon our existing technology. We then survey the current state of the art in the design of quantum hardware, especially technology based on trapped ions and neutral atoms.

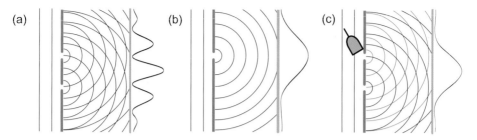

Fig. 1: A single particle passing through two narrow slits. (a) The probability distribution for the position of the particle on the screen if we do not know through which slit the particle passed: We observe a series of maxima and minima formed by quantum interference. (b) The probability distribution if only one slit is open: We observe a diffraction curve from a single slit, and no interference. (c) The probability distribution if the particle can pass through either slit, but we measure through which slit it passes: Again, there is no quantum interference, and the probability distribution is a sum of those from the two individual slits.

Quantum Mechanics

Quantum Mechanics was developed in the early 20th century as physicists sought to explain strange phenomena that had been observed in electromagnetic radiation, and in the properties of atoms and small particles. After the success of Planck's law of *blackbody radiation* in 1900, and Bohr's model of the atom in 1915, the concepts of quantum mechanics were developed by many physicists, including Schrödinger, Heisenberg and Einstein.

Quantum mechanics is inherently a statistical theory. It describes the preparation of a system in a particular *state*, and then predicts what the probability for different outcomes will be if some observable property of the system is measured. What is striking about this theory is that it allows for different probabilities to interfere constructively or destructively with one another, as waves do in classical physics. For example, consider a situation in which a single particle of light ("photon"), or any other microscopic particle is prepared in a quantum state where it travels towards two small openings, and if it passes through either of the openings, it will strike a screen where its position is measured (Fig. 1). According to quantum mechanics, a microscopic particle in this experiment acts like a wave, so that if we

do not know through which opening it passes, then the probability distribution will have maxima and minima as shown in Fig. 1a. This distribution can be measured by preparing the state and measuring the system many times. The pattern of maxima and minima which arises is exactly the same pattern that we would expect for light waves passing through a double slit. If we cover one opening (Fig. 1b), then the pattern disappears.

However, in the case of classical waves, we think of the pattern of maxima and minima arising because different parts of the wave pass through each of the slits, and then later interfere with one another. For classical waves there is always more than one particle involved in the process. By contrast, the probability distribution here arises even when only one particle passes through at a time.

The pattern of maxima and minima comes about because quantum mechanics says that the state of the particle exists in a superposition of the two possibilities – that it passed through the upper slit or the lower slit – and that these possibilities interfere with one another. This works physically as if the single particle had really passed through *both* slits! This theory can be tested by taking a measuring device (a microscope, for example), and trying to determine which slit the particle passed through before it hit the screen. If we measure with certainty which slit the particle passed through, then the quantum superposition state *collapses* into a single possibility, and the interference pattern disappears (Fig. 1c). In this sense we can really change the state of a system by measuring it!

The superposition of possible states in quantum system does not just occur in the path that a particle travels – superpositions of possibilities can occur for any property of a system described by quantum mechanics. This is also not restricted to a single particle. If there are multiple particles in a system, each of which can exist in several possible states, then the system can exist in a superposition of all of the possible combinations of the possible states for the individual particles. The implications of superposition states in quantum mechanics were found unintuitive from the outset. Despite the success of quantum mechanics in quantitatively predicting experimentally measured properties of small systems (in particular spectroscopic properties of atoms – the results of probing atoms with electromagnetic radiation), which is essentially unparalleled in physics, many physicists working in this area have expressed concern with the related philosophical questions it raises.

Famous examples include Schrödinger's construction of a thought-experiment in which a cat could be potentially placed as in a superposition state of "alive" and "dead," and Einstein's observation that two particles could be "entangled," so that no matter how distant they were from one another, a measurement on one could provide information and hence change the state of the other. These paradoxes have had significant impact on our understanding of the microscopic world.

The first of these, our non-observation of superposition states for large ("classical") objects such as Schrödinger's cat, is now generally explained by "decoherence" – the process of information about the state of the system leaking into the environment, causing a superposition of states of large objects to collapse and interference to disappear, as if we had directly measured the system. However, by contrast, it has been demonstrated experimentally that "entanglement" of multiple, separated particles is not only possible, but can be applied for practical use in the context of quantum computation.

Quantum Computing

A classical computer takes information, usually as a physical string of ones and zeros, i.e., *bits*, (such as electrical signals which can be at two different voltage levels), and manipulates it to produce an outcome, usually encoded as a different string of bits (Fig. 2). A quantum computer, on the other hand, would take information encoded on a quantum state, manipulate it according to the laws of quantum mechanics, and produce a new quantum state, from which information can be obtained by measurements. The difference between the two lies in the ability of a quantum state to represent the superposition of many possible classical states at once. A quantum bit, or *qubit* is not just a simple "0" or "1," but instead any possible superposition of "0" and "1," with complex numbers as coefficients. This is illustrated in Fig. 3a as a location on the surface of a 3D sphere, the "Bloch Sphere."

Of course, not only can each qubit be in a superposition state, but the system as a whole can be in a superposition of all possible combinations of qubit states at once. This is precisely what gives rise to

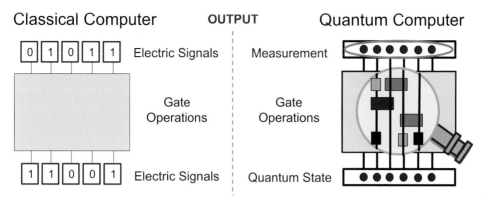

Fig. 2: A classical computer takes classical physical information, normally as a string of ones and zeros ("bits") characterised by electrical signals. It uses electronic circuitry to process this information, performing a set of pre-determined calculations, which can be broken down into "gate operations" in which the state of some bits is changed based on the known value of other bits. The computer then outputs the final result, again as a string of definite ones and zeros. A quantum computer takes a quantum state as an input, which can be a superposition of many possible states (see Fig. 3). It then performs gate operations, manipulating the state of certain qubits dependent on the state of others, and outputs the result as another quantum superposition state. This state must then be measured to extract information from this result.

the power of a quantum computer: Every possible state can be stored and processed in parallel with all the others (Fig. 3b). Moreover, the number of possible states that can be present in the superposition at once is huge – if we have N qubits then there are 2^N possible states in the super-position. If we had a quantum computer with 300 qubits, we would have 2^{300} possible states, or approximately the same number as the total number of atoms in the universe. Gate operations in a quantum computer – the single elements that make up a computation – then consist of operations on single qubits or two qubits, as they would in a simple classical computer. Two examples are illustrated in

Fig. 4. In the first, a *rotation* known as the Hadamard gate is performed on the state of a single qubit, and in the second a control NOT operation is performed on two qubits. The latter consists of swapping the state of the "Target qubit," 0_1 if and only if the "Control qubit" is in the "1" state. These gate operations are part of a minimal set which would make it possible to perform arbitrary computations on a chain of qubits. Combinations of such gate operations into quantum algorithms have a large potential impact on a class of problems considered to be hard in Computer Science. While everyday computational problems such as adding or multiplying numbers scale favorably with the

Fig. 3: Classical and Quantum Registers:
(a) A quantum bit can exist in a superposition state of "0" and "1."
(b) Superposition states allow quantum registers to store all possible values simultaneously.

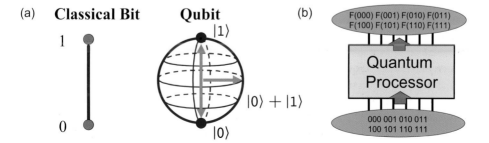

Single Qubit Gates

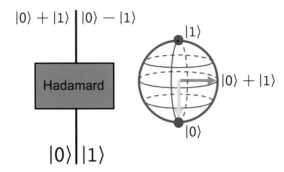

Fig. 4a: A single-qubit gate: The Hadamard operation.

Two-Qubit Gates

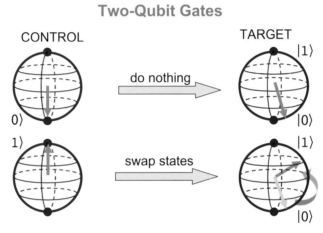

Fig. 4b: A two-qubit gate: The control-NOT operation (see text for more information)

size of the number n (they require on the order of $\log(n)$ operations), some scale less favorably (requiring on order n^k operations for some exponent k). One of the best examples of such operations is *factoring* a number. As a guide, if the fastest available supercomputers take about a year to factor a 150-digit number, then the same computers would take approximately the lifetime of the universe to factor a 400-digit number. The acceptance that factoring scales in this way is the basis of public key encryption systems, which are used every day for secure transactions made over the Internet. The security of the system relies on the fact that the "public key," essentially a large num-

ber, cannot be factored to find the "private key." However, as was first shown by Peter Shor in 1994 [3], an algorithm exists for a quantum computer with which a number could be factored using of the order of $\log(n)$ operations. This algorithm makes use of the special property that quantum computers are very good at finding the period of a periodic function, which can be related by number theory to factoring a number. If a quantum computer could be built which, using this algorithm, could factor a 150-digit number in about a month, then the same computer would take a few years to factor a 400-digit number. The main restriction on the algorithms designed for a quantum computer, which is overcome in the case of Shor's algorithm, is that when we measure the output state, the measurement *collapses* the superposition state. We thus only obtain one usable result, and so the algorithm has to be well designed to make use of the intrinsic power we have already discussed. Quantum algorithms are also difficult to engineer, because they are mathematically more complex and much less intuitive than algorithms for a classical computer. However, in addition to Shor's algorithm there are several other proposed algorithms, the most notable of which is Grover's search algorithm; using it the time required to search a list of n possible solutions to a problem scales as the order of $n^{1/2}$, instead of n on a classical computer. There is a high probability that more such algorithms will be found in the future, and together with them a wide array of applications for quantum computers.

Quantum Hardware: Basic Requirements and the Current State of the Art

The challenge of building a quantum computer is that of manipulating a large array of microscopic objects coherently, under the laws of quantum mechanics. The main difficulty with this arises in the fact that the objects must be as isolated from their environment as possible to prevent decoherence – the leaking of information from the quantum system that acts like a measurement process to destroy quantum interference. This leaking of information can also be seen as noise from the environment randomizing the state of the qubit.

As larger quantum computing systems are developed, we will essentially have small versions of "Schrödinger's Cat," i.e., relatively large systems which must be maintained in a coherent quantum superposition state. The larger they become, the

more difficult it will be to maintain the isolation. The basic criteria for the quantum hardware required to do quantum computing were formalized by Di Vincenzo [4] and are as follows:

1. There must be a scalable physical system with well-characterized qubits. We must have a quantum system consisting of an array of objects; these must have two available quantum states and be physically well understood. It should also be possible to make this system as large as is necessary to implement useful quantum algorithms. Typically this is of the order of 1000 Qubits, although for special purposes, such as simulation of other quantum systems, this number could be much smaller.

2. It must be possible to initialize the system to a simple feducial state. We must be able to place the system in a well-known initial state, for example, all qubits "0."

3. The decoherence times must be long, much longer than the gate time. The system must be isolated well enough from its environment that the environmental noise does not randomize the state of qubits before the quantum computation has been performed. The natural decoherence time can be improved upon to some extent using quantum error correction codes, at the expense of adding more qubits and more gate operations.

4. There must be a universal set of quantum gates. We require means to implement a sufficient set of gate operations that by using these gates we can perform any arbitrary combination of single qubit rotations and two-qubit gates.

5. There must be a qubit-specific measurement capability. This is required to read out the quantum state after manipulation of the system.

There are many existing theoretical proposals as to how such quantum hardware
could be constructed, and these proposals
are at various states in their experimental
implementations. Very successful early on
was the demonstration of quantum gates
using Nuclear Magnetic Resonance (NMR)
techniques with large molecules, and
Shor's algorithm has been used to factor
the number 15 as a proof of principle
exercise in this system [5]. Meanwhile,
two-qubit gates have already been demonstrated with trapped ions and neutral
atoms [6], and enormous progress has
been made in various solid-state devices,
especially qubits constructed using superconducting junctions. We discuss these
physical implementations below, focusing
in more detail on trapped ions and neutral
atoms as two example case studies. Regularly revised information on the state of
the art for all of these implementations
and to what extent they meet Di Vincenzo's
criteria is available in the USA Quantum
Information Science and Technology Roadmap [7].

i) Trapped Ions

There has been significant recent progress
in use of trapped ions (e.g., Ca^{2+} ions –
Calcium atoms with two electrons remov-
ed) for quantum computing purposes [8].
Such ions can be held in strings using
electric fields inside a vacuum chamber
(see Fig. 5), where they are typically separated by distances of a few micrometers.
Each ion in the string represents one
qubit, with the "0" or the "1" state encoded on two different long-lived electronic
states of the ion, and these states can be
initially set to "0" using techniques of
laser cooling and optical pumping, which
involve careful manipulation of the electronic state of the ions using laser light
of specific frequencies. Inside the vacuum
chamber, a string of ions is well isolated
from its environment. The main sources

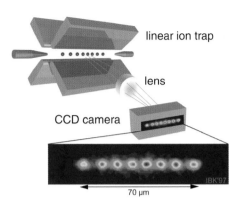

Fig. 5: A Paul Trap, in which a chain of ions is trap-ped
by a series of electrodes, which produce well-control-
led electric fields. The chain can be imaged on a CCD
camera by shining laser light on the ions at the correct
frequency, causing them to fluoresce. The image shown
here is from the group of Rainer Blatt in Innsbruck.
These ions can be addressed individually using tightly
focused laser beams, and their electronic states can be
manipulated to store qubit information.

of decoherence depend on the experimental setup but are typically randomization
of qubit states through interactions with
fluctuating magnetic fields, and spontaneous emission events, where an ion
absorbs a photon from the laser beam
and emits it in a random direction (the
normal interactions, via stimulated emission, involve photons being emitted back
into the same beam). While individual
qubit states can be rotated independently
of the others using tightly focused laser
beams of the correct frequencies, two-
qubit gate operations require more complicated operations.

All of the two-qubit gates demonstrated
to date follow a proposal made by Ignacio
Cirac and Peter Zoller in 1995, in which
information about the state of one qubit
is transferred to the state of the collective
motion (oscillations) of the entire string
in the trap, using a tightly focused laser.
Operations using another laser can then
be made on another qubit in the string,
dependent on the state of the collective
motion. Essentially, the oscillations of the
string of atoms are used as a "data bus"
for the computation!

There have been many successful demonstrations of two-qubit gates in ion traps [9], along with the publicly heralded demonstration of teleportation of a quantum state from one ion to another in 2004 by research groups at the National Institute for Standards and Technology in Boulder, Colorado, and at the University of Innsbruck in Austria [10].

Work is now in progress to scale up the number of qubits in the system, but fundamental limits to the length of the string that can be properly manipulated in this way means that a more futuristic design for an ion-trap quantum computer will have to involve separate storage and processing areas (see Fig. 6). Test versions of such devices are already under costruction, and while scaling ion traps to large numbers of ions is a significant task, the future of this technology looks very promising.

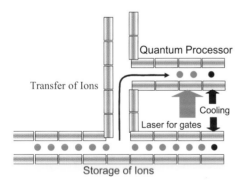

Fig. 6: Futuristic Ion Trap design: The trap setup consists of separate areas for storage of ions (with their encoded qubit information) and for performing gate operations. The ions are trapped and moved around the system by modifying the electric fields being used to trap the ions. Any one or two qubits may be selected from the storage area, and moved to the processor, where lasers are used to perform gate operations. At each stage, the system may be cooled using additional lasers, normally focussed on an additional ion, which acts as a refrigerator to sympathetically cool the rest of the chain.

■

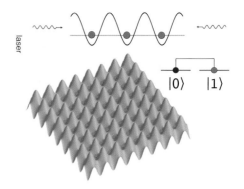

Fig. 7: Neutral Atoms can be trapped in "optical lattices," arrays of microtraps formed from standin waves of laser light, where the potential energy of the atoms depends on the intensity of the light. This system can be used for quantum computing, with qubits encoded on long-lived electronic states of the atoms, which are arranged in an array with one atom in each microtrap.

ii) Neutral Atoms

Possible technology for quantum computing with neutral atoms is similar in spirit to ideas with ions. Unlike ions, though, neutral atoms must be stored in magnetic microtraps [11], or in traps formed from laser light. Perhaps the most experimentally advanced of these ideas is the use of Bose-Einstein condensates (a new state of matter in which all atoms exist in the same motional quantum state) as a dense source of cold atoms which can be loaded into arrays of microtraps formed from standing waves of laser light (see Fig. 7). These arrays are known as optical lattices, and work because the standing waves have maxima and minima in intensity, and, depending on the frequency of the light, the atoms will be pushed either towards the dark or the light spots in the standing waves. Moreover, if the traps are sufficiently deep, then repulsion between atoms can be used to arrange the atoms so that there is exactly one atom in every site of the lattice (Fig. 7), a state that can be improved by various filteringtechniques. This state was recently produced in a seminal experiment by Immanuel Bloch and his collaborators [12], and

71

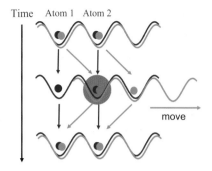

Time   Atom 1   Atom 2

move

Fig. 8: Two-qubit quantum gates for atoms in optical lattices can be engineered using collisions between the atoms themselves. Here, the lattice potential is shifted for one qubit state, so that neighboring atoms are brought together or not, dependent upon their qubit state.

forms the basis of the qubit register for quantum computing. As with ions, qubit states for atoms in an optical lattice can be encoded on two long-lived electronic states of the atoms in each microtrap, and the atoms are well isolated from their environment except for small decoherence effects due to field fluctuations, and spontaneous emissions of photons. Various proposals exist for performing two-qubit gates. One recently demonstrated in an experiment was based on collisions between neighboring atoms: the lattice was shifted for only one qubit state, so that atoms on neighboring sites would come together and interact if and only if the one on the left was in state "0" and the one on the right was in state "1" (see Fig. 8). This gate, known as a quantum phase gate, can, like the controlled-not gate discussed earlier, play the role of a two-qubit gate in a universal set.

There are now several experimental groups around the world, and many theoretical proposals for manipulating atoms in optical lattices for use in quantum computation [13]. Unlike with trapped ions, scalability of this system is not a problem – tens of thousands of atoms could be produced in a regular array for use as a quantum register. However, these atoms

cannot be simply addressed using tightly focussed laser beams because the separation between neighboring atoms (several hundred nanometers) is too small. Thus the requirement of individual qubit addressing is a difficult task to fulfil in this system.

However, atoms in optical lattices have another related use as a quantum simulator: these systems resemble many lattice-structure systems from solid state physics, and can be used to model those systems in a form of "special-purpose" quantum computing. Because there is great control over the lattice properties (it is created using laser beams), and because the states of the atoms can be probed using light, it is possible to make many measurements which cannot be made on real solid state systems, potentially giving us great insight to phenomena such as high-temperature super-conductivity.

iii) Superconducting Qubits

Another possible technology which may find application in quantum computing is circuits consisting of superconducting material. Such circuits are fabricated using thin film technology, and already have many applications, for example in the context of Superconducting Quantum Interference Devices (SQUIDs) used to make sensitive magnetic field measurements. There are various possibilities for encoding qubits using such circuits, exploiting the quantum coherence of a superconductor, where pairs of electrons (Cooper pairs) are *condensed* into the same quantum state. Possibilities include encoding information on the number of superconducting Cooper pairs (called a *charge* qubit), in the direction of a current and related magnetic field through a loop (a *flux* qubit) or in so-called oscillatory states (a *phase* qubit). Gates operations can be performed using Microwave or DC

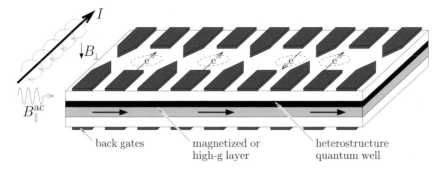

Fig. 9: An array of qubits encoded on the "spin" of electrons confined in quantum dots. The plates on the top surface (green) control the lateral confinement of the electrons, and the voltage on these can be adjusted to increase the interaction between two electrons by moving them closer together (e.g., here the two quantum dots on the right are coupled, but those on the left are decoupled). This makes possible two-qubit gate operations. The "back gates" can be used to pull the electrons closer to the central layer, which increases the coupling to applied magnetic fields and allows single-qubit gate operations to be performed.

pulses, and qubits in these systems could be measured using well-established devices such as SQUIDs, and Single Electron Transistors (SETs). Scaling of these systems to large arrays of integrated qubits is promising, but is technologically challenging because the quantum coherence is limited by defects in junctions between superconductors, and relies upon extremely accurate nano-fabrication. However, the small-size scales of these solid state devices result in a natural speed advantage for gate times, if these can be made shorter than the decoherence (dephasing) time scales.

iv) Quantum Dots and Solid State Spin Qubits

There are many possibilities for the use of electrons in solid state systems to encode qubit information. Individual electrons can be trapped and manipulated, for example, in so-called quantum dots, isolated islands separated from a conductor, which are fabricated using epitaxy or chemical synthesis [14]. Qubits are encoded on the quantum state of the electron "spin" (the direction of the electron's intrinsic magnetic moment), known as a "spin qubit," or on the existence ("1") or non-existence ("0") of an electron or an electron-hole pair in a quantum dot,

which is called a "charge qubit." Depending on the specific type of device used, these qubits can be manipulated using electrical gates (carefully positioned conductors near the quantum dots) or optically using lasers.

These systems are early in their development, and basic coherent operations have only recently been observed experimentally. While much is also still uncertain as to what coherence times are possible, there has been an enormous amount of development in technology for fabrication of solid state systems in the past ten years, providing much hope for the future of this technology. The major advantages of this approach are that, like superconducting qubits, the size scales involved in the system create a natural speed advantage for gate operations compared with ion traps and neutral atoms.

v) Nuclear-Magnetic Resonance

In NMR-based approaches, qubits are encoded on chemically distinct nuclear spins in a liquid phase, or on crystallographically distinct nuclear spins in a solid state system. These spins may be set and manipulated using radio-frequency-radiation, provided by NMR spectrometers which have been developed over the past fifty years for use in structure determination and imaging in chemistry, medicine, and materials science. The early success of liquid-phase NMR, where Shor's algorithm was implemented on a 7-qubit system has not rapidly led to further extensions, owing to fundamental limits in scaling these liquid-phase systems up to large numbers of qubits. However, recent proposals for solid state NMR quantum computing provide interesting future possibilities in this direction [15].

vi) Quantum Computing with Photons

Qubit states can also be stored on photon states, for example via the existence or nonexistence of a photon in a high-finesse optical cavity. Such systems are particularly useful in combination with qubits stored using neutral atoms present inside the cavity, where information can then be transferred between the atom state and the photon state through application of an appropriate laser pulse from the side of the cavity. If the photon is allowed to escape from the cavity it can be deterministically "caught" in another cavity by the application of a second laser pulse. In this way, gate operations can be performed among a network of such cavities.

Two-qubit gates have also been demonstrated using linear optics technology, in which the qubit state encoded on a photon (either the physical path of the photon or the polarisation state) can be manipulated using normal optical elements such as mirrors and beamsplitters. In most proposals and current experiments, two qubits gates performed on such photonic qubits are induced by changing the state using carefully designed measurements, as opposed to a direct interaction.

Photon-based quantum computing, even with a few photons, would have distinct advantages as part of quantum networking and quantum communication protocols, where information can be transmitted using photons among a distributed network of nodes.

vii) The Future: Error Correction, Quantum Networks, and Quantum Communication

One of the most important requirements for any implementation of quantum computing in the future will be quantum error correction mechanisms. Even in classical computing, mechanisms are required to make systems fault tolerant in the event that a bit is randomly flipped. The idea is that by encoding a single piece of information on several physical bits, redundancy can be built into the system so that if any one bit is wrong, the information will still be accurately extracted from the others. The nature of a qubit makes such fault tolerance more complex in the context of quantum computing, with schemes required to correct for the effects of environmental noise which can make any arbitrary adjustment to the state of a qubit. However, quantum information theorists have produced several schemes to introduce the necessary redundancy into qubit encoding, including a whole class of schemes which allow the transfer of classical error correction schemes into quantum systems. The implementation of such codes is now an important goal in experimental implementations of quantum computing. For more information, see John Preskill's *Physics Today* article on decoherence and fault tolerance in quantum computing [16].

Another challenge for the future of quantum computing technologies is the production of quantum networks – the ability to take several small-scale quantum computing devices and link them together, transferring quantum information among the nodes of the network. Such distributed networks would offer the ability to combine the strengths of different quantum computing technologies, and would facilitate the scaling of quantum computers to larger numbers of qubits. A quantum network fundamentally requires the ability to transfer quantum information from one place to another – which is limited in quantum mechanics, as the duplication of an unknown state is forbidden. However, transfer of such information with the original copy being destroyed, i.e., quantum teleportation, has been recently demonstrated in experiments for photon states and electronic states of ions.

Quantum Computer A

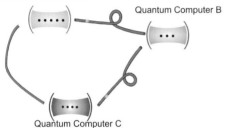
Quantum Computer B

Quantum Computer C

Fig. 10: A quantum network: quantum information (qubit states) is transferred among several separated nodes, each of which consists of a quantum computing device able to store and process such information.

The clearest route to a distributed network is provided by photon-based quantum computing, in which nodes consisting of quantum memories and small quantum processors are linked by "flying qubits" in the form of photons, which vary quantum information between the nodes [17].

These peculiar properties of quantum mechanics that make transfer of quantum information difficult and complicated also have their own technological application in the secure transfer of classical information. Quantum Communication, as this is known, will permit the generation of secret keys for encoding messages that cannot be intercepted by an eavesdropper. The fundamental principle involved is

quantum measurement – if person "A" sends information to person "B" encoded on the quantum state of a photon, then an eavesdropper must make a measurement on the photon in order to determine its state. However, such a measurement changes the state of the photon in a way that person "B" can detect and avoid. And the eavesdropper also cannot copy the photon and forward the original photon to person "B," as this is prohibited by quantum mechanics. Quantum cryptography with photons propagating in free space and optical fibers has already been successfully demonstrated, and there are even several companies commercially producing systems for such communication over distances of up to one hundred kilometers.

Conclusion and Outlook

In the end, it is always hard to predict the impact that any new technology will have in the future. History is covered with examples of visionaries who have tried to make such predictions, and found that advances in technology have either fallen well short of, or greatly surpassed those predictions. A well-cited example of the latter was the comment published in 1949 in the journal *Popular Mechanics* shortly after the construction of the ENIAC, one of the world's first computers: "Where a calculator on the ENIAC is equipped with 18,000 vacuum tubes and weighs 30 tons, computers in the future may have only 1000 vacuum tubes and perhaps weigh one and a half tons." This writer certainly could not have comprehended the incredible advance in technology that has occurred since that time.

While the current experimental systems have only a few qubits and gate operations compared with the tens to thousands of qubits and more than 10^6 operations which are required for useful algorithm implementations, the use of these systems as quantum simulators is likely to be significant even in the next few years. Moreover, improvements in current technology are extremely rapid, and although there are enormous technical and engineering challenges to the construction of large-scale quantum computers, no fundamental obstacles have yet been foreseen.

In the meantime, the quest to build large-scale arrays of isolated qubits will be a challenge to physicists, while the quest to develop new algorithms and methods to use such devices will challenge computer scientists and quantum information theorists. We stand to learn a lot about such quantum systems and their interaction with their environment in the process, which will no doubt lead to technological advances that is currently impossible to foresee. Whether large-scale quantum computing has an enormous direct impact on the world or not, its investigation is an exciting branch of science, and stands to bring about huge benefits to technology in the 21st century.

Acknowledgements: Work in Innsbruck is supported by the Austrian Science Foundation, EU Networks, and the Institute for Quantum Information. The authors thank R. Blatt for permission to reprint Fig. 5, and D. Loss for permission to reprint Fig. 9. The concept for Fig. 1 was based on similar drawings in presentations given by A. Ekert and R. Werner.

References

[1] For more information on Moore's law, see http://www.intel.com/labs/eml/.

[2] For more detailed information, see M. A. Neilson and I. L. Chuang, "Quantum Computation and Quantum Information," First Edition, Cambridge University Press, Cambridge, UK (2000), and references therein.

[3] Ibid.

[4] D. P. DiVincenzo, "The Physical Implementation of Quantum Computation," Fortschritte der Physik 48, (2000), p. 771.

[5] L. M. K. Vandersypen, M. Steffen, G. Breyto, C. Yannoui, M.H. Sherwood, and I. L. Chuang, "Experimental Realization of Shor's Quantum Factoring Algorithm using Nuclear Magnetic Resonance," Nature 414, (1999),p. 883.

[6] J. I. Cirac and P. Zoller, "New Frontiers in Quantum Information with Atoms and Ions," Physics Today 57, (2004), p. 38.

[7] "Quantum Information Science and Technology Roadmap," http://qist.lanl.gov.

[8] J. I. Cirac and P. Zoller, "New Frontiers in Quantum Information with Atoms and Ions," Physics Today 57, (2004), p. 38.

[9] F. Schmidt-Kaler, H. Häffner, M. Riebe, S. Gulde, G.P.T. Lancaster, T. Deuschle, C. Becher, C. F. Roos, J. Eschner, and R. Blatt, "Realization of the Cirac–Zoller controlled-NOT Quantum Gate," Nature 422, (2003), p. 408; and D. Leibfried, B. DeMarco, V. Meyer, D. Lucas, M. Barrett, J. Britton, W. M. Itano, B. Jelenkovi, C. Langer, T. Rosenband, D. J. Wineland, "Experimental demonstration of a robust, high-fidelity geometric two ion-qubit phase gate," Nature 422, (2003), p. 412.

[10] M. Riebe, H. Häffner, C. F. Roos, W. Hänsel, J. Benhelm, G. P. T. Lancaster, T. W. Körberl, C. Becher, F. Schmidt-Kaler, D. F. V. James, and R. Blatt, "Deter-ministic quantum teleportation with atoms," Nature 429, (2004), p. 734; and M. D. Barrett, J. Chiaverini, T. Schaetz, J. Britton, W. M. Itano, J. D. Jost, E. Knill, C. Langer, D. Leibfried, R. Ozeri, and D. J. Wineland, "Deterministic quantum teleportation of atomic qubits," Nature 429, (2004), p. 737.

[11] M. Greiner, O. Mandel, T. Esslinger, T. W. Hänsch, and I. Bloch, "Quantum phase transition from a superfluid to a Mott insulator in a gas of ultracold atoms," Nature 415, (2002), p. 39.

[12] M. Greiner, O. Mandel, T. Esslinger, T. W. Hänsch, and I. Bloch, "Quantum phase transition from a superfluid to a Mott insulator in a gas of ultracold atoms," Nature 415, (2002), p. 39; and M. Greiner, O. Mandel, T. W. Hänsch, and I. Bloch, "Collapse and revival of the matter wave field of a Bose–Einstein condensate," Nature 419, (2002), p. 51.

[13] D. Jaksch and P. Zoller, "The Cold Atom Hubbard Toolbox," Annals of Physics 315, (2005), p. 51, available at http://www.arxiv.org/abs/cond-mat/0410614.

[14] V. Cerletti, W. A. Coish, O. Gywat and D. Loss, "Recipes for spin-based quantum computing", preprint available at http://www.arxiv.org/abs/condmat/0412028 and M. Kroutvar, Y. Ducommun, D. Heiss, M. Bichler, D. Schuh, G. Abstreiter, and J. J. Finley, "Optically programmable electron spin memory using semiconductor quantum dots," Nature 432, (2004), p. 83.

[15] "Quantum Information Science and Technology Roadmap," http://qist.lanl.gov.

[16] John Preskill, "Battling Decoherence: The Fault-Tolerant Quantum Computer," Physics Today 24, (1999), p. 24.

[17] C. Monroe, "Quantum information processing with atoms and photons,"Nature 416, (2002), p. 238.

As a guide, if the fastest available supercomputers take about a year to factor a 150-digit number, then the same computers would take approximately the lifetime of the universe to factor a 400-digit number. However, as was first shown by Peter Shor in 1994, an algorithm exists for a quantum computer with which a number could be factored using of the order of log(n) operations. This algorithm makes use of the special property that quantum computers are very good at finding the period of a periodic function, which can be related by number theory to factoring a number. If a quantum computer could be built which, using this algorithm, could factor a 150-digit number in about a month, then the same computer would take a few years to factor a 400-digit number.

the architecture

intersections of real and virtual space in an authentic architecture of the digital era

Buildings were once materialized drawings, but now, increasingly, they are materialized digital information – designed and documented on computer-aided design systems, fabricated with digitally controlled machinery, and assembled on site with the assistance of digital positioning and placement equipment. Within the framework of digitally mediated design and construction we can precisely quantify the design content and the construction content of a project, and go on to define complexity as the ratio of added design content to added construction content. This paper argues that the emerging architecture of the digital era is characterized by high levels of complexity, and that this enables more sensitive and inflected response to the exigencies of site, program and expressive intention than was generally possible within the framework of industrial modernism.

William J. Mitchell is Professor of Architecture and Media Arts and Sciences, Head of the Media Arts and Sciences Program, and former Dean of the School of Architecture and Planning at MIT. He previously taught at UCLA, Cambridge and Harvard universities. His publications include City of Bits (1995), E-topia (1999), and Me ++ : The Cyborg Self and the Networked City (2003). He is a Fellow of the Royal Australian Institute of Architects and Fellow of the American Academy of Arts and Sciences.

William J. Mitchell:

constructing an authentic architecture of the digital era

CONSTRUCTING AN AUTHENTIC ARCHITECTURE OF THE DIGITAL ERA

Introduction

Perhaps you have wondered why the shapes of buildings seem to be getting more complex. Conceivably, it could be nothing more profound than an arbitrary flicker of architectural fashion. But it is worth asking whether the difference between, say, Frank Gehry's Bilbao Guggenheim and the characteristically rectangular slabs and towers of the late 20th century is due to something more fundamental? Does the curved shape of London's Swiss Re Building, the twisted profile of New York's proposed Freedom Tower, or the non-repetitive roof structure of the British Museum courtyard represent some significant change in the conditions of production of architecture?

The shift, I suggest, is a direct outcome of new conditions created by the digital revolution. Buildings were once materialized drawings, but now, increasingly, they are materialized digital information – designed with the help of computer-aided design systems, fabricated by means of digitally controlled machinery, put together on site with the assistance of digital layout and positioning devices, and generally inseparable from flows of information through global computer networks. Many architects have simply exploited digital technology to reduce the time and cost of producing buildings in the conventionally modernist mode, much as architects of the early industrial revolution took advantage of mass-production to inexpensively proliferate the ornament that had previously been created by craftsmen. But others have recognized that the digital revolution has opened up new domains of architectural form for exploration, and they have seized the opportunity to produce projects that break the old rules.

Breaking the Old Rules

To see precisely how new formal possibilities emerge from the interplay of information and materiality, we need to do some numbers. It will be helpful to begin with a homely example that should be familiar to anyone who has ever operated a computer graphics or computer-aided design system. Consider the task of inputting a *circle*. You need to give a circle command and specify three numbers – usually an *x-coordinate*, a *y-coordinate* and a *radius*, though Euclid tells us that there are other, equivalent ways to convey the same information. You can enter the circle's three parameter values by typing the numbers, or by graphically selecting and sizing a circle with a mouse, but the result is the same in any case. Now consider the task of inputting an irregular, jagged polygon with, say, 50 vertices. It is a lot more work. You need to explicitly enter the *x-coordinate* and the *y-coordinate* for each vertex – a *polygon* command, plus a total of 100 parameter values. Let us say, then, that the *design content* of a shape entered and stored in the system is the number of discrete items of information (that is, command words and parameter values) required to specify it. (A little more strictly, it is the number of bits in the input stream.) It is easy to see that design content of the circular shape is approximately three percent of that of the irregular, jagged shape.

The difference is not just a technicality. The higher the design content of a shape, the more opportunities it provides for adaptation to a specific context. If a designer needs to fit a circular shape into a tight space, for example, she can only shift its center point and vary its radius. But if she needs to fit the jagged shape, she can shift any combination of vertices to accommodate arbitrary nooks and crannies. This added flexibility comes at

Fig. 1: (top right) The Bush Building at MIT designed by Walter Netsch in the early 1960s – an elegant example of industrial modernism. The design content is low, since the entire form is generated by a few key decisions. Construction economies were achieved through extensive repetition.

Fig. 2: (bottom) The roof of the British Museum courtyard, London, below, by Norman Foster. Non-repetitive construction is enabled by efficient numerically controlled fabrication, but design content remains fairly low, since the varied shapes of the roof panels, structural members, and joints are controlled by simple rules and a few parameter values.

a price, however. There are more decisions to make with the jagged shape – more for the designer to think about.

To refine this definition of design content a little further, we can establish it relative to particular computer-aided design systems. Any such system has a set of input commands – enabling the user to specify a straight line, a circle, a rectangular box, a spline, and so on. Some systems have more specialized commands to facilitate the entry of objects like columns, walls, doors, windows, and the like. In interpreting a command, the system makes use of built-in design content – knowledge, expressed in computer code, of how to display a straight line defined by its end points, how to display a circle specified by three parameters, how to display a column proportioned as desired, and in general how to display anything in the system's shape vocabulary. Some systems encode very little predefined design content in this way, and have correspondingly restricted sets of input commands, while others encode a great deal, and provide extensive repertoires of commands for users to learn and utilize. Thus, when a designer inputs a shape using the commands of a particular system, the input that she provides is the *added* design content. This can be defined as the *smallest* number of discrete items of information (shortest string of bits, if you want to be precise) required to specify the shape fully. This modified definition allows for the fact that there will usually be efficient and inefficient ways to enter the same geometric information, and stipulates that we are only concerned here with the most efficient.

Designers can re-use not only content that they find pre-encoded in a system at the start of a design process, but also content that they have input themselves, at some earlier stage in that process. A common strategy in design of office towers, for example, is to lay out a standard floor then repeatedly translate vertically and copy to describe the entire building. Depending upon the specific circumstances, we might regard this either as elegant economy of means or as lazy self-plagiarism. A fully displayed design, then, is the joint product of the information already encoded in the system and the information added, in response to particular conditions and requirements of the context at hand, by the designer. The system automatically does the work of expanding the added design content into a complete display.

Another way to express this point using more traditional terminology is to say that any computer-aided design system encodes stylistic conventions. Many systems support a style derived directly from Euclid's *Elements* – one characterized by straight lines, arcs of circles, parallels, perpendiculars and tangents. Some encode the vocabularies and layout rules of particular industrialized component building systems. It would be a provocative but technically trivial exercise to implement a neoclassical system that encoded the vocabulary and syntax of the style specified by, say, Palladio's *Four Books*, or Durand's *Précis*. A designer working within the established intellectual framework of a strong tradition, as expressed in the commands of a computer-aided design system, needs to add only a small amount of content to specify a complete design, while a designer working within a more general tradition typically needs to add more. A designer who is content to operate within the bounds of encoded tradition needs to add relatively little, while a designer who wants to break radically with tradition needs to work harder. In design innovation, as in other domains, there are no free lunches.

Fig. 3: The Bilbao Guggenheim, by Frank Gehry. The forms are non-repetitive, and they are not controlled by simple rules. Design content is high, since the architect made many explicit choices.

The New Style Rules

Investment in computer-aided design software favors the associated style. Early computer-aided architectural design systems mostly privileged a very conventional style of walls, columns, doors, windows, extruded floor plans, floor slabs and so on, laid out with the help of grids, construction planes and skeletons of construction lines. In the 1980s and 1990s, though, the software industry invested in computer-aided design systems that encoded knowledge about the calculation and display of free-form curved shapes specified by a few parameters. As a result, these became widely and inexpensively available. They were mostly intended for use in the automobile, aerospace and animation industries, but were quickly appropriated by architects. They established and enforced the rules of a new style – one of splines, blobs and twisted surfaces. Before these systems, creation and display of an architectural composition consisting of free-form curved surfaces would have required a huge amount of added design content – impractically large in most practical contexts. After these systems, the same composition could be specified with a much smaller amount of added design content. Under these new conditions, it was hardly surprising that schools and avant-garde practices happily embraced curved surfaces – much as the schools, in previous eras, had followed Palladio and Durand. It was a matter of the shifting economics of information work.

But it is one thing to specify and render a curved-surface shape on a computer-aided design system, and quite another to materialize it, at large scale, on a construction site. Successful materialization requires some sort of construction machine that can efficiently translate the digital description of the shape into a tangible realization. (The process is analogous to that of performing a digitally encoded score on an electronic musical instrument.) It might, in principle, be a sophisticated CAD/CAM fabrication device such as a laser cutter or a multi-axis milling machine, or it might be an organized team of construction workers with the skills and tools needed to do the job. Let us, for the moment, make the simplifying assumption that it is just a black box that accepts a digital description as input and produces a material realization as output.

Now, like a computer-aided design system, a construction machine will have some set of commands that it can execute. A simple laser cutter, for example, might execute commands to *move* the laser from one

Fig. 4: The Stata Center at MIT, designed by Frank Gehry. The architect made many explicit choices in response to the demands of a very complex program and urban context, so the form has a corresponding level of complexity. Form follows function in a new sense.

specified point to another, and to *cut* from one point to another. To connect to such a device, a computer-aided design system needs driver software that translates an internally stored description of a shape into a corresponding sequence of *move* and *cut* commands. The **construction content** of a shape may be defined as the length of this sequence. (More strictly, it is the number of bits in the sequence.) A rectangle, for example, has little construction content; it can be generated by one *move* command followed by four *cut* commands. But a 50-sided polygon requires a *move* command followed by 50 *cut* commands, so it has much greater construction content. In each case, an additional *locate* command must be executed – by fingers, a robot, or a construction crane – to place the fabricated piece within an assembly of pieces.

The translation of a shape description into a sequence of commands to a construction machine is one of converting a *state description*, which specifies a desired end condition, into a *process description*, which tells

how to get there. The translation task may be quite trivial, as in generation of *move* and *cut* commands for a laser cutter. The translation of a complex 3D shape into tool paths for a multi-axis milling machine is, however, much less trivial. In general, state-to-process translation algorithms encode knowledge of construction materials and processes.

There are, however, supply chains for construction elements, and the definition of construction content should be established relative to position within a supply chain. If, for example, a designer has at her disposal a pre-cut rectangle of the right size for use in her project, then no further cutting operations are required; the only construction operation is to *locate* it in the desired position. This *locate* operation represents the *added* construction content at this step in the supply chain. In general, construction machines that start with elementary raw materials add a lot of construction content in the process of realizing elaborate designs, while construction machines that assemble sophisticated,

86

highly finished, prefabricated components add relatively little. This, of course, relates closely to the economist's concept of added value at each step in a supply chain.

Generally, construction operations can usefully be subdivided into *fabrication* operations (cutting, milling, stamping, etc.) that produce discrete elements, and *assembly* operations that combine discrete elements to produce systems. Since ancient times, for example, builders have fabricated discrete bricks by shaping and drying or firing clay, and then assembled bricks into walls, arches, and other structures. Similarly, in modern electronics, solid-state devices – very sophisticated building blocks – are fabricated in expensive and technologically sophisticated plants, and then robotically assembled into devices. A designer may assume prefabricated elements, or even pre-assembled complete subsystems. In doing so, she not only establishes a starting point for addition of construction content, she also inherits design content. This inherited design content may be represented explicitly and in detail in a computer-aided design system, as when selection of a component from a menu results in insertion of a detailed description of that element into the design, or it may be represented by an abstraction, as when an element is represented simply by its outline.

The ratio of fabrication operations to assembly operations may shift from project to project. When a cave is carved directly out of the living rock, or an adobe building is created from mud, the task is entirely one of in situ fabrication. Conversely, when a factory is assembled from precast concrete elements, or when a child creates a composition of Lego blocks, the task is entirely one of assembly. A standard strategy of industrial modernism has been to minimize in situ fabrication, and to do as much pre-fabrication and pre-assembly

as possible, under controlled factory conditions. Execution of a command by a construction machine has an associated time and a cost. Obviously the total time to fabricate a component is the sum of the times for the individual commands in the sequence, while the total cost is given by the cost of raw materials plus the sum of the costs for the individual commands. Similarly, the total time to assemble a subsystem is the sum of the times for the individual assembly steps, and the total cost is the sum of the individual costs. Thus the times and costs of executing a design rise with construction content, but can be reduced by machines that execute commands quickly and inexpensively. In practice, this analysis is complicated by the fact that errors occur in fabrication and assembly processes. They must therefore incorporate strategies for error detection and correction. Net efficiency depends upon reducing error rates, and upon effective detection and correction.

It follows from all this that fast, reliable, efficient construction machines allow designers more construction content within the same schedule and budget constraints. Industrial-era machinery typically achieved such efficiency through repetition, mass-production and economies of scale. In the digital era, numerically controlled machines have allowed similar efficiencies with *non-repetitive* operations.

Constructing Complexity

With the concepts of design content and construction content in hand, we can now formalize the intuitive idea of the *complexity* of a designed and constructed shape, an assembly of shapes, or a complete architectural project. Roughly speaking, it is the number of design decisions relative to the scale of the project. We can measure it as the *ratio of added design content to added construction content*.

87

If the entry of a few command words and parameter values to a computer-aided design system suffices to generate a great deal of construction content, then the project is of low complexity. If many parameter values are required, as in the case of a 50-sided irregular polygon to be produced by a laser cutter, the complexity approaches one hundred percent. Differences in complexity arise because a command given to a computer-aided design system may imply more construction content than immediately meets the eye.

	Repetitive construction	Non-repetitive
Low complexity	Industrialized component building systems	British Museum roof Swiss Re
High complexity	Habitat, Montreal	Craft construction Stata Center, MIT

The difference between building designs of low complexity and those of higher complexity is economically and culturally significant, and its implications have played out differently in different eras. This can conveniently be demonstrated by means of the above two-by-two table. Along one axis there is a distinction between projects of low complexity and those of high complexity, and along the other the distinction is between repetitive construction and non-repetitive. The entries list examples of each combination. The condition of low-complexity, repetitive design and construction is illustrated by the industrialized component building systems that were popular in postwar Europe. These radically reduced the time and cost of construction through efficient mass-production of standardized elements. Architects working within the frameworks of such systems could select and specify the positions of standard elements – adding relatively little design content as they did so. If the elements were available from stock at construc-

tion time, there was also little added construction content. So large buildings could be designed and built very quickly and economically, but the process provided little opportunity to adapt buildings sensitively to local site and climatic conditions, programmatic requirements, and cultures.

Mainstream architectural modernism more generally – particularly in its developer-driven manifestations – has frequently served as a strategy for simultaneously meeting challenges of scale, budget and schedule by reducing complexity (Fig. 1). A typical modern office tower, for example, might have a modular layout, symmetry about one or more axes, a repetitive structural frame and curtain wall, and a standard floor plan that repeats vertically. An urban complex might even be composed of repeating towers, as in the case of the ill-fated World Trade Center. At the design stage, replication of a floor or an entire tower by a *translate-and-copy* command is an operation that adds very little design content, but eventually generates a great deal of construction content. But you get what you pay for; this simplification of design (typically under budget and time pressure) reduces an architect's ability to respond thoughtfully to the exigencies of particular moments and spaces.

Typically, modernists have minimized complexity not only by standardizing components and subassemblies, but also by standardizing the spatial relationships among them – laying them out in repetitive arrays and grids. An alternative strategy was famously demonstrated by Moshe Safdie's Habitat in Montreal, where the box-like units were highly standardized, but the spaces and masses that they produced were varied. The efficiencies of mass production could still be achieved, but the resulting level of complexity was higher. Norman Foster's designs for the British Museum courtyard (Fig. 2) and the

Swiss Re tower in London illustrate the condition of non-repetitive geometry with relatively low complexity. In each case, the structural frame and skin system is topologically uniform but geometrically varied. The metal structural members are connected in a standardized way, but the lengths of the members, the joint angles and the dimensions of the glass panels that they support are varied. The variation is controlled by simple formulas and a few parameters, so the added design content is not much higher than for fully repetitive designs. This is variety, cleverly achieved through exploitation of numerically controlled fabrication, but without resulting in great complexity. Habitat and the British Museum courtyard combine standardization and variability in different ways – putting the capacity for res-ponsive variation in different places. In Habitat it is in the spatial relationships among standard physical elements, while in the British Museum roof it is in the lengths and connection angles of the physical elements themselves.

Under conditions of craft production, the versatility of craft workers makes it possible to produce buildings that contain very little repetition anywhere. But the operations performed by craft workers tend to be slow and expensive, so craft production does not scale – as illustrated by projects like Gaudi's Sagrada Familia, which has been in construction, at great cost, for many decades. Non-repetitive construction at large scale requires digitally controlled fabrication, positioning, and placement machinery that combines versatility approaching that of craft workers with efficiency approaching that of mass-production techniques. Frank Gehry's projects for the Bilbao Guggenheim (Fig. 3), the Disney Concert Hall in Los Angeles, and the Stata Center at MIT (Fig. 4), vividly demonstrate this new possibility of scaling up variety. Both the shapes of the material components and their spatial relationships are non-uniform. Efficient construction required both numerically controlled fabrication and use of advanced electronic surveying and positioning techniques to assemble fabricated elements on site. Added design content is very high, since each space, element and detail had to be considered individually. This gave the architect enormous scope to respond to the demands of complex programs and surrounding urban conditions, and provided a great deal of expressive freedom. The result is correspondingly complex form, at large scale, achieved through clever exploitation of the possibilities of non-repetitive but efficient construction.

It does not follow that buildings with very high design content, produced under conditions that allow varied construction at large scale, will always be spectacularly irregular in their forms. It is logically possible for many carefully considered design decisions to add up to an elegantly minimal, tightly disciplined response. But this is now a deliberate design choice, not a side effect of industrial-era construction technology and inherited design content.

Conclusion

New technological capabilities are not always wisely used. Our new capacity for digitally enabled variety and construction of strange and irregular shapes has sometimes been deployed merely for its sensational effect. But thoughtful architects are beginning to see beyond the short-lived seduction of the surprising, and to find new ways of responding – without the compromise of Procrustean simplification – to the demands of the complex conditions they engage. As they do so, an authentic architecture of the digital era is emerging.

Designing with rules, algorithms and with running the process builds the foundations for a new kind of building. These buildings are based on the behavior of an intelligent flock of swarming points, each of them executing a relatively simple rule, each of them acting according to local awareness of their immediate environment. The outcome of this process can be a class of simple rules generating visual complexity, which is highly appreciated by the public since it feels rich and communicates the feeling of freedom. This paper explores a major paradigm shift in the way we connect to buildings as running processes: the New Kind of Building is not only designed through computation, it is a computation.

Kas Oosterhuis is the principal of ONL (Oosterhuis_ Lénárd), a multidisciplinary practice in Rotterdam, and Professor of Architecture at TU Delft, Head of the Hyperbody Research Group. He is the co-founder of the Attila Foundation (1994), which pursues the electronic fusion of art and architecture. He delivers lectures around the world and publishes his works internationally. His recent writings include Hyperbodies – Towards an E-motive Architecture (2003), Architecture Goes Wild (2002), Programmable Architecture (2002).

kas oosterhuis:

a new kind of building

A NEW KIND OF BUILDING

Mass-customization

Traditional vernacular building is accomplished by executing the process. There are no intermediate phases like a set of drawings, working drawings, drawings of details. The communication is direct from person to person. In modern computing lingo: through a peer-to-peer wireless sensor network. Peer-to-peer since people connect directly to their own kind, wireless since they are not physically connected and sensor network since they immediately absorb, process and propagate information. People put their minds together, discuss and take action. Exact measurements and other relevant numeric details are decided along the process of building. The end result is unpredictable in detail, but is performed according to a agreed upon set of simple rules.

Now at the beginning of the 21st century machines have taken the place of humans for the production and actual execution of the building elements. And now, relying on digital techniques we are able to establish a very similar peer-to-peer network of machines communicating with each other to produce an endless variety of different building elements, visually rich and complex, but still based on a set of simple rules. Humans connect to machine-to-machine communication through conceptual interventions and through a variety of input devices. This process is called mass-customization, based on file-to-factory (F2F) production methods. Now everything is different in absolute size and position, not because of human non-accuracy, but thanks to computational processing of diversity.

Building as the public knows it is based on the industrial mass-production of building components. The elements are produced as generic material, which will be customized later in another phase of the life of the product. The half-products are produced in a limited range of sizes and measurements, then stored and cataloged, waiting to be taken up by the next party, eventually ending up in an assembly in the factory or on-site as part of a building. The mass-produced elements are categorized and have specialized into discrete classes: doors, beams, windows, columns, tiles, bricks, hinges, wire, piping, etc. Production according to the principle of mass-customization follows a completely different path. There is no catalog, the products are produced starting from raw material (which in most cases still is mass-produced) for a specific purpose, to become a unique part in a unique setting in a specific building. That mass-produced part would not fit anywhere else, it is truly unique.

Architecture based on this new paradigm of mass-customization will be essentially different from the art of designing buildings as we have seen it until now. Completely new tools for creating diversity and complexity are being developed now to produce visual and constructive richness and diversity, yet based on simple rules being applied on conceptual procedures to generate behavioral relations between all constituting building elements. The driving forces to organize

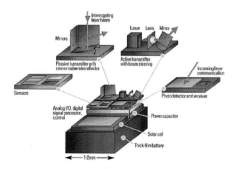

Fig. 1: Smart Dust, Kristopher Pister et al., 2004, Multifunctional Micro-Mote

Fig. 2: Utility Fog, John Storrs Hall, nano-scale Foglets shaking hands

the behavior of the control points of the geometry come from both external and internal forces communicating with the evolution of the 3D model.

Looking at the worlds from within the paradigm of mass-customization (MC), we see that it includes all possible products along the production lines of mass-production (MP). By setting all parameters to the same value we can easily step one level down from MC to MP. The other way round is impossible. MC does include MP, while MP definitely does not include MC. Think of the inhabitants of Flatland: they are not able to experience – let alone conceive – Space. But Space inhabitants do have a notion of Flatland, as a section sliced out of Space.

A true understanding of the peer-to-peer network of machines communicating to machines connected by a flow of information leads to a complete new awareness of the architect/designer. We must go one level up, and start designing the rules for the behavior of all possible control points and the constraints of their behavior, instead of thinking of the rich and complex as exceptions to a given standard. The swarm of control points will be referred to as the Point Cloud in the context of this paper. All possible positions of the control points are no longer seen as exceptional states but as implicit possible states in the flocking relations between the points. The Point Cloud may be seen as sort of a Quantum State of geometry. There are no exceptions to a given standard; non-standard computation rules the control points. The exception has become the rule. Stepping one level up can be understood as stepping out of a world of plans and sections into a truly 3D space. Now we step out of mass-production and repetition into the realm of mass-customization and complexity, made possible by computational programming. We will step one level up and look at the world from there. As we will see later, I will propose to step another level up to enter the world of swarming behavioral space, leaving frozen 3D space like an experienced time-traveler would, or leaving Flatland like an inhabitant of Space.

Programming the Point Cloud

The recent ONL (Oosterhuis_Lénárd) projects like the WEB of North-Holland, the Acoustic Barrier and the Cockpit building are based on the new building paradigm of mass-customization and the new design paradigm of programming soft design machines. Simple rules put into the machines are designed as to create a visually complex geometry. Through a peer-to-peer communication the data are transferred from the 3D model to the executing machines. Cuttinig, bending, drilling, welding machines are operated by numbers and sequences, which are produced by scripts, routines and procedures written by ONL and executed on the points of the Point Cloud. ONL organizes the points of the Point Cloud through a variety of design strategies, using a variety of programming tools. Each project has followed a slightly different path, but shares the principle of programming the Point Cloud. To fully understand the nature of the Point Cloud I must place it in the context of recent developments outside the working field of architecture. There are three concepts I want to discuss here, all of them having to do with what you see when you are looking at the world from the level of complexity, i.e., Smart Dust, Utility Fog and Flocking Behavior. After that I want to dive deeper into the new kind of science as proposed by Stephen Wolfram, and draw conclusions from the implications it has for the architectural programming of the Point Cloud.

Fig. 3: Boids, Craig Reynolds 1987, Flocking Behavior

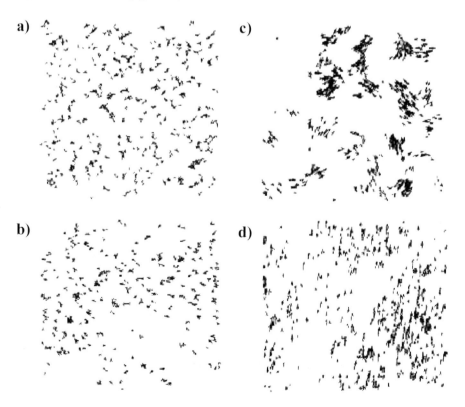

a)

b)

c)

d)

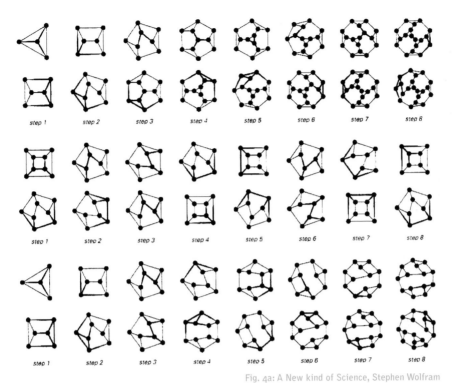

step 1   step 2   step 3   step 4   step 5   step 6   step 7   step 8

step 1   step 2   step 3   step 4   step 5   step 6   step 7   step 8

step 1   step 2   step 3   step 4   step 5   step 6   step 7   step 8

Fig. 4a: A New kind of Science, Stephen Wolfram 2002, Substitution system: Simple rules generate complex results

After that, I want to take you one more level up and discuss the Real Time Behavior of the recent ONL projects Trans-Ports, Handdrawspace and the MUSCLE. The behavior of the control points has become in these projects a running process, which keeps running when it has been built. These constructs keep reconfiguring themselves, and produce complexity and unpredictability in real time. These projects are executable.

Building Relations between the Nodes

The concepts of Smart Dust, Utility Fog and Flocks are all based essentially on the concept of building local relations. One node looks at the neighboring node, but has no awareness of the whole swarm of nodes. Intelligence is not something that can be programmed from the top down in a manner of reverse engineering, but is an awareness that emerges from

the bottom up through a process of evolution by building relations between the nodes of the system. Intelligence is not necessarily aware of itself as being intelligent. Intelligence can very well emerge from relatively stupid swarming components. Together they perform as something complex, which humans may interpret as intelligent. Intelligence as I use it here is not seen as human intelligence. It is regarded as emergent behavior coming up from the complex interactions between less complex actuators. It seems possible to apply the same definition of intelligence to the functioning of our brains, traffic systems, people gathering together, and the growth and shrinking of cities. And, as I wish to discuss here, it seems also possible to apply to the relations that are built (both in the design process and in the actual operation of the construct) between all actuators/components assembled into a building.

95

Building relations in the concept of Smart Dust (Fig. 1) is done through a peer-to-peer wireless sensor network [1]. The concept of Smart Dust is developed by Kristofer Pister at Berkeley University and working prototypes are being put together. Each micro-electromechanical mote sends and receives signals from and to other micro-sensors. They have a sensor in their backpack, all of it no bigger than a grain of sand. The sensor is designed to pick up signals, smells, chemical substance, molecules according to the purpose of the Smart Dust particle. There is no PCU governing the swarm of Smart Dust particles. They basically sense, send and receive, propagating data and information like a rumor propagates through people in society. In the end people are sensors, senders and receivers also. It is my hunch – after having taken the step to see the world from one or two levels up – that we must start designing from the awareness that buildings and all constituting building elements are sensors, senders and receivers in the end, locally communicating with other specimens of their own and other species. Smart Dust is an operational system, although production costs of one mote still amount to something like $ 100 instead of the intended $ 1 to make it commercially applicable.

The concept of Utility Fog (Fig. 2) by John Storrs Hall is based on the speculative assumption that we could build programmable molecules [2]. If so we could program these Foglets to configure into any shape or substance we might desire. The description of the possibilities goes beyond any sci-fi movie you have seen. Since the Utility Fog particles are not visible – you can even breathe them freely in and out – they can spontaneously appear and disappear. They can swap from visible and tangible to non-visible and ephemeral. Utility Fog builds the ultimate bridge between the gaseous and the solid state of stuff. It can transform itself from one state into the other based on its programming. Utility Fog is seen by their author as an array of molecular robots looking at each other, and eventually connecting to each other to form solid material. No one could predict how it will feel or look like, but in principle it should work. The question here is if we can learn from the concept of Utility Fog when thinking of complex structures for buildings. The way ONL has developed their latest projects shows that this is indeed the case. ONL basically regards each node as an intelligent point which is "peer-to-peer" looking to neighboring points, and acting according to a simple set of programmed rules to form a complex consistent structure.

The constructive concept of points looking actively to each other brings us immediately to the concept of Flocks, Flocking Behavior and Boids (Fig. 3). Boids as developed by Craig Reynolds [3] are active members of a flock calculating in real time their positions in relation to each other. Simple rules are underpinning their behavior. Each Boid computes a limited number of simple rules: Do not come too close to your neighbors, match your velocity with your neighbors, try to move towards the center of the mass of Boids. None of these rules says, form a flock; the rules are entirely local, referring to what a local Boid can see and perform in its immediate vicinity. And yet the flock forms and is recognizable as a complex whole. The importance for the procedure of architectural design here is that one does not need to define the exact overall shape beforehand in order to group the individual members into a consistent whole. Boids can be interpreted as the flocking nodes of a constructive mesh. The designer could work with simple rules starting from the related positions of the nodes to generate the relevant data for mass-customized production. Also, the behavior of the nodes might be used to form the shape of the building. Placing a bouncing box around the flock to limit their room to move remains a valid possibility since each building has to take into account the presence of other objects in their urban context.

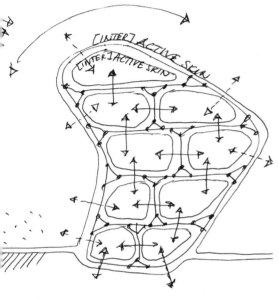

827 /KO

Fig. 4b: TORS, ONL [Oosterhuis_Lénárd] 1995-2004, Specialization of the detail

A New Kind of Building

Building on existing machines called Cellular Automata (Fig. 4a–4b), Stephen Wolfram recently declared his research in this field to form the foundations for a new kind of science, which he has also chosen as the title of his 1 kg heavy book [4]. Running a cellular automaton means creating generation after (line after line) generation following some simple rules. By performing years of runtime on thousands of possible rules, Wolfram found out that some rules lead to visually complex and unpredictable beings. Other rules tend to die out or would lead to uniform

and predictable generations. And yet the rules leading to complexity are not more complicated then the other rules. Wolfram expects that these rules form the driving force behind all evolution, be it natural organisms or products induced by the interventions of humans, including scientific theories and mathematics. In theory everything that is complex and behaves unpredictably must be based on simple rules generating this complexity. If this is indeed the case then the development of cellular automata will outrun traditional science as the basis for further progress in all scientific fields, and, which is relevant in the framework of this paper, it will turn out to cause a paradigm shift in the way buildings are conceived, geometry is generated and the constituting parts are produced. In essence all points – comparable to the cells in a cellular automaton – are looking to its previous generation to decide what the next step will be, following some simple rules. Only by running the system can one find out to what class of result the simple rules will lead.

Designing becomes running the computation, generation after generation, checking it, making changes, and running it again. Designing becomes to a much lager extent than it ever was an iterative process. In a traditional design process one iterates a limited number of times. When setting up a set of simple rules in a computation machine, one iterates in real time, that is, many times per second. In turbo lingo this is designing with the speed of light, designing like a Formula 1 driver. Designing with rules, algorithms and with running the process creates the foundations for a new kind of building. These buildings are based on the behavior of an intelligent flock of swarming points, each of them executing a relatively simple rule, each of them acting according to local awareness of their immediate environment.

Specialization of the Building Detail

Local rules executed by the nodes create not only their behavior, but also the complexity of their configurations. The nodes evolve through running substitution systems, following simple rules as: substitute this node by three nodes with small distances between the three new nodes. This leads to a local specialisation of the node. Or in architectural terms, to the building detail. Building details need more points, and those new points may be generated by a script describing some simple rules executed on the nodes. In the case of the Acoustic Barrier (Figs 5a–5d) each node of the Point Cloud has been multiplied to hundreds of new points in order to describe the geometry and generate the data needed for the production of all the thousands of unique elements [5].

It may be obvious that some of the data received by the script come from the behavior of the points of the overall Point Cloud, and that other data used in the script come from the top-down styling interventions of the designer, the characteristics of the applied materials, structural calculations and a variety of environmental constraints. Thus the complex swarm of flocking particles is evolving until a decision has been made to produce them.

Reading *Scientific American* (SA) regularly as my favorite architecture magazine (I do not read traditional architectural magazines since it is my strong belief that you have to experience the built reality architecture of your fellow architects in order to understand the essence of it, and read their theoretical texts), I stumbled upon an article [6] on the specialization of skin into hair (Fig. 6). This seemed to resonate well with my attitude towards the specialization of the node into the detail as ONL has developed and built over the last few years.

Hair and skin seem to be two completely different discrete elements, eventually assembled and cooperating as two separate families of elements, similar to embedding the headlights of a car in the car body. But where did hair come from, when did it start to be hair? The theory as described in SA speculates on the concept of the specialization of the skin into a folded rim. This folded rim proved to have qualities that remained in the process of evolution. Then, in the deepest recesses of the rim a new micro-climate arose, where certain cells would become harder, yet kept growing and evolved into something hard sticking out of the skin. It soon became clear that a hair had advantages for protecting the skin against environmental

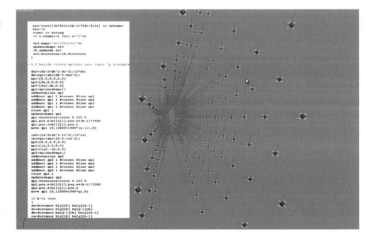

Fig. 5a: Acoustic Barrier, ONL [Oosterhuis_Lénárd] 2004, Point Cloud and generic script

Fig. 5b: Acoustic Barrier, ONL [Oosterhuis_Lénárd] 2004, File to Factory process of Mass-Customization generates 10.000 different nodes

conditions, and on its evolutionary path skin folded into hair on many parts of the body.

Replace now the cells by the nodes of a construct, and replace hair by the building detail. This is exactly what happens during the evolution of the 3D model of ONL projects like the WEB, the Acoustic Barrier and the Cockpit. Just as hair covers the body in principle at most places, the specialized node in the form of the building detail is in principle present where it is useful. Basically at all places the specialization from node to detail is everywhere the same, but circumstantial differences in orientation create the variety of appearances of the specialized detail. Technically speaking, the detail is fully parametric; its parameters change with the changes in orientation. The end result is that of a visually rich complexity. Not a single detail out of hundreds (WEB) or thousands (Acoustic Barrier) is the same. All is different, and that illustrates the way we look at the world from one level up.

The detail of the WEB (Figs 7a–7c) is directly derived from the Point Cloud organized according to an icosahedron mesh mapped on the double curved NURBS surface [7]. Just like needles stuck into a needle cushion, ONL generated normals perpendicular to the surface pointing inward. This action doubled the number of points and generated a new Point Cloud. The points are instructed to look at their immediate neighbor and construct flat planes between the double set of points. These planes are given a thickness, and that leads to another doubling of points.

From there the bolted joints are developed, leading to another multiplication of the total number of points needed to describe the geometry and hence to send those data to the cutting machines. By receiving data from interventions by the designer, in the manner of cloning and adding points according to a simple local procedures, the detail evolves from the node.

Since the doubling of the nodes is not executed along parallel lines, the connecting planes are placed at an angle in relation to each other. This leads to an evolutionary constructive advantage since the fold increases the strength of the folded plates. It turns out that with this constructive parametric principle ONL can virtually construct the support structure of any complex double-curved surface, no matter if the curvature is round and smooth or sharply folded, no matter if the surface is convex or concave. The parametric detail of the WEB counts for a major invention in the construction technique for double-curved surfaces. Moreover it immediately connects the styling of the surface to the construction and the manufacturing of it. Architecture, construction and manufacturing are one, in much the same way as body, skin and hair are one.

The Point Cloud of the Acoustic Barrier is generated through a different procedure than was used for the WEB. A long stretched NURBS surface on both sides of the barrier is bombarded by 10,000

Fig. 5c: Acoustic Barrier, ONL [Oosterhuis_Lénárd] 2004, Building site progress, 15 September 2004. The Cockpit will connect to the left end.

parallel lines. The 20,000 intersection points form the nodes of the Point Cloud. Executed on the nodes a number of scripts are evolved to develop the detail, and to generate the data needed for the production of the 40,000 unique structural members and the 10,000 unique triangular glass plates. By no means could this have been performed by traditional drawing techniques or by traditional production methods.

The Point Cloud of the Cockpit is directly related to the Point Cloud of the Acoustic Barrier. The stretched volume of the barrier is inflatable and gives space to over 5,000 m^2 floor surface for the Rolls Royce garage and showroom. The points are controlled along supple curves, which in turn are controlled by a single reference curve, built in parametric ProEngineer software.

Fig. 5d: Cockpit Hessing ONL [Oosterhuis_Lénárd] 2004, Specialization of group of points to form the Cockpit

Inside, ProE ONL has applied a "pattern" for the parametric detail using the points on a surface. The architectural, structural and production concept of the Acoustic Barrier means another major innovation. ONL has proved in close cooperation with the steel manufacturer Meijers Staalbouw that within a regular budget large complex structures can be built and managed without the intervention of a general contractor. Thanks to the direct link between the evolved 3D model and the manufacturing, thanks to connecting the design machines to the production machines through scripting based on simple rules, ONL has proved that a complex building can be developed as a intelligently engineered product.

Nature and Products are Computations

Based on my experiences with building the WEB, the Acoustic Barrier and the Cockpit, I do now strongly believe that all of nature and all evolution seen in products are the result of a complex set of simple computations. Computations can be seen as building relations between nodes applying simple rules. The relation can vary from tracing a line (shortest connection) to exchanging data in real time (Smart Dust).

Making architecture is setting up a set of computations. ONL has a definite preference for working with raw products like sheet metal. The WEB is made completely out of sheet metal, both steel for the construction and Hylite aluminum for the cladding panels. The TT Monument (Fig. 8)

is made exclusively from very pure cast aluminum [8]. The more ONL can introduce the F2F process into raw material, the simpler the rules can be to generate the outcome of the design and manufacturing process. Then the outcome of the process can be based on simple rules generating visual complexity, which is highly appreciated by the public since it feels rich and communicates the feeling of freedom.

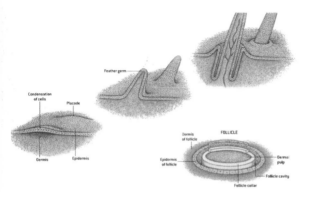

Fig. 6: Specialization from skin into hair, Scientific American, March 2003

While everything we see around us in every room, in every car, on every street, in every city is based on simple computations creating complex behavior, it is virtually impossible to trace back the rules. The only way to find out is to run the system, to design a system which is based on simple rules generating complexity. This awareness potentially turns designers into researchers. Designers must set up systems and run them in order to perform. Performative architecture brings the architect and the artist back into the genetic center from which everything we see around us is generated.

Buildings are Complex Adaptive Systems. This means that building relations between the nodes represents only one class of relations among many other possible and necessary relations. To evolve something as complex as a building involves

many truly different actors. It is not just one system that runs in real time. It must be seen and designed as a complex set of many interrelated systems, all of them performing simple rules. In something as complex as a building, the nodes communicate not only to other nodes, but even more to other product species. They receive information from other systems as well, and include those data in the processing of the information and in their behavior. In other words, a Boid is not moving in an empty world, a Cellular Automaton can not live as an isolated machine, Smart Dust particles do have contact with other systems. All machines feed on information, and all machines produce information of some sort. All machines are a small player in a complex structure of many interacting machines.

But the necessity remains that in order to see the world from the next level, designers must start from simple rules placed in a complex environment rather then starting from a superficially complex structure without a clear concept of how to generate

Fig. 7a: Web of North-Holland, ONL [Oosterhuis_Lénárd] 2002, Autoslip routine for F2F process

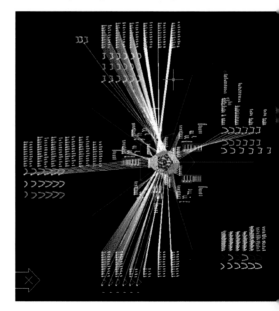

the data needed for customized production. In the end we must think of building and evolving networks relating all the different players in the dynamic process of the evolution of the 3D model. Each player in the process can be seen as having its own specific view on the data. The different constituting elements of the building have different views on the evolving 3D model. Each of them sends signals to the model which receives the signal, processes it and acts accordingly.

From other disciplines the model would receive another class of signals leading to adjustment of the model for completely different reasons. In essence this awareness leads to a process of Collaborative Design and Engineering. All players in this process – people, materials, forces, algorithms, money and energy alike – are in their own way connected to the evolutionary 3D model. Each of them performs some simple set of rules, without complete awareness of what the other parties are doing or capable of. They all contribute from their own systems to the complex set of related systems as a whole. In this sense, even a traditional building process behaves like a swarm. But now we can learn from the new kind of science that we must build design processes on swarming intelligent particles in the Point Cloud communicating with each other. As humans we must learn to relate to the dynamics of super-fast real-time computational processes. We must build the computational tools for Collaborative Design and Engineering in order to meet the rich expectations created by looking at the world from one or two levels up.

Based on my work with the Hyperbody Research Group at the TU in Delft, which I will discuss later in this paper, I have started the Protospace Lab for Collaborative Design and Engineering. We are now entering our second operational year,

Fig. 7b: Web of North-Holland, ONL [Oosterhuis_ Lénárd] 2002, Generic parametric detail

Protospace 1.2. Next year we hope to continue with Protospace 2.0 (Fig. 9) in the resurrected WEB which is intended to be placed right in front of the Faculty of Architecture [9].

One of the issues we are dealing with is how to develop the design in collaboration with other disciplines (construction, ecology, economy) and with the client from the Point Cloud. The Point Cloud is the raw design material, comparable to the Foglets of the Utility Fog, the Smart Dust particles and Neumann's Cellular Automata. Starting from this universe of particles we can start building rules and watch the worlds develop.

From the Point Cloud to the Soap Bubble Construct

Wolfram's New Kind of Science includes studies on substitution systems for the evolution of networks. The building of networks is a very appropriate tool for organizing the points of the Point Cloud. The

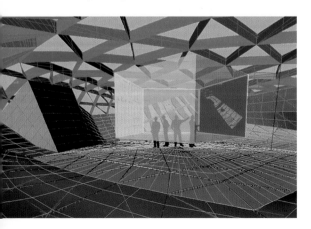

notion of the network can almost immediately be translated into the constructive system of a building. The rule starts like this: Replace the one point of the T-crossing with the four points of a tetrahedron. Make sure that the distance between the four new nodes are substantially smaller than the distance between the primary nodes of the constructive system. Repeat this process with slightly adapted rules to organize the number, the direction and the positions of the new generations of the node. In this way the new generations are nested in or patterned on the 3D array of primary nodes.

Repeating this procedure along the same substitution rule generates a 3D model resembling a soap bubble structure with smooth rounded off transitions from floor to wall and from wall to roof. In fact the connection between floor and roof becomes completely equivalent to the connection between wall and roof, between wall and another wall. The complete structure of a multistory building can thus be developed from one universal Point Cloud of structural nodes, each of them specialized in the building detail via a limited number of simple rules.

Point Clouds Running in Real Time

For the Architecture Biennale 2000 ONL created the Handdrawspace interactive painting (Fig. 10), one of the worlds running in the installation Trans-Ports [10]. This work shows with what material ONL is redefining art and architecture. ONL uses game development software (Nemo then, Virtools now) to run the system. Games are by definition running in real time; the game unfolds, the game is played by the rules. Game software is also capable of setting up multi-player worlds, which promises to be very appropriate for the process of Collaborative Design and Engineering.

Fig. 10: Handdrawspace, Architecture Biennale Venice 2000, Interactive painting installation

In Handdrawspace particles are continuously emitted from invisible 3D sketches. The number of particles, the size of the particles, their position in the universe, the colors are input values set through infrared sensors by the visitors walking around in the central space of the installation. The people connect to the Point Cloud universe. The always changing values for the particles make sure that the same configuration will never be repeated. Each time you visit the Handdrawspace Universe you experience a fresh unique world. The outcome of the real-time computation is rich and complex, and never predictable in detail. The people walking around step by step learn how to cooperate with the running system; they teach themselves how to play with the rules (without changing them). Some people watch the running environment as if it were an instant movie, while others involve themselves actively and change the course of the universe. Now extrapolate this concept to the realm of architecture. When we can involve the very movements of people in the running process of architecture itself, we are really changing the static foundations architecture has been built upon. And when we can involve the

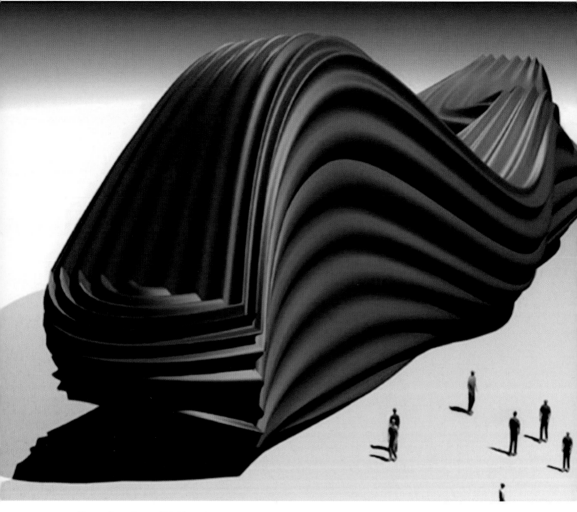

Fig. 11: Trans-Ports, ONL [Oosterhuis_Lénárd] 2000,
Architecture Biennale 2000, Programmable architecture

changing circumstantial conditions of the weather and other contextual data in the running process of the building itself, we can start looking at the world again from another level. Then we are at least two levels up from where we are now. Extrapolating Handdrawspace into architecture leads to a major paradigm shift in the collaborative evolution of the 3D model and it leads in the same manner to a major paradigm shift in the way we connect to buildings as running processes. Looking at the world from there means looking at the Point Cloud as a swarm of intelligent

beings communicating with each other in real time and all the time, as long as it takes them to live their process.

The installation Trans-Ports in self-explaining mode (Fig. 11) gives us another clue to building the relations between the points themselves, the people among themselves, and finally the people and the points [11]. People and points are two different Point Clouds interacting with each other. Trans-Ports self-explaining mode introduces a third active Point Cloud in the form of the pixels mapped as information on the

106

interior skin. These pixels can be seen as a Point Cloud which can be programmed to communicate many visual complexities ranging from letters and language through signs and images to movies and real time Web-cams connected to other active environments.

Walking around in Trans-Ports changes values of the positions of the nodes of the construction. The nodes are connected between each other by a building block called Cool Cloth, bought by ONL via Internet from an Australian gamer. The algorithm of Cool Cloth organizes their nodes in a 7x7 frequent mesh in such a way as to simulate the movements of a waving flag. ONL connected the active flag mesh to a shape that recalls the shape of the Saltwater pavilion, an inflated tunnel body with open ends.

While the nodes of Trans-Ports communicate through Cool Cloth, the interaction with the users is built by ONL through a MIDI building block especially developed for Trans-Ports. Triggering the sensors is translated into MIDI numbers (between 0 and 12) which are inked to certain actions of the connected node-structure. ONL has programmed the actions in such a way that all actions can take place simultaneously, leading to complex behavior that never repeats itself.

Looking at the Trans-Ports machine in operation one gets the feeling that it displays free will, a will of its own. Since the free will of people in the end is the result of a complex set of rules that are simple in themselves being executed by human brains in close cooperation with the human body, it seems perfectly reasonable to postulate that it is a simple form of free will indeed. It is unpredictable by the people who have scripted it, and unpredictable by the people playing with the running system. If it is not them predict-

ing what Trans-Ports will do exactly, then it can only be the running system called Trans-Ports itself that decides in real time. The Trans-Ports machine digests the randomness of the people navigating in the installation arena.

For ONL Trans-Ports had become an anchor point for Programmable Architecture. From then on ONL was ready to lift the conceptual designers mind up to the next level, that of all possible interactions between all players in the game of building and architecture. Looking at the world from there no building can be seen as static; they all move, albeit most of them extremely slowly and extremely stupidly. Since 2000 ONL has embarked on an architecture where all players (including all building materials) are seen as potential senders, processors and receivers of information, and where all players communicate with members of their own flock and with other flocks in real time.

MUSCLE at Non-Standard Architectures

Built especially for the NSA show in Paris for a budget of EUR 70,000 ONL has applied the knowledge of the theoretical vehicle Trans-Ports into a working prototype called the MUSCLE (Fig. 12). The MUSCLE consists of 72 pneumatic muscles connected to each other and forming a consistent mesh wrapped around a blue inflated bubble [12]. In this prototype for a programmable structure it is not the nodes that are informed to move but the connecting muscles. Variable air pressure is sent in an endless stream of millisecond pulses to each individual muscle. When air pressure is pumped into the muscles they become thicker and shorter (muscles are a product of FESTO). When air pressure is let out again of the muscles they relax and regain their original maximum length. By varying the air pressure in real time (which in our physical

Fig. 12: MUSCLE, ONL [Oosterhuis_Lénárd] 2004,
Non-Standard-Architectures, Pompidou Center Paris
Interactive Installation with 72 actuators

world means, many times per second, and not absolutely continuously per se) for each individual muscle the Point Cloud of nodes starts moving like the birds in a swarm.

The real time Virtools game as developed by ONL together with student-assistants of the HRG sends out signals to the I/O boards, which are connected to the 72 valves opening or closing the airlocks. The MUSCLE game graph also receives input in real time from 24 sensors on eight sensor boards attached to eight nodes of the constructive muscular mesh. The public can touch the sensors (infrared sensors, touch sensors and proximity sensors) as to interfere with the MUSCLE running system.

The flock of muscles is programmed in such a way that all muscular actuators co-operate to perform a change. It is impossible for one muscle to change place without cooperating with the other connected muscles. Programmed by assembling the

graphs in the Virtools software, the nodes are set to look at each other when changing positions. The change is communicated to the neighboring nodes. From there the desired length of the connecting muscles to accurately perform the displacement of the nodes is calculated. The calculation is based on experimental values found from testing the system with the chosen air pressure, the chosen sizes of the air pressure tubes, and the chosen capacity of the valves.

The nodes are looking at each other all the time. While the muscles are changing their lengths, the MUSCLE is hopping, twisting, bending and rotating constantly. As long as the program runs and the air pressure holds it is alive. The MUSCLE is ONL's first materialized construct as a running system acting out of its own free will and at the same time interacting with the public. The process of interaction can only take place when there are at least two active parties involved, when there are at least two running systems

108

communicating with each other, the MUS-CLE being one running system, the human person the other, both with a will of their own. The MUSCLE is a "quick and dirty" built prototype for the New Kind of Building as introduced in the title of this paper. This new kind of building is not only designed through computation, it is a computation. The New Kind of Building never stops calculating the positions of its thousands of primary and its millions of secondary nodes, based on input values from both the users of the building and from environmental forces acting upon the structure. The New Kind of Building is a Hyperbody.

911 Hypercube

Asked by Max Protetch to contribute to the Ground Zero exhibition showing architects' response to the 9/11, ONL proposed a large fully programmable cubic volume, a Hypercube. ONL proposes here an Open Source Building approach, in contrast to the defensive Pavlovian reaction the US took as their policy. Only by setting up an open political system based on mutual respect can one build a society that is not based on threat, hate or fear. To this open global society belongs an open global architecture. An architecture that is a running process and feeds on streaming information from all sides of the globe. ONL came up with a 3D lattice structure where all structural members are data-driven programmable hydraulic cylinders. The pistons act as actuators for the data-driven building. If all pistons are at their extreme position the building can shrink 50% of its size along all three axes. As a net result the building can shrink or expand to eight times its original volume.

The 911 Hypercube Building (Figs 13a–13b), responds to changes triggered by its users, and also proposes changes by itself according to a set of simple rules

generating a complexity of possible configurations [13]. Furthermore, the Hyperbody would respond to changing weather conditions, the behavior of people in the street, and signals and patterns received from other buildings and other information processing vehicles from all over the world. The 911 Hypercube is designed to be a giant interface between many different behavioral swarms, ranging from people of every culture to other built structures, both ephemeral (programs, organizations, the Internet) and tangible (buildings, cars, microwaves, air conditioning, cell phones) information processing machines. The presentation of the 911 Hypercube comes in 12 modes, corresponding to the 12 months of the year, 12 exemplary types of weather and 12 typical NY events.

Peer-to-peer architecture means communicating between equivalent computing machines. Just like in Smart Dust, we look at the nodes of the 911 Hypercube as small computing devices. Some form of intelligence has been built into the node. The nodes do at least perform some form of sensing, processing and propagating of signals. They send signals to the actuators, the hydraulic cylinders. Thus the construction of 911 Hypercube is a peer-to-peer network. People can be peers, spaces can be peers, they all connect in simular peer-to-peer networks. A simple conversation between people establishes a peer-to-peer communication. It is actually this basic level of communication I am considering when thinking of programmable pro-active hyperbuildings.

Protospace 1.1 Demo

Now that I have explained the nature of the New Kind of Building and looking at the world from there, I want to discuss how the different disciplines might work together in order to get there. At the DUT my HRG has built a first rough concept for the Protospace 1.1 Demo [14]. As in a complex set of peer-to-peer networks working inside Protospace the various disciplines want to communicate in their own way with their own kin. In a process of Collaborative Design and Engineering one wants to express oneself to the highest level of knowledge and intuition of one's discipline. One expert in a specific field does not want to limit him/herself to constraints set by other disciplines which are either "not obviously" or "obviously not" relevant to one's own discipline.

The HRG has built a simple demo where the different players in the evolution of the 3D model each have their own view on the 3D model. For the demo I have chosen the role of the construction engineer, the stylist, the ecologist, the economist and the tourist. Each of them actually sees the 3D model differently. The construction engineer sees nodes and connecting members; the stylist a surface model, which can be shaped; the ecologist the surfaces separating different micro-climates; the economist numbers and spreadsheets; while the tourist navigates through the model as it visually will appear. Each of the players sees something different but is still looking at the same thing. It is important that they see the essence of their own disciplines since that effectively shows the working space where they are authorized to propose changes.

Each discipline has another view of the same thing, just like every single person looks differently at the same scene. Ask two people to describe what they have seen, and you end up with two different stories. But still they were watching the same scene. Similar to the birds in a flock, to the behavior of cars on the highway, to people in a meeting round the table, the experts in Protospace are looking to each other to adjust their positions

in real time while they are actively participating in the developing scene. In Protospace one is looking at the 3D model through his/her own pair of disciplinary eyes, while the other players may have a different look at things. The central theme of building tools for Collaborative Design and Engineering (CD&E) is to develop the 3D model by focused disciplinary input, synchronous with the input of the other disciplines. The ultimate goal of Protospace is to improve the speed and quality

Fig. 13a: 911 HYPERCUBE, ONL [Oosterhuis_Lénárd]
2002, Max Protetch Gallery New York, Open Source
Architecture, March mode

of the design process based on parallel
processing of the knowledge of all disciplines involved from the very first stages
of the design. The players will have immediate insight into the nature of the changes
the other party is putting through. And it is
then up to the flock of players to decide
whether these changes are improving or
damaging the 3D model.

To facilitate this the HRG is working on
intuitive validation systems to validate the
changes that occur in the CD&E process.
None of the disciplines takes the absolute
lead. Just like in a peloton of cyclists, the
players lead by turns to advance as fast
as possible as a swarm, a whole. And to
be perfectly honest, just like in a real
tournament someone's contributions will
turn out to be advantageous and respect-
ed, and this person will eventually attach
his or her name to the project.

One would be quite justified in comparing the process of CD&E with a game that is enfolding. The rules of the game are set from the beginning. The players play by the rules. Good players play an interesting game, inexperienced players a boring one. The question which arises here is, Who sets the rules? The architecture of any outcome of the game resides inside the rules. Simple strong rules create a higher form of complexity than shabby rules. Good architecture builds upon the strength of the set of rules. The true game of architecture in a CD&E setting creates situations where the rules are verified, tested and eventually improved. Only then can one speak of a true evolution of the 3D model – as opposed to enrolling and developing. The one who improves the project rules can be any player at any time in the CD&E process.

Conclusion

Architecture has become a rule-based game played by active members of a flock, communicating with other swarms. As proven above this is true for the F2F process of mass-customization, for the New Kind of Building based on Real Time Behavior (RTB) of programmable proactive structures, and for the interactive process of CD&E. To be able to develop the F2F process of mass-customization we must step one level up and look at the world from there. Not looking from the top down, but from within into the new dimension of complexity. To be able to deal with the RTB of programmable constructs we must step another level up and look at the world from the point of view that all nodes are executing their systems in real time and communicating in real time with their own kin and other species. And in order to be able to get there – two levels up – we need to beam ourselves up into the running process of CD&E, and look at the world from within

the process. The information architect works inside evolution. To summarize the attitude of ONL in the design and production process of the New Kind of Building:

A
One level up to Mass-Customization (MC):
¬ MC means not a single repetetive component in the built structure
¬ MC includes traditional mass-produced [MP] building, while traditional building excludes MC

ONL achieves MC by:
¬ Developing the generic parametric detail
¬ Establishing the File to Factory (F2F) process
MC and F2F are based on:
¬ Point Cloud
¬ Scripts, routines and procedures to instruct the control points

B
Two levels up to Real Time Behavior (RTB):
¬ Constructs are developed as running processes
¬ The building reconfigures itself constantly
¬ RTB includes traditional static architecture, while traditional architecture excludes dynamic RTB

ONL achieves RTB by:
¬ Defining building components as actuators
¬ Feeding the actuators with data in real time
¬ Relating the actuators to the game program
RTB is based on:
¬ Swarm behavior
¬ Game Theory
¬ Collaborative Design and Engineering (CD&E)

This text was originally written for the Non Standard Praxis Conference in September 2004 at MIT, Cambridge, USA.

References:

[1] Smart Dust:
B. A. Warneke, K. S. J. Pister, "An Ultra-Low Energy Microcontroller for Smart Dust Wireless Sensor Networks," Int'l Solid-State Circuits Conf. 2004, (ISSCC 2004), San Francisco, Feb. 16-18, 2004.
"The goal of the Smart Dust project is to build a self-contained, millimeter-scale sensing and communication platform for a massively distributed sensor network. This device will be around the size of a grain of sand and will contain sensors, computational ability, bi-directional wireless communications, and a power supply, while being inexpensive enough to deploy by the hundreds. The science and engineering goal of the project is to build a complete, complex system in a tiny volume using state-of-the art technologies (as opposed to futuristic technologies), which will require evolutionary and revolutionary advances in integration, miniaturization, and energy management." Website: http://robotics.eecs.berkeley.edu/~pister/SmartDust/.

[2] Utility Fog:
J. Storrs Hall, "Utility Fog: The Stuff that Dreams Are Made Of."
"Imagine a microscopic robot. It has a body about the size of a human cell and 12 arms sticking out in all directions. A bucketfull of such robots might form a 'robot crystal' by linking their arms up into a lattice structure. Now take a room, with people, furniture, and other objects in it – its still mostly empty air. Fill the air completely full of robots. The robots are called Foglets and the substance they form is Utility Fog, which may have many useful medical applications. And when a number of utility foglets hold hands with their neighbors, they form a reconfigurable array of 'smart matter'." Website: www.imm.org.

[3] Boids:
C. W. Reynolds (1987), "Flocks, Herds, and Schools: A Distributed Behavioral Model," in Computer Graphics, 21(4) (SIGGRAPH '87 Conference Proceedings), pp. 25-34.
"The aggregate motion of a flock of birds, a herd of land animals, or a school of fish is a beautiful and familiar part of the natural world. But this type of complex motion is rarely seen in computer animation. This paper explores an approach based on simulation as an alternative to scripting the paths of each bird individually. The simulated flock is an elaboration of a particle system, with the simulated birds being the particles. The aggregate motion of the simulated flock is created by a distributed behavioral model much like that at work in a natural flock; the birds choose their own course. Each simulated bird is implemented as an independent actor that navigates according to its local perception of the dynamic environment, the laws of simulated physics that rule its motion, and a set of behaviors programmed into it by the 'animator'. The aggregate motion of the simulated flock is the result of the dense interaction of the relatively simple behaviors of the individual simulated birds." Website: www.red3d.com/cwr/boids/.

[4] S. Wolfram, "A New kind of Science," Wolfram Media, Inc., 2002, ISBN 1-57955-008-8.
"But my discovery that many very simple programs produce great complexity immediately suggests a rather different explanation. For all it takes is that systems in nature operate like typical programs and then it follows that their behavior will often be complex. And the reason that such complexity is not usually seen in human artifacts is just that in building these we tend in effect to use programs that are specially chosen to give only behavior simple enough for us to be able to see that it will achieve the purposes we want." Website: www.wolframscience.com/.

[5] Acoustic Barrier, architect ONL [Oosterhuis_Lénárd], date of completion December 2004, client: Projectbureau Leidsche Rijn, product manufacturer: Meijers Staalbouw.
"The rules of the game.The brief is to combine the 1.5 km long acoustic barrier with an industrial building of 5,000 m². The concept of the acoustic barrier including the Cockpit building is to design with the speed of passing traffic since the building is seen from the perspective of the driver. Cars, powerboats and planes are streamlined to diminish the drag. Along the A2 highway the Acoustic Barrier and the Cockpit do not move themselves, but they are placed in a continuous flow of cars passing by. The swarm of cars streams with a speed of 120 km/h along the acoustic barrier. The length of the built volume of the Cockpit emerging from the acoustic dike is a ten times more than the height. The concept of the Cockpit building is inspired by a cockpit as integral part of the smooth body of a Starfighter. The Cockpit building functions as a 3D logo for the commercial area hidden behind the acoustic barrier." Website: www.oosterhuis.nl/quickstart/index.php?id=302.

[6] Richard O. Prum and Alan H. Brush, "Which Came First, the Feather or the Bird?", Scientific American, March 2003, pp. 60-69.
"Hair, scales, fur, feathers. Of all the body coverings nature has designed, feathers are the most various and the most mysterious. How did these incredibly strong, wonderfully lightweight, amazingly intricate appendages evolve? Where did they come from? Only in the past five years have we begun to answer this question. Several lines of research have recently converged on a remarkable conclusion: the feather evolved in dinosaurs before the appearance of birds. The origin of feathers is a specific instance of the much more general question of the origin of evolutionary novelties – structures that have no clear antecedents in ancestral animals and no clear related structures (homologues) in contemporary relatives. Although evolutionary theory provides a robust explanation for the appearance of minor variations in the size and shape of creatures and their component parts, it does not yet give as much guidance for understanding the emergence of entirely new structures, including digits, limbs, eyes and feathers." Website: www.sciam.com [and type in the title in the search engine]

[7] Web of North-Holland, architect ONL [Oosterhuis_Lénárd], completed 2002, client Province of North-Holland, product manufacturer Meijers Staalbouw.
"One building one detail. The architecture of ONL has a history of minimizing the amount of different joints for constructive elements. Fifteen years ago this attitude led to minimalist buildings like the Zwolsche Algemeene and BRN Catering. At the beginning of the '90s Kas Oosterhuis realized that extreme minimalizing of the architectural language in the end will be a dead end street. Hence in the office a new approach towards detailing was developed: parametric design for the construction details and for the clad-ding details. Basically this means that there is one principal detail, and that detail appears in a multitude of different angles, dimensions and thicknesses. The parametric detail is scripted like a formula, while the parameters change from one position to the other. No detail has similar parameters, but they build upon

the same formula. It is fair to say that the WEB is one building with one detail. This detail is designed to suit all different faces of the building. Roof, floor and facade are treated the same. Front and back, left and right are treated equal. There is no behind, all sides are up front. In this sense parametrically based architecture displays a huge correspondence to the design of industrial objects. Parametric architecture shares a similar kind of integrity." Website: www.oosterhuis.nl/quickstart/index.php?id=117.

[8] TT Monument, artist ONL [Oosterhuis_Lénárd], completed 2002, client TT Circuit Assen, product manufacturer Aluminiumgieterij Oldenzaal.
"We wanted to fuse the motorbike and the driver. The speed of the bike blurs the boundaries between the constituting elements. Each part of the fusion is in transition to become the other. Each mechanical part is transformed to become the mental part. The wind reshapes the wheels, the human body fuses into the new man-machine body. The fusion creates a sensual landscape of hills and depressions, sharp rims and surprising torsions. The fused body performs a wheelie, celebrating the victory and pride like a horse. The TT Monument is the ultimate horse: strong and fast, agile and smooth, proud and stubborn." Website: http://www.oosterhuis.nl/quickstart/index.php?id=169.

[9] Protospace is a Laboratory for Collaborative Design and Engineering in Real Time, directed by Professor Ir Kas Oosterhuis, at the Delft University of Technology.
"The transaction space for collaborative design is an augmented transaction space. Through sensors and actuators the senses of the designers are connected to the virtual prototype. The active view on the prototype is projected on a 360° panoramic screen. Active worlds are virtual environments running in real time. The active world is (re)calculating itself in real time. It exists. It represents a semi-autonomous identity developing a character. The active worlds are built according to a game structure. A game is a rule-based complex adaptive system that runs in real time. The rules of the game are subject to design. The collaborative design game is played by the players. Eventually the structure of the design game will co-evolve while playing the game." Website: http://130.161.126.123/index.php?id=5.

[10] Handdrawspace, artist ONL [Oosterhuis_Lénárd], Architecture Biennale, Venice, 2000, interactive painting installation in the Italian Pavilion.
"Handdrawspace is based on seven intuitive 3D sketches which continuously change position and shape. The trajectories of the sketches are restlessly emitting dynamic particles. The particles are appearing and disappearing in a smooth dialog between the 3D Handdrawspace world and the visitors at the biennial installation Trans-Ports. When you step into the cave and go right to the centerpoint, a new color for the background of the Handdrawspace world is launched. The inner circle of sensors triggers the geometries of the sketches to come closer, and thus to attract the particles. They become huge and fill the entire projection. Stepping into the outer ring of sensors the particles are driven away from you, and you experience the vastness of the space in which the particles are flocking." Website: http://www.oosterhuis.nl/quickstart/index.php?id=197.

[11] Trans-Ports, architect ONL [Oosterhuis_Lénárd], Architecture Biennale, Venice, 2000, interactive installation.
"The active structure Trans-Ports digests fresh data in

real time. It is nothing like the traditional static architecture which is calculated to resist the biggest possible forces. On the contrary, the Trans-Ports structure is a lean device which relaxes when external or internal forces are modest, and tightens when the forces are fierce. It acts like a muscle. In the Trans-Ports concept the data representing external forces come from the Internet and the physical visitors who produce the data which act as the parameters for changes in the physical shape of the active structures." Website: http://www.oosterhuis.nl/quickstart/index.php?id=346.

[12] MUSCLE, architect ONL [Oosterhuis_Lénárd], interactive installation in Forum des Halles, Pompidou Center, Paris, 2004.
"For the exhibition Non-Standard Architecture ONL realizes a working prototype of the Trans-Ports project called the MUSCLE. Programmable buildings can reconfigure themselves mentally and physically, probably without considering completely displacing themselves like the Walking City as poposed by Archigram in 1964. Programmable buildings change shape by contracting and relaxing industrial muscles. The MUSCLE is a pressurized soft volume wrapped in a mesh of tensile Festo muscles, which can change their own length. Orchestrated motions of the individual muscles change the length, the height, the width and thus the overall shape of the MUSCLE prototype by varying the pressure pumped into the 72 swarming muscles. The balanced pressure-tension combination bends and tapers in all directions." Website: http://www.oosterhuis.nl/quickstart/index.php?id=347.

[13] 911 Hypercube, Ground Zero exhibition, Max Protetch Gallery, New York, 2002.
"The war in Afghanistan took more lives than the attack on the WTC. Why do most people feel different about the death toll in Afghanistan than about the sudden death of the WTC and 3000 users? Are some killings more just than others? Are the winners always those who kill the most people? If you examine crime movies you will find out that the 'good' ones are always licenced to kill many 'bad' ones. Is that why the US had to kill more Afghans and Saudis than there were citizens killed on 9/11? Come on America, wake up and find a way to take revenge in a more intelligent way. Do not waste our precious time on the easy killing of poorly armed people. Let's face it. Everybody was fascinated by the 9/11 event. Everyone was thrilled to watch the movie, over and over again. Only extremely disciplined individuals could resist watching. Quickly destroying things is naturally much more appealing than   slowly synthesizing things. How can we as architects appeal to people's fascinations by building new stuff?" Website: http://www.oosterhuis.nl/quickstart/index.php?id=155.

[14] Protospace 1.1 Demo, directed by Professor Ir Kas Oosterhuis, built by the Hyperbody Research Group, Delft University of Technology, 2004.
"How do stakeholders collaborate in real time? Imagine the following scene. The game leader opens a file, the active world. Each file has a specific set of rules on how to propose changes in the file. However, there will be developed a detailed Protospace protocol on how to play by the rules. The referee explains to the players how to play the game. Each stakeholder chooses a view on the file. One player may choose dif-ferent roles at the same time. The players enter the action according to the rules of the game when it is their turn to propose a change. When playing the role of a specific stakeholder only that

particular view on the database is displayed. While
delivering the input through sensors and numpads the
players are free to walk and chat in the group design
room. The group design room is an open design studio,
a social transaction space. The other players watch the
active player and respond immediately like in a normal
conversation." Website:
http://130.161.126.123/index.php?id=5.

Fig. 13b: 911 HYPERCUBE, ONL [Oosterhuis_Lénárd]
2002, Max Protetch Gallery New York, Open Source
Architecture, March mode

special reports

models of mixed-
Reality
Environments

Today, the world of information understands the human being at the center of a wirelessly linked world, which comprises all networks. We study different concepts of integrating digital processes into the space of everyday life. Instead of ignoring the physical space, like in traditional Virtual Reality (VR) approaches, we create interfaces and processes, which link human perception to the computer's program and the real/virtual Mixed Reality space. In our focus is the human being with his/her sensual, cognitive and culturally coded experiences in order to create contact between people via perceptive, performative and mobile interfaces.

Monika Fleischmann is a research artist and head of the department MARS - Media Arts and Research Studies at the Fraunhofer Institute for Media Communication in Sankt Augustin, Germany. In 1988 she co-founded with Strauss Art + Com, Berlin, one of the first transdisciplinary research institutes for computer-assisted media research.

Wolfgang Strauss, architect and media artist, studied Architecture and Visual Communication. He is a researcher, lecturer and teacher in Interactive Media Art and Design, and co-director of the MARS Lab. Strauss & Fleischmann artistic work has been presented in exhibitions and festivals widely throughout the world e.g. at ZKM Karlsruhe, Nagoya Science Museum, SIGGRAPH, ICC - Tokyo, Imagina - Monte Carlo, ISEA and was awarded the Golden Nica at Ars Electronica 1992.

wolfgang strauss, monika fleischmann:

implosion of numbers — performative mixed reality

The digital implosion is the basis for an aesthetics of the unpredictable data space. In this generative space, which is constantly mutating at random, there is no fixed position, neither for the user nor for the objects.

IMPLOSION OF NUMBERS _
PERFORMATIVE MIXED REALITY

Introduction

"The traditional concept of space is a concept based on perspective. It was developed half a millennium ago and perceived space from a fixed and absolute viewpoint as being an endless, homogeneous and three-dimensional expansion. The decisive novelty brought about by cubism was the displacement of this absolute perspective by a relative one. Artists experience the space's unreal comprehensiveness as its essential element ... and that one has to move through space to be able to really experience it as being three-dimensional" [1].

Berlin 1988 – generative transformations of space: "I say cubes and you visualize a cube with six surfaces, eight corners and 12 edges. Cubes, cubes, cubes – a vast amount of cubes. I feed cubes into my computer and it reacts by producing a digital crash! Instead of Euclidean geometry, it presents the implosion of numbers, which changes perspective dynamically with each cursor-movement of the viewpoint. In our first experiments working with computer graphic workstations, the computer screen displays images of

numbers between Zero and One. Like in real-time morphing, we see a continuous transformation of shape. Perspective, proportion and scale of space are transformed into a matrix of free floating numeric data, which points out the mathematization of space and architecture" [2].

The screenshots "Between 0/1" represent interpretations of one and the same set of data. Simple cubes transform into a myriad of elements and figures. It is like Alexander Dorner was saying: each movement of the viewpoint radically changes the view of space. Here, the digital implosion is the basis for an aesthetics of the unpredictable data space. In this generative space, which is constantly mutating at random, there is no fixed position, neither for the user nor for the objects. The snapshots "Between 0/1" demonstrate the transformation of figure and form similar to Eadweard Muybridge's motion studies. The individual pictures show the connection of human sight and perspective to a virtual camera viewpoint. In fact it is a digital camera obscura, which presents images from inside an artificial 3D model-world. Vilém Flusser supposed these images to be representations of his vision: "I dream of a house with walls that can be changed at any time, of a world whose structure is no more than an expression

Fig. 1: Murmuring Fields – staging the space of mixed reality

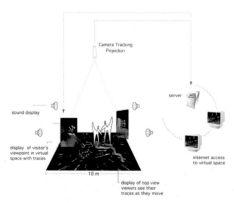
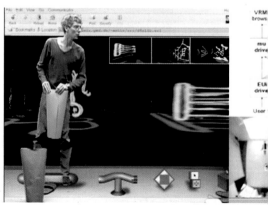

of my ideas" [3]. It is a body-adaptive architecture. It turns space into a space-suit, which is tailor-made camouflage for its user.

Mixed Reality Space to Perform with

A decade later the world of information understands the human being at the center of a wirelessly linked world, which comprises all networks [4]. It is our aim to gain an understanding of the link between man, machine and space. We extend the notion of "Mixed Reality," which Paul Milgram defined as a spectrum extending from real to virtual experiences [5]. We study different concepts of integrating digital processes into the space of everyday life. Instead of ignoring the physical space, like in traditional Virtual Reality (VR) approaches [6], we create interfaces and processes, which link human perception to the computer's program and the real/virtual Mixed Reality space. Our focus is the human being with his/her sensual, cognitive and culturally coded experiences in order to create contact between people via perceptive, performative and mobile interfaces [7]. Due to its superposition with the digitally networked environment, physical space appears to be an information and knowledge space. The term knowledge space [8] refers to an architectural

rapprochement to digitally stored information – for example a digital archive of sounds. The question is, How can information space become physically perceptible beyond a metaphoric sense in the form of a space one can walk into?

Murmuring Fields

"Murmuring Fields" (1999) [9] is based on a mixed-reality environment for performers on different real and virtual stages (Figs 1–4). It is oriented towards the experience of spatial knowledge [10] like the Theatre of Memory [11] or mnemonics, that is, methods of memory training. Mnemonics are a medium, which manifests itself in graphic or space-related interfaces and can be characterized as the interface to memory. Neuroscience today refers to our thinking as a theater play, just as philosopher Giulio Camillo Delmino had transformed the "Art of Memory" [12] into a practical means for constructing a "Memory Theater" in 1550 [13]. This theater was described as a fan-shaped building with a wooden structure, which would allow one or two individuals at a time within its interior to play with memory and to train discourse. The Memory Theater was an aspect of a science of the imagination which was practiced from Antiquity up to the Renaissance.

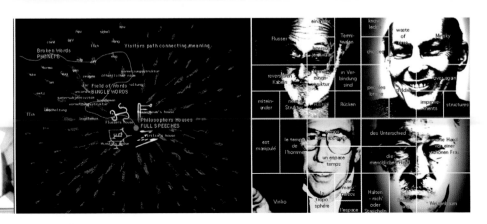

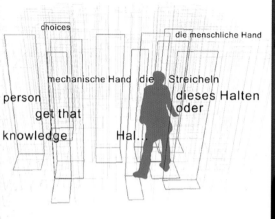

Fig. 2: Murmuring Fields – interaction and movement on the mixed-reality stage

It was used for the development of memory, and also as a mind-map, a connected symbolic space, often represented as a building.

In the soundscape of Murmuring Fields we study collaborative Mixed Reality space. It is explored in a performance by two dancers, using Memory Theater principles of spatially arranged information. The stage of the dancers and the virtual stage environment are linked with each other via optical tracking [14]. The performers literally move in an imaginary landscape of audiovisual signs. Surrounded by voices and words, syllables and sounds, the dancers act in a sphere of digital data which are mixed by their movement. The information space is structured in four zones with acoustic samples in different languages and talks from media thinkers, such as Vilém Flusser, Marvin Minsky, Joseph Weizenbaum and Paul Virilio. The virtual stage is a landscape of iconic signs and archaic pictograms, which are linked to the theories of the individual thinkers. Depending on the speed and direction

of movement, the performers create re-readings for the audience. As the temporal structure of digital signs and sounds appears in a different way, the audience perceives a re-collection of statements. Through the performative use of the Mixed Reality environment a battle of words unfolds. Sound follows movement and thus generates a dynamic circuit of bodies engaged in space. The digital material is re-sampled, re-written and re-composed. The performer's body becomes a musical instrument. The almost audible experience communicates the feeling of something that is created with the body, e.g. playing sounds through body-movement. The dancers' experience is that interactive space creates "a novel understanding of presence, time, duration and space" [15].

The neurologist Hinderk Emrich put forward his thoughts on Mixed Reality by experimenting on stage: "The audience experience everyday events as no longer in harmony with their impressions of their internal and external world. The electronic

space stands for the inner reality, the physical space can be equated with the external world." He describes the process of interaction on different levels. First, he mentions the stage technology – the electronic multi-user stage environment eMUSE, 1998 – as being an enormous "sensitive system" that one can experience via one's own body. Then he refers to the perception the actor has of him/herself: "I do not only see myself from my usual perspective. At the same time, I also watch myself from the exterior, from a second perspective. I observe myself. This is a phenomenon that can also be used for therapeutic purposes. We never live exclusively in the external world; we always live in an imaginary world created by ourselves, too. And, maybe this is the most important task of this installation, to make people understand, that we always live in Mixed Realities" [16].

Murmuring Fields presents a model for an electronic stage. Here Mixed Reality is like a room furnished with data in a multistory box for overlapping spaces of polar consis-

tency. The notion of the room stands for physical interaction space. Data-furniture is an embodiment of digital information allocated to a real object. Data-furniture connects experience of mnemotechnics and cognitive science to the interface. In Murmuring Fields, the body, materiality, mediality and interactivity are placed at the center of observations under the aspect of performance. The body is not only the point where all experience takes place. It is also the interface and the link to all things in the world. These considerations follow the understanding that sensual experience and conceptual reflection are coming together in the "body's sensual thinking," which is a view that has been discussed by the epistemologist George Lakoff in *Philosophy in the Flesh* [17].

Energy Passages:
Reading and Writing the City

"Energy_Passages" (2004) [18] is an art installation in the public space that generates a linguistic space of the city in the form of a data flow (Figs 5–11).

Fig. 3: Murmuring Fields – layers of the mixed-reality stage.

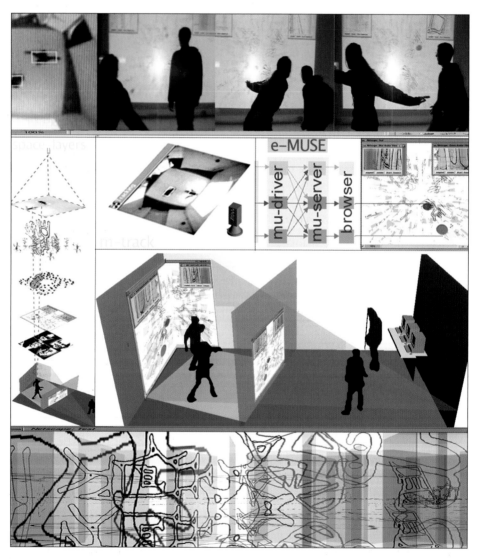

Fig. 4: Murmuring Fields – the electronic stage of transparent polygons and drawings

Hundreds of catchwords taken from current newspapers appear via RSS-Feeds [19] in a projected "information flow." They are spoken by artificial computer voices. As soon as passers-by select individual words, thematically related networks of terms start to perform in this flow. Thus, text is detached from its linear context and is staged as a media reading in urban space.

An automated software analyzes the news everyday and reduces it to the 500 most-used words. The 27,000 words contained in current news are reduced to the 500 relevant ones. The words filtered according to this process appear in a large projection as information flow at Salvatorplatz in front of the House of Literature in Munich. This data flow represents a spectrum of information that usually accompanies us unnoticed throughout the day and which forms our cultural conscience. The words mentioned most frequently in this performative public installation are percent and million. Whereas words such as truth, friendship or love are quite rare, mostly chosen by passers-by.

The public performance process works as follows: Visitors to the installation select individual terms from the information flow via microphone or touch screen. Then a network of terms appears which, in the newspaper, were linked to the chosen terms by content. Computer voices directly react to their selection and accompany these terms in the form of a polyphonic echo. By selecting specific terms, passers-by "rewrite" the newspaper and a "Living Newspaper" thus develops. Their selected catchwords also lead to the retrieval of the corresponding passages from the daily press. The information cube displays a world map indicating the geographical origin of each individual message. This highlights the partnership links that the city has with other urban centers as well as those that do not appear on the map. Whereas some terms contained in the information flow allow for associational links, the fragmented enumeration of individual pieces of text, as they appear in the Living Newspaper, refers to the loss of context that we experience due to the acceleration and mass of information [20]. As a public and experimental stage for the perception and experience of a Mixed Reality, the installation offers a test area, in which those present have a decisive say in shaping the public space. The large projection in the street creates a cheerful space for verbal communication and gestures. Things are turned public. Public items are discussed publicly.

The technical carrier constructions for "Energy_Passages" are the physical architecture for the virtual environment. The construction consisting of aluminum cross beams forms one unit together with the information cube. They serve to contain the projection and the audio technology. The cube is the entry gate and the information interface. It contains all the hardware equipment. Blocks of concrete are

Fig. 5: (top)
Energy_Passages – context based generated cluster, related to the word "Kunst" (art)

Fig. 6: (right)
Energy_Passages – information flow of SZ newspaper, 29.11.2004

necessary for static purposes; looking like cliffs, they frame the information flow. The installation's physical parts have an independent space-shaping impact and are at the same time a symbol for the audio-visual installation that can be heard throughout the day but only becomes visible after dawn. The installation's architecture forms an ensemble of external buildings, an electronic front garden in an urban space. Together with the existing furniture in the form of stone tables and benches by Jenny Holzer, this reading garden has developed into an external space for the House of Literature, which specifically relates to it.

Under the heading of the "Local appointments – The arts in the public space" [21] in Munich, a virtual, sensual and cognitively perceivable urban space was developed, which was mainly created by the electronic medium and algorithms. This new space is clearly understood to be different from spaces existing in the world of goods with its advertising messages and images. The theme of the flow in the form of a large image creates a public and media space which is designed by text, language and light, and which is directly in one's way. It is the moment of time that occurs in the information river onsite. It is as good as real water because it comes as a refreshing instant flow of consciousness.

For the audience the information projected in public space is not difficult to read. The projected text and words represent daily public short-term memory as dispersed by the media. The installation also serves as a media protocol when ranking and filtering the most prominent words used at a place in a given time. Thus the installation mirrors and reflects reality. This process is digitally stored and the data provide the pigment for painting the final imagery of the archived status of this urban intervention, including the

Fig. 7: (top) Energy_Passages – the Living Newspaper created by visitors

Fig. 8: (below) Energy_Passages – in overlay with Jenny Holzer

Fig. 9: (bottom) The physical architecture of Energy_Passages

Fig. 10: Energy_Passages – hundreds of catchwords taken from current newspapers appear via RSS-Feeds in a projected "information flow"

complete four-week proceedings and data tracking of the visitors' activities. This image in fact looks like an architectural iconic abstraction of the city (at a certain time).

Conclusion

We use the term Mixed Reality for different scenarios of body, space and time. In Murmuring Fields digital information is positioned on stage. Body and spatial sound environment are linked. Space is extended in virtual space. In Energy_ Passages media reality like the newspaper creates an interactive and time-based public space. The collective mind of the daily newspaper is displayed in public space for digital and subjective transformation. This allows a re-reading of reality by building one's own associative topic maps. With Energy_Passages we support the formation of opinion in public discussion. Our strategies mentioned above are inspired by the Renaissance Memory The-

ater, which we are developing further into a Mixed Reality Experience. In today's Mixed Reality Memory Theater the notion of memory is extended in many ways: the memory of the body, the memory of space, the memory of time, the memory of thoughts. In the future, Mixed Reality applications will be integrated in everyday life as touchless, invisible or ambient immaterial interfaces. Therefore we have an interest in experimenting with new technologies from an artistic point of view. With our "Interactive Experience Lab" we provide a basis for a debate on experiments and prototypes, which we prove and reflect in playful learning scenarios or as artistic installations in public space. Memory Theater, digital archives, information space and spatial structuring of knowledge are some of the topics we have identified as important issues for new architectural concepts.

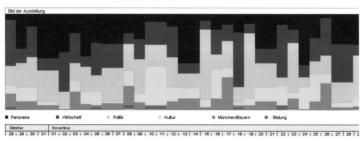

Fig. 11: Energy_Passages – city energy protocol from 28. 10. – 29. 11. 2004

130

References

[1] Monika Flacke-Knoch, "Museumskonzeptionen in der Weimarer Republik. Die Tätigkeit Alexander Dorners im Provinzialmuseum Hannover," Marburg, 1985, Vol. 3, pp 73ff.

[2] Wolfgang Strauss, Monika Fleischmann, "Virtuelle Architektur und Imagination," in Film + Arc 1, Artimage Graz 1993; and Wolfgang Strauss, Monika Fleischmann, "Space Of Knowledge: Zur Architektur Vernetzter Handlungsräume." URL: http://netzspannung.org/cat/servlet/CatServlet/$files/150567/Strauss.pdf.

[3] Vilém Flusser in "Home of the Brain" (1992) by Fleischmann/Strauss. URL: http://netzspannung.org/database/home-of-the-brain/en.

[4] With regard to this topic, see the initiative of the "Wireless World Research Forum." URL: http://www.wwrf.org/ founded by Alcatel, Ericson, Nokia, Siemens etc. in 2001.

[5] This term was first used by Paul Milgram and Fumio Kishino in 1994 and coined in "A Taxonomy of Mixed Reality Visual Displays," IEICE Transactions on Information Systems, Vol. E77-D, No.12, 1994.

[6] Steve Bryson of NASA Ames describes how the history of the term VR = Virtual Reality developed in "Virtual Reality: A Definition History." URL: http://www.fourthwavegroup.com/fwg/lexicon/1725w1.htm (12. December 2004).

[6] See Wolfgang Neuhaus' contribution "Der Körper als Schnittstelle" [The body as interface] in Telepolis on the conference organized by us cast01. URL:http://www.heise.de/tp/r4/artikel/9/9668/1.html (12. December 2004).

[8] See "Von Der Information Zum Wissensraum ... Der Begehbare WissensRaum: Eine Architektonische Annäherung an Digitale Archive," in Global J. of Engng. Educ., Vol. 7, No. 3, Published in Australia, © 2003 UICEE, URL: http://www.eng.monash.edu.au/uicee/gjee/vol7no3/StraussW.pdf.

[9] Murmuring Fields, 1999, URLs: http://www.erena.kth.se/murmur.html, http://www.medienkunstnetz/werke/murmuring-fields/, http://netzspannung.org/database/murmuring-fields/.

[10] Knowledge presentations do not refer to knowledge in the sense of wisdom, but in the sense of knowing.

[11] See Peter Matussek, "Computer als Gedächtnistheater" [Computer as Theater of Memory]. URL: http://www.sfb-performativ.de/seiten/b7.html; and Peter Matussek, "Der Performative Turn: Wissen als Schauspiel," published on netzspannung.org, knowledge room for digital art and culture. URL: http://netzspannung.org/positions/digital-transformations/ first published in Monika Fleischmann, Ulrike Reinhard (Editors), "Digitale Transformationen – Medienkunst als Schnittstelle von Kunst, Wissenschaft, Wirtschaft und Gesellschaft," whois verlags- und vertriebsgesellschaft, Heidelberg 2004.

[12] Francis A. Yates's "The Art of Memory" is the classic study of how people learned to retain vast stores of knowledge before the invention of the printed page (Francis A. Yates, "The Art of Memory," The University of Chicago Press, 1966).

[13] Ibid, p. 157.

[14] See zeitenblicke 2 (2003), Nr. 1; and Monika Fleischmann, Wolfgang Strauss, "netzspannung.org: Kollektiver Wissensraum und Online-Archiv" [Collective Knowledge Space and Online Archive], URL: http://www.zeitenblicke.historicum.net/2003/ 01/fleischmann/fleischmann.pdf.

[15] Wolfgang Strauss, Monika Fleischmann et al., "The eRENA Report: Linking between real and virtual spaces," 1999, http://www.imk.fraunhofer.de/ images/mars/erena99_D6_2.pdf.

[16] eMUSE – electronic Multi User Stage Environment, 1999, URL: http://www.erena.kth.se/ emuse.html.

[17] George Lakoff, Mark Johnson, "Philosophy in the Flesh. The Embodied Mind and Its Challenge to Western Thought," Basic Books, New York 1999.

[18] See the project description and technical explanation, URL: http://www.energie-passagen.de/projekt.htm.

[19] Really Simple Syndication = XML-based format to synchronize content.

[20] See the simulation and the installation's archive, URLs: http://www.energie-passagen.de/webinstallation.html., http://www.energie-passagen.de/presse2.html.

[21] German title of the exhibition: "Ortstermine 2004 – Kunst im öffentlichen Raum", URL: http://www.ortsterminemuenchen.de/seiten/projekte_2004/energie_passagen.html.

Take a ten-minute trip round the world or visit the 16th century and tour Siena Cathedral. Glide through underwater realms without getting wet or effortlessly scale the Himalayas . Give your imagination free reign, stretch your mind. Have fun learning. Cybernarium makes all that possible. It is a place where seeming opposites come together: research and fun, theory and passion, the real and the virtual. Cybernarium is the first experience and learning center that uses novel media technologies to bring together innovative teaching strategies and constantly changing content.

Torsten Fröhlich studied Computer Science at the Technical University in Darmstadt, Germany. Before joining the Fraunhofer Institute for Computer Graphics as a researcher in 1996, he worked at NASA's Johnson Space Center implementing a shared virtual environment for astronaut training. In 2002 he organized a first public exhibition on virtual and augmented reality, the Cybernarium Days 2002. After finishing his PhD thesis in 2002, he joined the Cybernarium Projektgesellschaft as managing partner and technical director (CTO).

Rolf Kruse studied Architecture at the Technical University in Darmstadt. During his studies he teamed up with the Fraunhofer Institute for Computer Graphics (IGD) for various virtual reality projects. In 1994 he became head of the City and Architecture Department of Art+ Com - Interactive Media Solutions in Berlin, before founding the Laboratory for Media Architecture (LAMA) in 1997 to develope new spatial interfaces. In 2002 he took over the development of Cybernarium as Managing Director (CEO).

torsten fröhlich, rolf kruse :

cybernarium_ a mixed- reality edutainment center

Whoever visits Cybernarium explores unknown worlds.
You change time, space, proportion and perspective, meet
limits and move beyond them.

CYBERNARIUM _A MIXED-REALITY EDUTAINMENT CENTER

Cybernarium is a spin-off enterprise of the Fraunhofer Institute for Computer Graphics in Darmstadt, Germany. Its mission is to employ mixed-reality technologies for public education and entertainment. After proving the potential and applicability of mixed realities at very successful temporary exhibitions, the Cybernarium has moved into its own building in Darmstadt, presenting a permanent exhibition since the summer of 2004. In 2007, Cybernarium will move into the Science and Convention Center Darmstadt, which has been under construction since the fall of 2004.

Mixed Reality as Medium for Knowledge Transfer and Entertainment

The origin of mixed realities is industrial and military visual simulation. Virtual reality had been developed since the late '80s of the last century and was being applied in training simulators and to support rapid prototyping for industrial production. Virtual reality creates interactive spatial audiovisual environments for a single or multiple users. The ultimate goal is to immerse visitors as much as possible into a virtual world. Equipped with special glasses, visitors of all ages explore novel worlds of knowledge by interactive study trips. 3D graphics immerses visitors into virtual environments, which allow the user to actively influence what is going on.

While virtual reality consequently blanks out the real environment, augmented reality combines real and virtual images. Continuous motion tracking of the locations of spaces and objects makes it possible to overlay the real environment with synthetic images. A room can be "augmented" with virtual objects, characters or annotations. Both technologies are summarized by the term mixed reality. Mixed-reality contents are never just re-produced from pre-recorded material but generated by powerful computers at the time of use. Bringing the user into the simulation loop allows real-time interaction. Users turn from spectators to actors. That makes mixed reality a perfect medium for knowledge transfer. It enables people to explore spaces of knowledge actively, play an active role in a simulation, try things out, experience the consequences and finally gain a deeper under-

Fig. 1: The Siena virtual cathedral, developed for EXPO 2000 and now permanently visible at Cybernarium

Fig. 2: Interior study of Cybernarium (Panorama)

standing of complex systems. However, the application of mixed realities in public education and entertainment is still not well investigated. Mixed reality technology was simply not available outside R&D laboratories due to the immense costs of hardware and software. With the advent of cheap commodity computer hardware (graphics cards, video cameras, projection systems etc.) and 3D modeling and authoring software, that situation changed.

Group Interaction

People visit public institutions in groups such as families, peer groups, school classes etc. Sharing their experiences with others is part of the fun. While the interaction between humans and computers normally happens "one on one" (one computer screen, one user), mixed realities can serve multiple users. But today most scenarios allow only a single person to be (inter)active at a time. The other visitors

Mixed reality enables people to explore spaces of knowledge actively, play an active role in a simulation, try things out, experience the consequences and finally gain a deeper understanding of complex systems.

Fig. 3: (top left, top right) Visitors exploring Cybernarium's Interactive Planetarium in 3D: While one
visitor navigates the others watch fascinated

Fig. 4: (bottom left) Spraying virtual graffiti on the
walls of the global village

Fig. 5: (bottom right) A trip to a car factory of the
future

remain passive spectators until it is their turn to take control. Consequently, group interaction is an area of research and development. How can we involve groups into a mixed-reality environment and enable each member to interact? How can we represent and support group dynamic processes like cooperation, competition or finding mutual consent? Cybernarium has already developed exhi-bits for up to eight users – the goal is to cover audien-ces of more than 100 visitors.

Interactive Cinema

That research will lead to an interactive immersive cinema for large audiences, which is the main attraction of the Cyber-narium at its new location at the Darm-stadt Science and Convention Center. At the end of the path group interaction

and modern technology for audiovisual presentations will merge: Breathtaking stories can be experienced together and in more than three dimensions. The goal is to make this attraction the "cinema of the future" and to export it globally.

Fig. 6: Swimming with the sharks in the Virtual Oceanarium

Fig. 7: Interior study of Cybernarium (Panorama)

A Diverse Sojourn

Whoever visits Cybernarium explores unknown worlds. You change time, space, proportion and perspective, meet limits and move beyond them. Those who leave take questions and answers, ideas and inspiration with them. They will see the world with new eyes, look closer and come again. A theatrical interplay of the various attractions is building the success of Cybernarium. Visitors are offered a balanced range of various possibilities, from individual discoveries to evocative experiences in small groups to active participation in the show at the interactive cinema. The range of small and large attractions, individual and group events, educational and entertaining moments ensures a stimulating, diverse visit.

Fig. 8: Virtual Graffiti: Not adoring the creativity of others but being creative oneself

New Spaces

The understanding of space as a mixed-reality environment offers an enormous and fascinating opportunity to convey knowledge to the Cybernarium visitors in an unprecedented way. Emerging technologies and those already available are enabling the integration of the physical space provided by the building and its furnishings with the simulated spaces created by the interactive installations. Physical movements of people and real objects seamlessly merge with animated virtual environments that are potentially enlivened with avatars. Based on the current exhibits and already gathered know-how, Cybernarium and its partners will develop these next-generation mixed realities incorporating all aspects of technical design, spatial design, continuous interaction and multi-user dramaturgy.

Fig. 10: Foyer of the future Science and Convention Center Darmstadt (Panorama)

Fig. 11: Augmented Man (avatar)

Fig. 9: Exterior design of the future Science and Convention Center Darmstadt, into which Cybernarium will move in 2007.

T_Visionarium is an immersive, interactive, multi-modal environment made of inflatable fabric. By enabling viewers to immerse themselves in virtual modalities, it explores the expressive potential of transcriptive as opposed to conventional interactive narrative. Navigation through the data sets dramatizes the televisual information archived in T_Visionarium's database. This strategy allows viewers to experience the sense of a wholly personalized authorship.

Dennis Del Favero has had numerous solo shows and has participated in various major international exhibitions, including Münchner Stadmuseum, Neue Galerie Graz, Sprengel Museum Hannover, ZKM I Center for Art and Media Karlsruhe and many more. He holds an Australian Research Council QEII Fellowship and is co-founder and co-director of the Center for Interactive Cinema Research (iCinema) at the University of NSW and Artist-in-Residence at ZKM.

Neil Brown is a leading researcher in the areas of cognitive theory of art, creativity and art education and a member of the Center for Cognitive Issues in the Arts (CCIT) at the University of Bristol, UK. Professor Brown's research is centered on two projects. The first aims at establishing theoretical grounds for a philosophically neutral ontology of the artifact. The second seeks empirical evidence for the way in which children and adults' vernacular theory of art conditions their understanding of works and informs their practice.

Jeffrey Shaw has pioneered the use of interactivity and virtuality in his many art installations since the late 1960s. His works have been exhibited worldwide at major museums and festivals. From 1991–2003 he was director of the Institute for Visual Media at the ZKM I Center for Art and Media Karlsruhe, Germany. Since 2003, he has been founding co-director of the Center of Interactive Cinema Research (iCinema) at the University of New South Wales, Sydney, Australia.

Peter Weibel was appointed professor of visual media art at the University of Applied Arts, Vienna in 1984. He was head of the digital arts laboratory of the Media Department of NY University from 1984–1989, and founded the Institute of New Media at the Academy of Fine Arts, Frankfurt/M in 1989. From 1986–1995, he was artistic consultant and later artistic director of the Ars Electronica in Linz, and from 1993–1999 curator at the Neue Galerie am Landesmuseum Joanneum, Graz. He commissioned the Austrian pavilions at the Venice Biennial from 1993–1999. Since 1999, he has been Chair and CEO of the ZKM I Center for Art and Media Karlsruhe.

Dennis Del Favero, Neil Brown, Jeffrey Shaw, Peter Weibel:

T_Visionarium_Towards a Dialogic Concept of Digital Narrative

T_Visionarium augments existing research into narrative as a form of dialogical inter-action within virtual space, by the addition of viewer-generated transcription of cine-matic information within virtual time.

T_VISIONARIUM _TOWARDS A DIALOGIC CONCEPT OF DIGITAL NARRATIVE

Concept of the Dialogic

Currently the dominant position in aesthetics conceptualizes narrative as mono-temporal or linear. The digital, by contrast, is conceptualized as a-temporal or non-linear. This monochronic explanation reduces narrative to a mono-temporal process that fails to account for not only the potential of interactive digital narrative but also the workings of conventional cinematic narrative itself. In contrast the *concepts of dialogic and transcriptive* provide an understanding of narrative as a multi-temporal process operating beyond the structuralist notions of linearity and non-linearity. The dialogic refers to the interactive multiplicity immanent within the digital, while the transcriptive describes the cinematic capture and reconstruction of multimodal forms of information within virtual environments. Recently the authors explored these concepts as a model for the production of interactive narrative by means of an experimental study entitled T_Visionarium, Cinemas du Futur, Lille Cultural Capital, 2004.

T_Visionarium – Experimental Design

T_Visionarium is an immersive, interactive, multi-modal environment set within a dome 12 m in diameter by 9 m in height made of inflatable fabric [see Fig. 2]. It allows viewers to spatially navigate a televisual database in virtual time. On entring the dome viewers place a magnetic position tracking device, connected to cableless stereo headphones, on their heads [Figs 1, 3]. By means of a remote control interface, viewers are able to select from a range of parameters which arrange the televisual database according to thematic categories such as "dialog" and "crowds." The projection system is fixed on a motorized pan-tilt apparatus mounted on a tripod which projects televisual data onto the interior skin of the dome. The projection system is articulated to the tracking device so that viewers, by shifting their heads, move the large projected viewing window across the interior surface. This tracking device identifies the exact orientation of an individual viewer's point of view, which in turn controls the orientation of the projector so that it presents an image directly in front of where the viewer is looking. The audio-visual data streams are virtually distributed over the entire surface of the dome, so that the movement of the projection windows enables the viewer to navigate between these multi-modal data streams. The delivery software creates a spherical distribution of all the televisual data by their real time texturing onto a virtual polygonal model of the dome. In other words the stored televisual data sets are physically mapped over the dome surface such that each data set is allocated a specific window grid on the dome's surface. This enables viewers to navigate between each data set by merely shifting their point of view. This mapping strategy applies to both image and sound.

Seamless transitions between discrete image and sound events are handled by specific design parameters of the audio-visual delivery system. The acoustic delivery system is based on the use of RF (radio frequency) cableless headphones, which each visitor wears while inside the dome. Multiple audio channels are interactively mixed down for stereo RF delivery to all the headphones. The mixing of these channels is handled dynamically in immediate relationship to the movement of the pan-tilt projection system so that a fully spatialized sound-scape can be defined inside the dome architecture. This is directly linked to the distribution of the visual content. The mixing of the audio, synchronized with the movement of the pan-tilt projection system, allows a fully spatialised soundscape inside the dome to be synchronized with the distribution and experience of the visual content. These same satellite data streams are recorded onto a hard disc system and sorted within a database. By the application of a recombinatory software matrix, unprecedented narratives are reconfigured from this database by the viewer. By means of their interaction with the matrix interface and simultaneous the movement of their heads and projection window individual viewers originate unique performances on behalf of a larger viewing public of up to eighty persons. This strategy allows viewers to experience the sense of a wholly personalized authorship. To this extent the recombinatory matrix produces a deeply interactive authorship, emergent in the encounter between the viewer and matrix in multi-temporal time.

Fig. 1: Viewers, by shifting their heads, move the projected window across the interior skin of the dome.

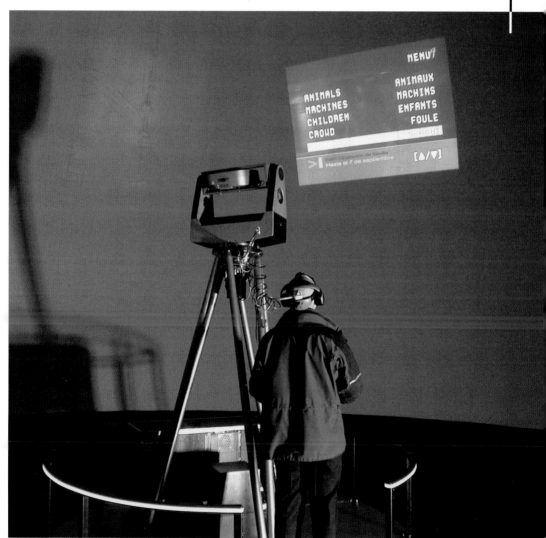

T_Visionarium – Experimental Methodology

T_Visionarium, by enabling viewers to immerse themselves in virtual modalities, explores the expressive potential of transcriptive as opposed to conventional interactive narrative. It allows new recombinatory narrative content to be generated by the viewer. Navigation through the data sets dramatizes the televisual information archived in T_Visionarium's database. These data sets are reconstituted across the interior skin of the dome under the converging impetus of viewer and matrix and are encountered as emerging multitemporal events. Processing is animated by the recombinatory parameters of the interactive software. It is based on recorded broadcasts from 48 global satellite television channels recorded sequentially in 30-minute intervals over a single 24 hour period. This data is post-processed by the matrix in ways that hyperlink the variegated data sets in virtual time to form a large scale database. Based on deep content authoring, which allows high levels of semantic and abstract classification, the matrix sorts the data according to characteristics of language, movement, color, speech, composition, lighting and pattern recognition as organized by identifiers originating as functional agencies within a conceptual framework [1]. The viewer explores the results of these recombinatory searches by moving the projection window across the dome screen. Selecting the parameter "dialog," for example, ushers forth intersecting cascades of current affairs, sports, features, life style, historical, scientific, musical and anthropological episodes of "dialog" across 48 channels, a multiplicity of languages, numerous time zones, and a heterogeneity of cultures within the simultaneous timeframe of the visualization apparatus.

The recombinatory matrix unravels these convergences of multi-modal data at temporal levels of intensity, archival density and extensiveness that only become recognizable as they coalesce in the complex time projected across the dome. Thus, with changes to their point of view, viewers activate a powerful navigational matrix that produces a directional flow of information in which the expressive meaning of the data is boundlessly transcribed. The profoundly multi-temporal logic echoes the theoretical architecture implicit in digitized audio-visual data [2]. This logic is imperceptible in conventional viewing frameworks, which can only recover time analogically by scanning and juxtaposing whole fragments. At best, conventional viewing establishes symmetrical patterns of temporal resemblance among broadcast items that are based on syntactical properties patent within the data [3]. T_Visionarium's narrative moves beyond this logic of resemblance.

Fig. 2: T_Visionarium is set within a dome 12 m in diameter by 9 m in height made of inflatable fabric.

It is able to unfold new content within a virtual infosphere of digitized images and sounds whose patterning is freed from the constraints imposed by the analogical, or representational, redelivery of information. Sifting through digitized televisual data the viewer unravels sub-visible links. By cutting the multi-modal structure of prerecorded information at a number of aesthetically significant joints the recombinatory matrix coalesces new audio-visual streams into episodes that can be functionally reassigned a narrative. Reassignment is made at the discretion of the viewer within the infinite latitude extended by virtual time. As a consequence narrative becomes a complex event which interlaces a number of intersecting temporal and physical navigations. The viewer, by selecting a specific parameter, can refine these streams by zooming into a specific current within the streams. Once these new virtual time currents are projected across the dome, the viewer can then process them in real time by physically navigating the projection window across the surface of the dome. This interweaving of matrix and viewer navigation precipitates the emergence of unprecedented narratives. In this respect T_Visionarium opens interactive cinema to a multi-modal aesthetic of a kind that is currently confined to the uni-modal contexts such as text-based chat rooms. It augments existing research into narrative as a form of dialogical interaction within virtual space by the addition of viewer-generated transcription of cinematic information within virtual time.

Meta-model Strategies

The T_Visionarium methodology provides a meta-model for dialogic and transcriptive strategies that is appropriate for the semantic and aesthetic reformulation of databases that contain any and all kinds of audiovisual information. By sifting

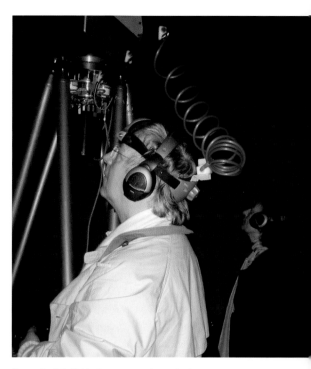

Fig. 3: Each individual viewer originates his/her personalized narrative by navigating a televisual database in virtual time.

through heterogeneous and seemingly inchoate and unrelated data, its transcriptive narratives create original and often unexpected logics of data interrelationships. This "media ecology" recycles waste data into new sensory fields of experience and communication. At an individual level applying transcriptive narrative to materials that are already bound together in proto-narrative formations – such as family-photo and moving-image archives – reveals the profound recombinant potential of transcriptive narrative, especially revelatory to those who are its protagonists.

References

[1] Howard Wactlar, Michael Christel, Yihong Gong, Alexander Haputmann, "Lessons Learned from Building a Terabyte Digi Library," 1999, http://www2.cs.cmu.edu /~hdw/IEEEComputer_Feb99.pdf.

[2] Elizabeth Grosz, "Becomings: Explorations in Time, Memory and Futures," New York: Cornell 1999.

[3] Juan Casares, "Silver: An Intelligent Video Editor," 2001, http://www.2.cs.cmu.edu/~silver/CasaresShort Paper.pdf.

From HardWare to SoftForm is a 3D digital interactive installation dealing with the generative aspects of integral architectures. It investigates the transformation of the virtual object into an environment of light, speed and sound. The generative aspects of integral architectures activate surfaces into a hybrid system of layering. The politics of layering, creasing and wrapping activate zones and environments where boundaries are negotiated and distinctions are blurred. Architecture becomes a responsive medium – appliance, information and environment. Architecture as process.

Winka Dubbeldam is the principal of Archi-Tectonics NYC founded in 1994. She is a graduate of the Faculty of Architecture, Rotterdam, and holds a Masters Degree from Columbia University NYC (1992). In 2002, she received an Emerging Voice Award from the New York City Architectural League. Dubbeldam is an Adjunct Assistant Professor of Architecture at Harvard University and Associate Professor of Practice at the University of Pennsylvania. Archi-Tectonics was a participant in multiple exhibitions, among which at the Museum of Modern Art in New York (The Unprivate House, 1999), the Archi-Lab conferences in Orléans, France, and at the Venice Biennale of Architecture in 2004.

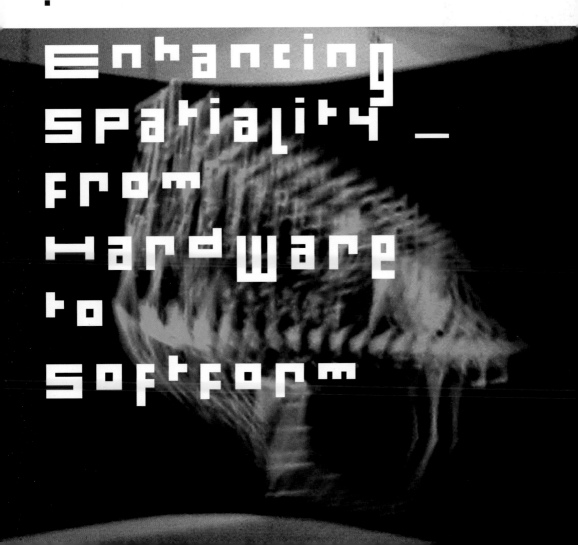

Winka
Dubbeldam
:
Enhancing
Spatiality _
From
Hardware
to
Softform

Direct interaction and feedback to coded data generate a sequential of animate architectures. As an interactive device, enscripted code translates its data from the virtual world to the "real," its sets of higher-dimensional worlds collide, connect and overlap, and boundaries dissolve.

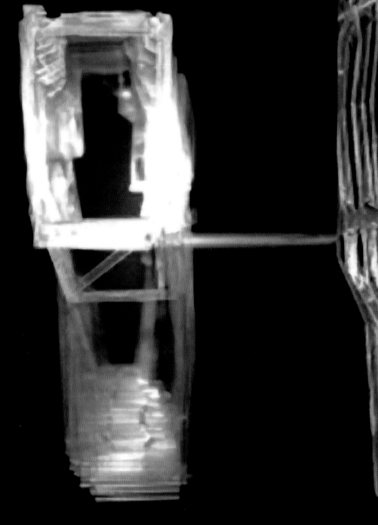

ENHANCING SPATIALITY _
FROM HARDWARE TO SOFTFORM

Interactive Installation

From HardWare to SoftForm is a 3D digital interactive installation of an "armature" exhibited in the Frederieke Taylor Gallery in Chelsea, NYC (Sept. 2002), and the "Art & Idea" Gallery in Mexico City (Sept. 2004). It investigates the transformation of the virtual object into an environment of light, speed and sound. Sensors, or triggers, in the interactive floor, developed by MIT Media Lab, activate the projected construct as a dissection of an organic unit that expands, contracts and envelops. The interaction challenges the relationship of the viewer and the object, constantly re-investigating its "objectness." An ambiguous animated environment ensues, enveloping the visitor and the gallery's confines.

Detlef Mertins writes in "Lyrical Architectonics": "As image, it is imbued with an additional intelligence that allows it to respond to the stimuli of visitors while shifting and mutating according to its own inner rhythms and choreography. Rendering its volume in slices interlaced with plumbing suggests the structural ribs of a battleship or a starship. At once anachronistic and futuristic, it evokes both the mechanical past and the neurological future of an infrastructural conception of architecture. Plastic and interactive, responsive and synergistic, this architecture will not only serve us but also dance with us and envelop us" [1].

The armature, in its true form, originates as a modulated core for a residence, functioning not only as an infrastructural unit but also as a circulatory and generative core. Its organic shape distorts the geometry of the house as "pure box"; it softens, tilts, and fragments. The genera-

tive aspects of the armature are based on its performance and are distilled in its precise configuration and operation. Its positioning in the residence creates overlapping programmatic zones with different environments around and adjacent to it. Architecture as process.

The idea of the "interactive floor" developed by the Context-Aware Computing Group at the MIT Media Lab became an integral part of the gallery installation and enhanced or "triggered" the visitor's interaction with the armature. The trigger is both an activator and a violator of the visitor's interaction with what is animated, i.e., the armature. Once triggered the sensor data are fed back to the computer, launching projected animations and thus creating mixed-reality environments. A special prototype of a modular steel floor, sponsored by Steelcase, incorporates the MIT Media Lab sensor technology of the PIC micro-chip, which analyzes changes in the capacitance of the interactive floor due to the compression of the foam dielectric. The sound technology further enhances the affect; localized hypersonic sound beams developed by Robotics International scramble sound until the sound waves hit a surface; hence the sound will seem to be projected from that surface and not from the speaker, thus creating a super spatial environment. They are integrated seamlessly and invisibly into the architecture of the space, to further enhance the spatiality of the 3D-projection space.

Perception and Interactivity

The difference between frame and interface lies in the distinction between passive *perception* and active *participation*. Where the frame defines, the interface mediates. Objective perception operates through *interactivity*, which exists only through the interface, not the frame.

156

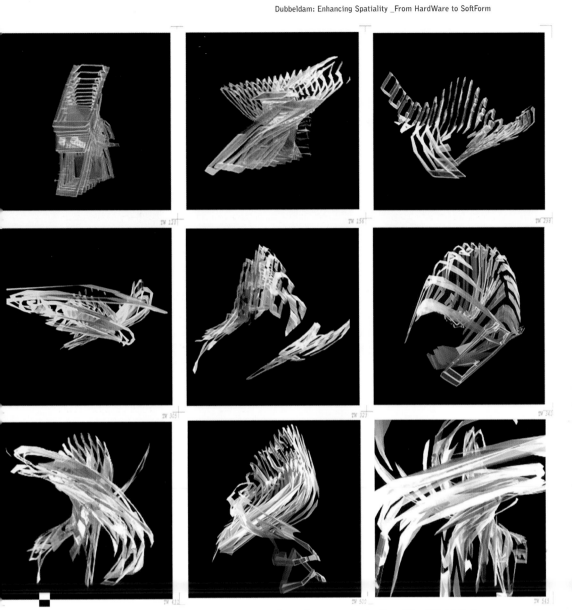

Fig. 1: Sequence of animation stills of "Twist Me."
Once triggered it sends a signal to the cpu to transform the "armature" in an environment of light,
speed and sound.

Framing is a filmic device; it merely creates a geometric and physical boundary, thus defining a distant viewpoint. The frame is meaning, has emotions. The interface on the other hand is neutral, situates itself between the virtual and the viewer, negotiates. As in animation, its analog is to be found in an informational system, its elements in data. But where in animation form is created by time, the interface performs over time.

Direct interaction and feedback to coded data generate a sequential of animate architectures, to be activated by the viewer. As an interactive device, enscripted code translates its data from the virtual world to the "real", its sets of higher-dimensional worlds collide, connect and overlap, and boundaries dissolve. Always already infor-med, it calculates through code and data, in order to generate the data-scapes we now inhabit, unfinished, adapting, flexing, reacting.

Interactive animate architectures thus call into question the permanence of built form, (mind over matter), the importance of the whole and the part (matter and memory) and the exogenous character of all urban life. As Husserl says in *The Origin of Geometry*: "Precisely in this activity of free variation, and in running through the conceivable possibilities of the life-world, there arises, with apodictic self-evidence, an essentially general set of elements that go through all the variants. These endless modulations, these spatio-temporal shapes, imply the generation of spatial constructs not as static devices but as a set of transformations over time" [2]. The notation of perceptions of dreams, memories and time in surface registrations of force fields, smart systems and programmatic mappings are indeed a combination of art, science and luck.

Fig. 2: (top, bottom) The interactive projection space wraps the visitor in an animated environment, constantly changing and adapting as one triggers.

Archi-Tectonics sees architecture as a series of inventions. The studio operates not unlike a laboratory in which research is an important segment of the design process and the computer is an active agent in that process. Each project is seen as a challenge in itself, as well as possible further research on the subjects we are interested in. We integrate the computer as a *generative tool* and not solely as a re-presentational or technical drawing implement. Here "dynamic structures" in architecture are not seen as "moving objects" but surface registrations of force fields, smart systems and programmatic mappings. The inflection of surfaces transforms the 2D plane of the facade and/or wall into a 3D spatial device, to be occupied, inhabited and trespassed. The question of movement is in essence an expression of the traditional, still pervasive mechanistic way of thinking, as opposed to a generative,

process-oriented organismic approach.
The basis of the organismic paradigm –
the notion that an organism is characterized by its immanent patterns of organization – is similar to the notion of spirit,
also described by Leibniz as monads
and by Hegel as *Begriff* or Absolute Idea.
These organizing phenomena occur on all
levels: in society, in behavioral processes,
and in nature. On all levels, time and
space relationships are inseparable.

Conclusion

Now, at the beginning of the 21th century, the computer has accelerated mass
media into digital electronic communication – whose tendency toward specialization and individualization has fragmented
mass society of the postwar period into
a *society of niche cultures* (Alvin Toffler),
whose de-massified niches commandeer
the space of the Internet. The net operates not only on this microscale but also
on a macro one, increasing globalization
is transforming our cities into physical
expressions of global economies in which
local cultures remain only as traces.
Within this global network, a new hybrid
condition proliferates, in which the relationship between local and global is constantly adjusting. Situated precisely
between the real and the virtual, architecture is challenged, yet resists...

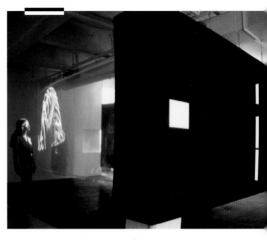

Fig. 3: The gallery installation shows both the real-
time projection space as well as the abstract computer generated animations in a recessed monitor,
a "window" to the virtual world beyond.

The From HardWare to SoftForm Installation was
made possible through a grant of the Dutch Foundation of Art, Architecture and Design, Amsterdam.

Credits

Design
Archi-Tectonics

Project Team
Winka Dubbeldam, Michael Hundsnurcher,
Ana Zatesalo, Susanne Bellinghausen, Leo Yung.
In cooperation with Ted Selker, MIT Media Lab

Digital Programming
Als Design, Seiichi Saito

Interactive Components Consultant
Beatrize Witzgall

Interactive Floor Surface
MIT Media Lab, Ted Selker

Sound Design
Jesus Colao Martinez

Sponsors
The Dutch Consulate of New York,
Steelcase Inc.

References

[1] Detlef Mertins, Lyrical Architectonics, in From
HardWare to SoftForm (catalog), 2002.

[2] Edmund Husserl's Origin of Geometry, Nebraska
University, The Bison Book Edition, 1989.

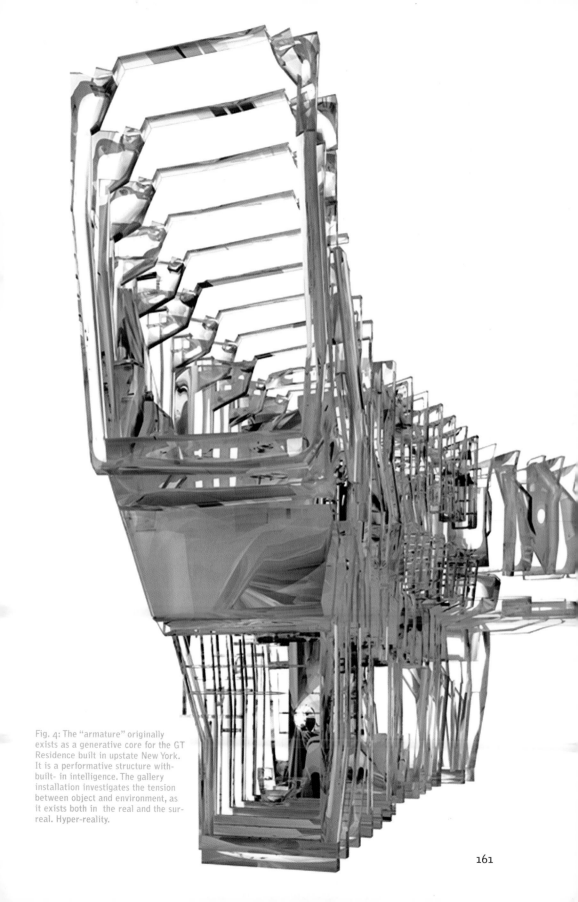

Fig. 4: The "armature" originally exists as a generative core for the GT Residence built in upstate New York. It is a performative structure with-built- in intelligence. The gallery installation investigates the tension between object and environment, as it exists both in the real and the sur-real. Hyper-reality.

161

The link between analog and digital fields concerning the relationship between architecture and virtual media demands new functional and typological concepts: Our concept of space revolves around the movement of space. The aim is the decontextualization and recombination of the media, remediation and new design of informative physical spaces. In order to think and even practice new type of architecture new instruments are needed. The existing software is insufficient and in most cases not even programmed for a new vision of architectural space. The code of architecture, its alphabet, needs to be changed.

Ivan Redi and Andrea Schröttner are principals of ORTLOS architects in Graz, Austria, founded in 2000 as a network of interdisciplinary partners. With their strong commitment to the on-line working methods, ORTLOS has focused on expanding classical architectural tasks by simulating virtual environments to be applied to future realities and by using cutting-edge computer technologies. Their work has been published and exhibited world wide, among others at Venice Biennale 2000. Ivan Redi and Andrea Schröttner are currently teaching at Graz University of Technology.

ivan redi, andrea schröttner :

The Relationship between architecture and virtual media

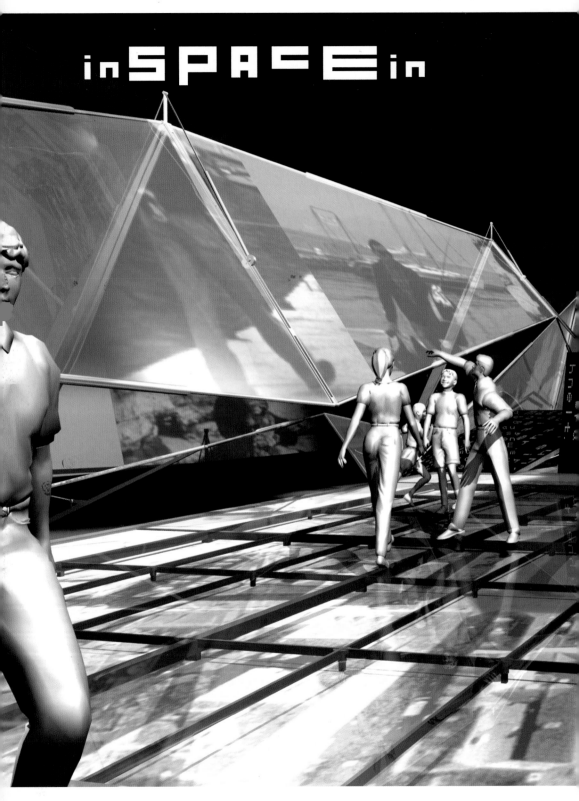

inSPACEin

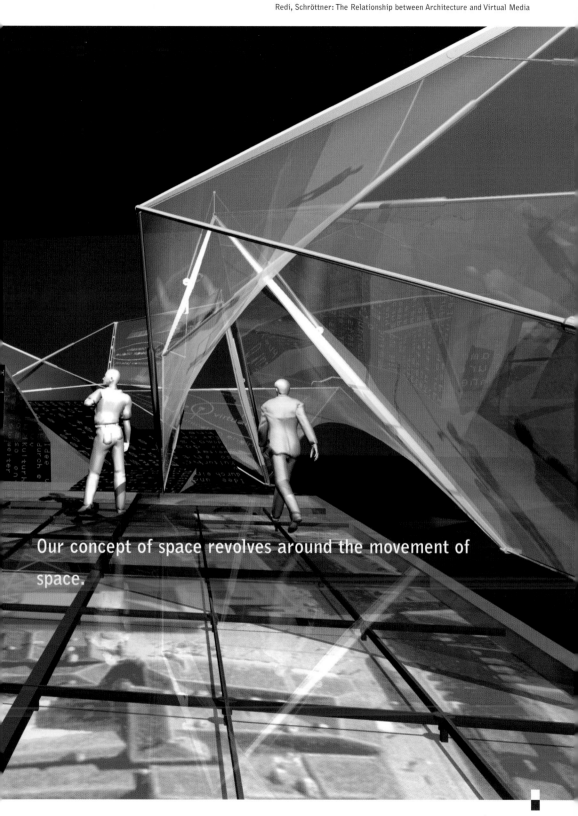

Our concept of space revolves around the movement of space.

THE RELATIONSHIP BETWEEN ARCHITECTURE AND VIRTUAL MEDIA

inSPACEin

In 2002, one year before Graz became the cultural capital of Europe, we were asked by the director Wolfgang Lorenz to design a way to show all aspects of the cultural impact existing in the city through a mobile exhibition touring in major European capitals. It should be a preview of all cultural events in 2003, covering various topics: architecture, art, literature, music, theater, dance and others. Above all it should visualize the spirit of Graz as a major attractor for visitors. In other words the task was to minimize and pack the whole city in a bag and send it on its journey. In 2004, inSPACEin reached the final round of the competition for the Austrian pavilion for EXPO '05 in Japan and was honored as the runner-up entry.

The main intention was to create an architecturally formulated information-communication environment filled with a cultural content based on the program for the representation of any city. With this installation we are teletransporting one "urban atmosphere" to another. The link between analog and digital fields concerning the relationship between architecture and virtual media demands new functional and typological concepts: Our concept of space revolves around the movement of space. Spaces inbetween, "media cloths" as projection surfaces for cutting-edge information technology and hardware, defined by the parametric structure, are able to adjust themselves to the user's programmatic wish with various choreographies.

As a first thought, we define an area in the area. The superimposition of captured parallel realities and media should occur. "Moving walls," "video floor," image projections, "broken information strips" are elements that should form this area and shape it unpredictably and constantly through change. "Moving walls" is a construction of eight aluminum profiles, pneumatic "arms" with three joints each, connected to each other with pneumatic telescopes, since the change in the position of one arm causes the change of all. The series of IK (Inverse Kinematics) simulations are done to find out all possible positions, since the profiles are defining the space through membranes for the projections spanning between them with 30% stretchable material, where the folds in the material should be avoided. Five projectors are used for the sharp backplane projection controlled by the special synchronizing software developed by the Ars Electronica team (one of the consulting partners during the development phase). The movement is very slow and the change of the space is barely noticeable for the user. Video floor is about 60 m^2 modular steel construction with security glass on the top. Plasma screens mounted under glass are controlled as well through sync software which simulates video splitting, so the user has the feeling that he is going through the main street of the desired city or flying over a programmed scape. On the end of the video floor are broken "information strips" which are four folded steel fingers with LEDs on top, where the video signals will be translated into texts. This structure supports another level of information, which should be provided to the user. So, the inSPACEin information-communication environment shifts from "moving bodies through space" into "moving space with bodies." Further on, there are space behaviors and effects which can be activated by sensors (light, sound, smells, fog, etc). The information that parametrically defines the form of this area is grasped by telecommunication means and can be pre-ordered by the users, for example – over the Internet or through input-stations distributed in the city.

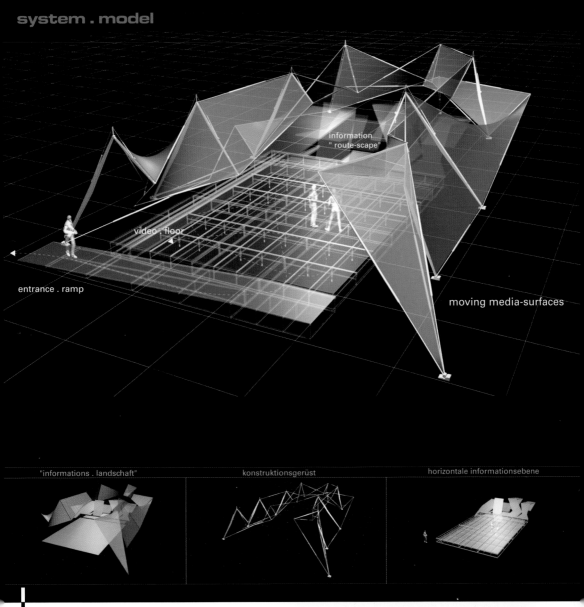

information
" route-scape"

video . floor

entrance . ramp

moving media-surfaces

"informations . landschaft"   konstruktionsgerüst   horizontale informationsebene

Fig. 1: (top) System model explains the elements of inSPACEin: moving aluminum pneumatic "arms" connected by the spanning projection membrane, video floor with the ramp and four steel "fingers" with running-text LED surface.

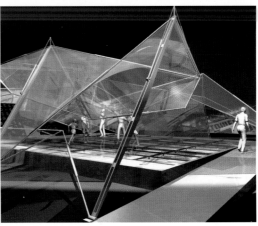

Fig. 2: (right) inSPACEin – a rendering of the system model above

a·n·d·i

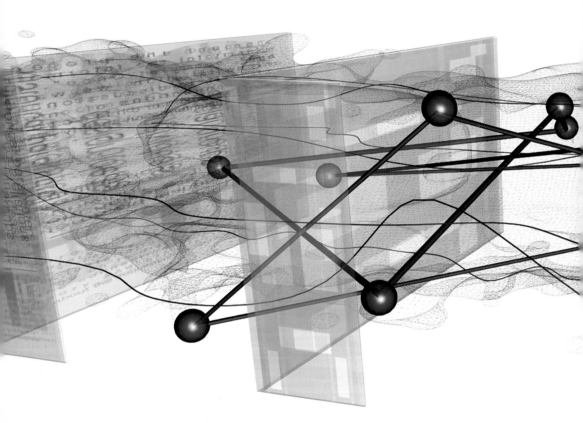

The only way to bring about decisive changes in the practice of architecture is to change the "architectural code."

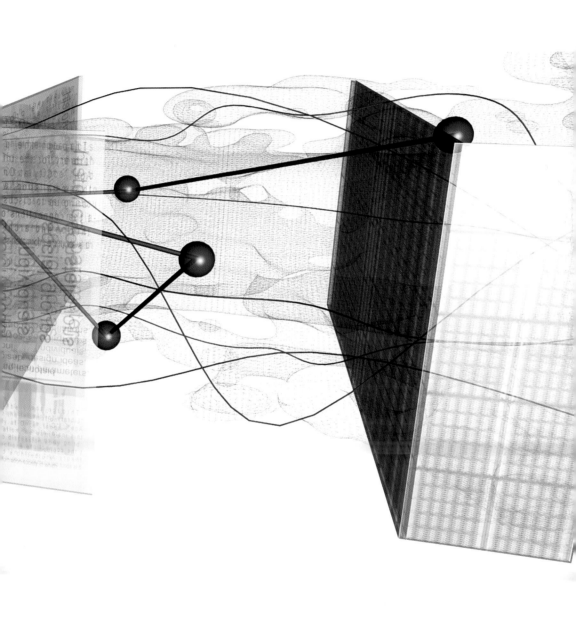

A.N.D.I.

In order to think and even practice new type of architecture new instruments are needed. The existing software is insufficient and in most cases not even programmed for a new vision of architectural space. Secondly, the architectural code, its alphabet, needs to be changed! In order to be able to change it, we will have to liberate it first and then make it publicly accessible. Open-source architecture, the development and use of A.N.D.I. (A New Digital Instrument for creative networked collaboration) is definitely the most immanent innovative future scenario and will change the situation significantly.

This working method will make a new generation of projects possible. It is an operating system based on the Internet which works interdisciplinary and internationally during each architectural or art project to solve complex urban, sociological and architectural problems, to increase the creative dimension of proj-

ects, and to improve communication during the process of conception, designing, planning, production and realization of projects. Again, the only way to define new architectural strategies and thus bring about decisive changes in the practice of architecture is to change the "architectural code." In order to enable a discourse that is all-embracing, comprehensive and sufficiently complex, this source code needs to be open and free. Then it will be possible to win over a large community for actively discussing relevant topics in forums and to motivate them to be highly involved in the creative processes.

A.N.D.I. has two basic features. On the one hand, it is a database-driven collaborative environment and, on the other hand, it will enable the development of future software and tools for networked creative collaboration. Initially, "A.N.D.I." will address a group of people and partners who are highly motivated and looking for individual ways of participating and interven-

Fig. 3: Design of the user interface with navigation based on "focus + context" method.

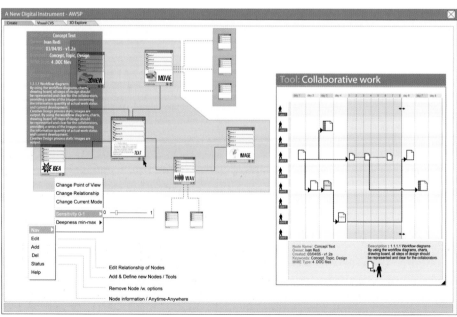

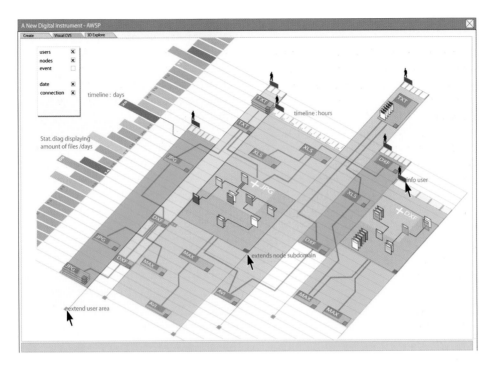

ing in their local and global urban situations. The main actors will be architects, urban planners, net artists, sociologists, media theorists, technology partners and developers, economy experts, production firms, service companies and, last but not least, clients. The ultimate objective and our vision will be to bring all those users together and create the virtual working space for the projects in their first creative conceptual phase.

The first steps in this direction are as follows: improved communication between the user and the developer, as well as the generation of complex systems of parametric procedural decisions. The changes of architectural production are linked to changes in thinking about architecture and architectural practice. A work will no longer be an expression of a single individual; it is an expression of the collective. Moreover, it is an expression of a virtual platform – one of a network of influences which are continuously being reorganized by all the participants involved.

Fig. 4: User interface for multiple authorships – a part of AWSP (Active Work Server Pages) supporting synchronous working methods. In this module every project participant is able to view his or her particular input in the context of the whole process and keep a clear overview of every design step. This interface must be usable for interdisciplinary partners, Web-oriented and runnable on every OS.

Fig. 5: AWSP (Active Work Server Pages) is a part of A.N.D.I. system – a digital environment supportive for the connected intelligence and creative networked collaborative work.

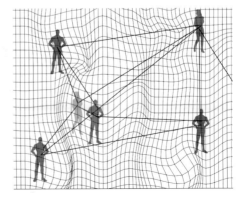

About ORTLOS

ORTLOS must be a kind of matrix, an infinite, constantly changeable field of the creative entries of those who shape it. From a certain size on, constructs show the first signs of self-organization. And so it has been with ORTLOS right from the beginning. It is a kind of virus that is spreading, and although it is in the background, it makes you gradually sink into a world whose laws correspond to a different logic. ORTLOS is an instrument for nomadic working methods.

Credits

inSPACEin – 2002-2004
Mobile Information - Communication Environment

Client: Graz Cultural Capital 2003 & Republic of Austria
ORTLOS architects: Ivan Redi and Andrea Schröttner with Martin Frühwirth, Djorde Kitic, Bernd Graber, Viola Rein,
Consulting: Ars Electronica Linz – Future Lab

A.N.D.I. - A New Digital Instrument for networked creative collaboration 2001-2004
Open source project - http://www.ortlos.at

ORTLOS architects: Ivan Redi and Andrea Schröttner with Vincent Cellier, Martin Frühwirth, Kira Kirsch, Peter Holzmann, Katrin Knass; Programmer: Neboja Dinic, Dragan Jovanovic, Aleksandar Stojiljkovic, Milos Stamenovic; Project Management: Ference Schröttner.
ORTLOS network: Martin Krusche, Net.Author; Maja Engeli & Kerstin Högger, Research Architects

Supported by: the Republic of Austria, KUNST.Bundeskanzleramt; Stadt Graz.Kulturamt; Land Steiermark, Abteilung Kunst & Abteilung für Wissenschaft und Forschung; Kultur Kontakt – Austria

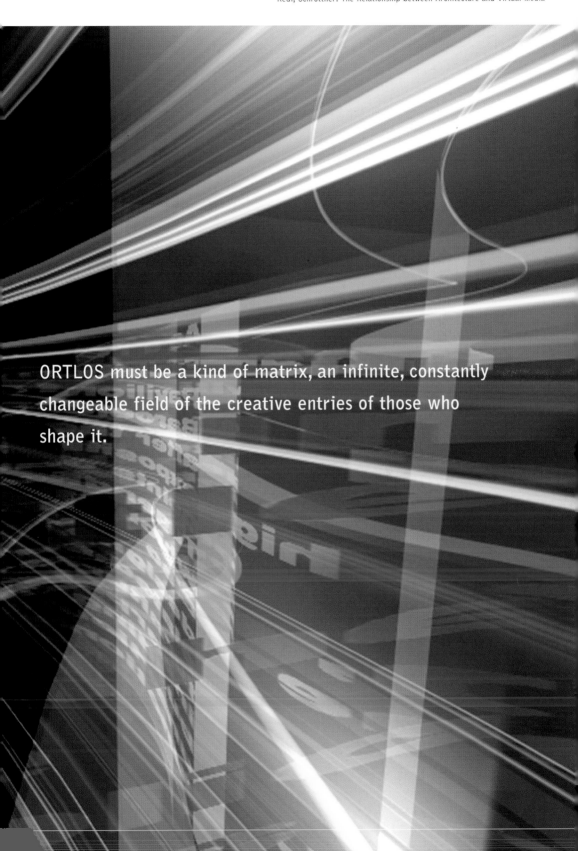

ORTLOS must be a kind of matrix, an infinite, constantly changeable field of the creative entries of those who shape it.

Architecture is beginning to steer away from the static compilation of separate parts and move toward an integrated system of dynamic and interactive components and interfaces. The shift toward organic, responsive and fluid designed forms, structures and materials is blurring the boundaries between analog and digital worlds. The virtual/real and real/virtual equilibrium means a more dramatic change in which the design process has no beginning and no end and can also be reversed if needed to enhance the overall product.

Stuart A. Veech is the principal of veech.media.architecture, founded in 1993 in Vienna, Austria as an interdisciplinary unit of architects, media designers and artists. He studied architecture at the University of Cincinnati, the Architectural Association, London, and the University of Applied Art, Vienna. Currently part of an international team conducting research on "Ambient and Augmented Environments" in London. From 1998-2001 he was guest lecturer at Vienna University of Technology, Department of Architecture, Professor William Alsop. Veech is the recipient of multiple awards, the most prestigious ones being Award in Gold at Adolf Loos Staatspreis Design 2003 and Eyes + Ears of Europe Award in Gold 2002 for his project Zeit im Bild (Newsroom).

stuart a. veech

:

architecture as a media catalyst

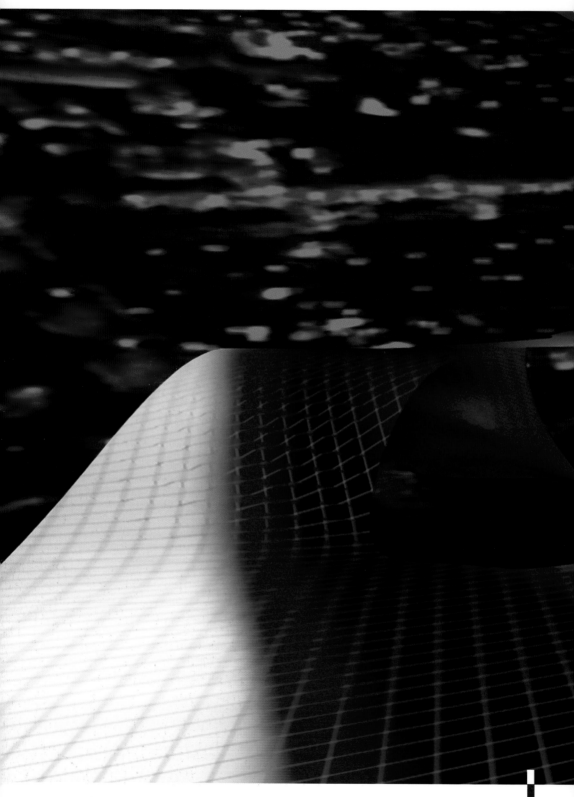

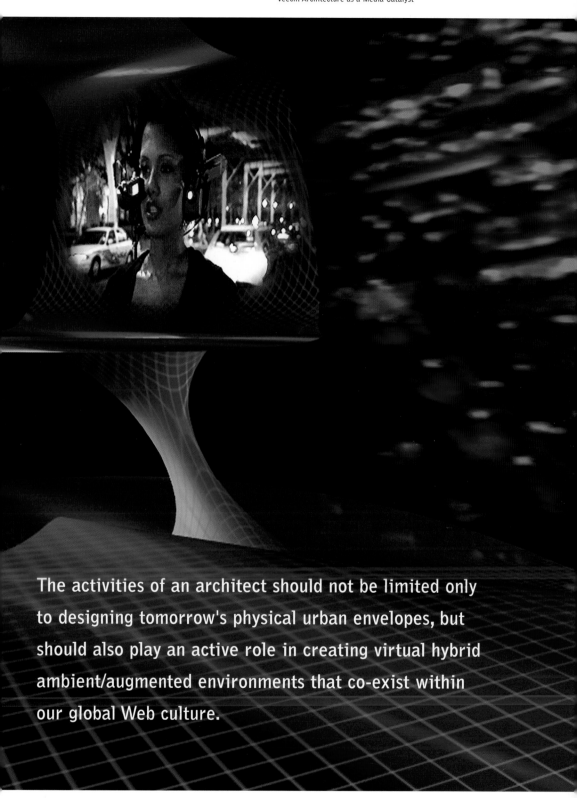

The activities of an architect should not be limited only to designing tomorrow's physical urban envelopes, but should also play an active role in creating virtual hybrid ambient/augmented environments that co-exist within our global Web culture.

ARCHITECTURE AS A MEDIA CATALYST

Introduction

Marshall McLuhan's famous terminology "the medium is the message" and "the global village" accurately anticipated today's digital culture. One could argue that his observations appear to be more in tune with the Web world and cyberspace hype that we are experiencing today and not limited to talking exclusively about television and its impact on society. Transformed by the rapid spread of electronic media and global communication networks, McLuhan's argument for understanding new media and its impact on society is in tune with the IT revolution. New information technologies have been successfully integrating art, design and advertising, and are making an impact on our urban environments, forcing architects to adapt their methodologies to embrace the newer forms of communication and tools. The digital world provides a fertile ground for the exploration and development of the next generation of tools which creative individuals can use to create tomorrow's multimedia environments.

Media.Architecture

Although broadcasting of live events and simultaneous satellite transmission worldwide has become a part of daily life since the Apollo moon landing, we recognized that architects are needed to explore the future of creating responsive communicative environments for a global mass-media culture. Our investigation into media spaces began in 1993 as we moved our office to Vienna to begin work on a corporate design strategy for ORF – Austrian Broadcasting Corporation. The first television studio designs began as an experimental exercise in the fusion of information technology and graphics into a hybrid architectural media environments. This opened up a completely new opportunity to explore areas that were previously excluded from traditional architectural practice.

It became the laboratory where we analyzed digital vs. analog architecture, virtual spaces 2D/3D space, on-air/live events, camera movements and choreography, theatrical lighting, perspective distortion and illusion, flexible and adaptable spaces, material research and testing, etc. By implementing high-end 3D software tools and coordinating a team of modelers, animators and specialists in video production, we are moving toward a more fluid approach to the design process where the collaborative input/output is stimulating continuous research and exploration into the relationship between media cultures and architecture environments. The new collaborations highlight what Buckminster Fuller prophesized as the need for the "comprehensive designer," that is, "the synthesis of artist, inventor, mechanic, objective economist and evolutionary strategist."

Virtual/Real and Ambient/Augmented

The IT revolution and the introduction of high-end 3D computer software into the design phase has significantly altered the way in which architects and designers have represented their ideas in the past ten years. The digital revolution has increased the flexibility to analyze a rather complex set of elements through the development of new tools that accelerate the decision-making process. As a result, architecture is beginning to steer away from the static compilation of separate parts and move toward an integrated system of dynamic and interactive components and interfaces. The shift toward organic, responsive and fluid designed forms, structures and materials is blurring the boundaries between analog and

Fig. 1: ORF "Zeit im Bild" Studio wide-angle view of the illuminated table, floating plasma screens, and the satellite image printed background to form the spatial identity.

digital worlds. The virtual/real and real/virtual equilibrium means a more dramatic change in which the design process has no beginning and no end and can also be reversed if needed to enhance the overall product.

The activities of an architect should not be limited only to designing tomorrow's physical urban envelopes, but should also play an active role in creating virtual hybrid ambient/augmented environments that co-exist within our global Web culture. It is here where the creative implementation of innovative technologies support the utopian visions of the architect/designer which will result in an explosion of new ideas and information exchange.

"Schauplätze der Zukunft"
Virtual Studio Architecture
ORF – Austrian Broadcasting Corporation,
1999–2000

The virtual studio architecture, powered by live 3D real-time texture mapping, was created for a six-part "Science and Technology" television program. The animated wireframe circumvented the technical limitations on modeling and texturing complexity for live broadcasting and superimposed contrasting elements which increased color and lighting variations, camera positioning, visual movement and perspective spatial depth.

Figs 2–3: (left, bottom) ORF "Schauplätze der Zukunft" Dynamic virtual studio architecture developed for a simultaneous live broadcast environment – "on-air" architecture.

A_World: Multimedia Center
Allianz Group, 2002–2003

The design team proposed a prototype urban building, a "liquid body" enclosed in a glass volume, positioned in major urban centers worldwide that can adapt to the specific site characteristics without losing its strong brand identity and programmatic content. The central organic shape, a flexible multimedia/exhibition space, is contained in a rectangular transparent glass envelope with a vertical public urban plaza distributed over a series of lightweight elevated platforms suspended from the roof structure. The platforms dissect the interior volume at various levels creating overlapping interior circulation patterns and accomodating supporting services such as galleries, entertainment units and cafe/restaurants. Multimedia projections and interactive screens located on the surface of the curved shape and media terminals positioned on the transclucent vertical platforms link the interior activities of the user in the enclosed media environment to the outside viewer. The notion of a physical navigation system, or architecture as "interface," develops where the content of the enclosed interior multimedia spaces, events, and activities is visually communicated to the surrounding urban context. A new urban plaza is formed from the vertically overlapping open spaces, which mirrors the complex modern urban lifestyles.

Group

Figs 4–6: (top, bottom left and right) A_World
A prototype urban building – a "liquid body"
enclosed in an rectangular transparent glass
envelope develops architecture as "interface."

183

To "blur" is to make indistinct, to dim, to shroud, to cloud, to make vague, to obfuscate. Blur is equated with the dubious. A blurry image is typically the fault of a mechanical malfunction in a display or reproduction technology. For our visually obsessed, high-resolution, high-definition culture that measures satisfaction in pixels per inch, blur is understood as a loss. Yet blur can also be thought positively – as de-emphasis. The Blur Building for Swiss EXPO 2002 is an experiment in the construction of de-emphasis and the immersive potential of blur on an environmental scale: while architecture is dematerialized, media becomes physically tangible.

Elizabeth Diller and Ricardo Scofidio are artists/architects and founding principals of Diller Scofidio + Renfro NYC. Since the formation of their partnership in 1979, they have produced a large body of prestigious work including architecture, planning, public art, museum- commissioned art works, experimental theater and dance works, books, and Web projects. Elizabeth Diller is professor of Architecture at Princeton University; Ricardo Scofidio is professor of Architecture at Cooper Union School of Architecture. Currently the main DS+R architectural projects are the Eyebeam Museum of Art and Technology NYC, and the Boston Institute of Contemporary Art.

Elizabeth Diller, Ricardo Scofidio:

architecture as a habitable medium

blur

Unlike entering a building, Blur is a habitable medium – one that is spaceless, formless, featureless, depthless, scaleless, massless, surfaceless and dimensionless.

ARCHITECTURE AS A HABITABLE MEDIUM

The Blur Building is an exhibition pavilion built for Swiss Expo 2002 on Lake Neuchatel in the town of Yverdon-les-Bains. It is an architecture of atmosphere. Its lightweight tensegrity structure measures 300 ft wide by 200 ft deep by 75 ft high. It streches over a total of 80,000 square feet. The primary building material is indigenous to the site, water. Water is pumped from the lake, filtered, and shot as a fine mist through a dense array of high-pressure mist nozzles. The resulting fog mass produced is a dynamic interplay of natural and man-made forces.

A smart weather system reads the shifting climactic conditions of temperature, humidity, wind speed and direction, and processes the data in a central computer that regulates water pressure to an array of 31,500 nozzles. Four hundred visitors can occupy the building at any time. Upon entering the fog mass, visual and acoustic references are erased, leaving only an optical "white-out" and the "white-noise" of pulsing nozzles.

Blur is an anti-spectacle. Contrary to immersive environments that strive for high-definition visual fidelity with ever-greater technical virtuosity, Blur is decidedly low-definition: there is nothing to see but our

dependence on vision itself. Unlike entering a building, Blur is a habitable medium
– one that is spaceless, formless, featureless, depthless, scaleless, massless, surfaceless, and dimensionless. On the platform, movement is unregulated and the
public is free to wander in an immersive
acoustic environment by Christian Marclay.

From the platform, the public can ascend
a stair to the Angel Deck at the summit.
Emerging through the fog is like pierc-
ing a cloud layer while in flight to the
blue sky. Submerged one-half level below
the deck is the Water Bar, which offers a
broad selection of bottled waters from
around the world.

Figs 1–3: (top, above, bottom) Blur – An exhibition pavilion built for Swiss Expo 2002 on Lake
Neuchatel in the town Yverdon-les-Bains.

blur/babble

It is an immersive environment in which the world is put out of focus, and so provides a perfect context to put our visual dependency into focus.

Babble

The originally planned but eventually not realized part of Blur Building was Babble – a media event that was to use wireless transmission and the challenge of navigation. This project was to be made in collaboration with IDEA of Palo Alto. It was never realized because of the loss of our sponsor, a telecommunications company after a corporate takeover.

Involuntary actions and reactions such as body language, blanching from shock and blushing from embarrassment have great communicative power, particularly when conventional language fails. What if these wireless technologies acquired more intelligence to expand telecommunications beyond conventional language, spoken or written? What if they could transmit emotions, expressions, personal attraction, aversion, or embarrassment?

The project introduces proxi-communications: a telecommunications network recalibrated to a human scale and used to enhance communication in our immediate surroundings. As the visitor in Blur is deprived of the clues typically used to gauge both the physical environment and social relations within, the media project compensates with a social communication system that extends the body's natural system of perception.

A prosthetic skin in the form of a raincoat, equipped with a sixth sense, allows each visitor to navigate the cloud and interact with other visitors without speech. This new form of "social radar" produces a condition of anonymous intimacy. As the human skin is a sensory organ that picks up and also broadcasts involuntary reactions beyond an individual's control such as blushing from embarrassment or goose bumps from the cold, cannot this prosthetic skin do the same?

All visitors to Blur-Babble enter at the Log-In station at the base of the entrance ramp and are given a questionnaire while they wait in a queue. Answers to the questions will be used to produce a response profile for each visitor that is continually added to a database. Each visitor is also given a "braincoat," a smart raincoat with embedded technologies in its skin. These technologies include an imprint of the visitor's response profile that enables the coats to communicate with one another once the visitors reach the media platform. The basis for this communication

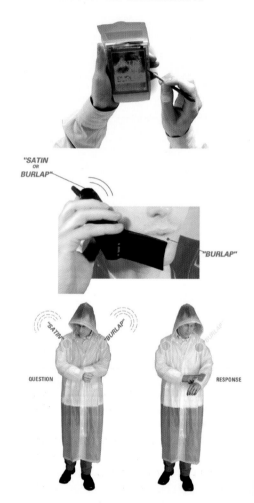

Fig. 4: "Braincoat" – a smart raincoat with embedded communication technologies in its skin allowing the visitors to communicate with one another and navigate thecloud (see also Fig. 6).

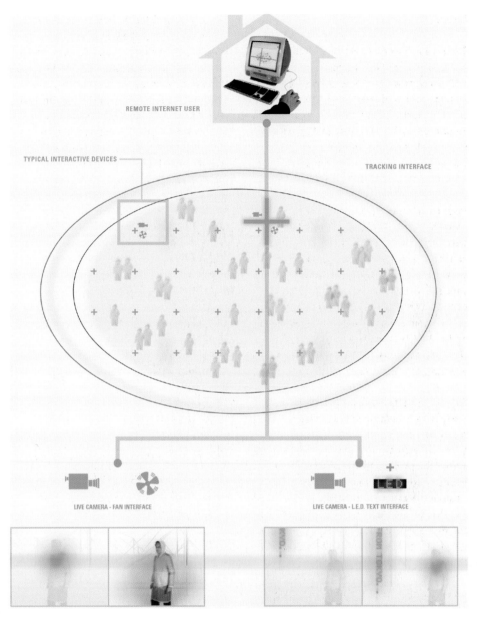

REMOTE INTERNET USER

TYPICAL INTERACTIVE DEVICES

TRACKING INTERFACE

LIVE CAMERA - FAN INTERFACE

LIVE CAMERA - L.E.D. TEXT INTERFACE

is the cumulative database. This multidimensional statistical matrix comprises a data cloud that complements the fog cloud. The questionnaire is an integral part of the creative project and is conceived in collaboration with a fiction writer. Visitors' responses (their profiles) are collected in a multidimensional data matrix that governs the experience of the project. To ensure proper interpretation

Fig. 5: Intoducing proxi-communications – a telecommunicatins network recalibrated to a human scale and used to extend the body's natural system of perception.

and statistical correlation we worked closely with a psychological profiler and a statistician. Though each visitor responds to only 20 questions there is a question set of several hundred. With the aid of a clustering program used for Web profiling, such as Firefly, visitors' profiles can be compared and evaluated by establishing correlations among the entire range of questions. Near the Log-in station visitors are each handed a PDA preprogrammed with a series of questions on successive screens. The visitor answers the questions at whatever pace he/she chooses. The PDA is then passed to an attendant who links it with the central database and synchronizes the visitor's profile with his or her coat. We also considered a mobile phone and the braincoat itself as input devices.

The braincoats have the capacity to display three types of responses. First, a visual response. As visitors pass each other on the Blur platform, their coats can compare character profiles and change color indicating their degree of affinity, much like an involuntary blush. When stimulated, the chest panel of the translucent braincoat displays a diffused colored light that glows in the fog. The coat functions like a sophisticated Lovegetty, a matchmaking device popular with Japanese teenagers. The color range is coded so that a shift toward cool blue-green represents antipathy and a shift toward warm red, affinity. The degree of color shift intensifies in proportion to the strength of the match.

The coat can also render an acoustic response. With the knowledge of visitors' profiles, the communication network can identify visitors that have the highest affinity and assign each visitor a statistical match. An acoustic pulse, like a sonar pinging, sounds from a speaker embedded in each coat. The pulse is audible only to the wearer. Like sonar, as matched visitors approach one another the steady pulse accelerates, reaching a peak when they are very near. Slow or rapid, the sound pulse constantly identifies the relative location of this statistical match. Each visitor may choose how to navigate with this social sonar by either avoiding an encounter, or tracking his/her match, or by remaining indifferent.

There is also a tactile response. Occasionally, visitors in Blur may have a 100% affinity. To register this rare occurrence, a third response system is integrated into the coat. A small vibrating pad, modeled after the vibrating motor of a pager, is located in the rear pockets of the braincoat. When two perfectly matched visitors encounter one another in the fog, the motors send a vibration through the coat, mimicking the tingle of excitement that comes with physical attraction.

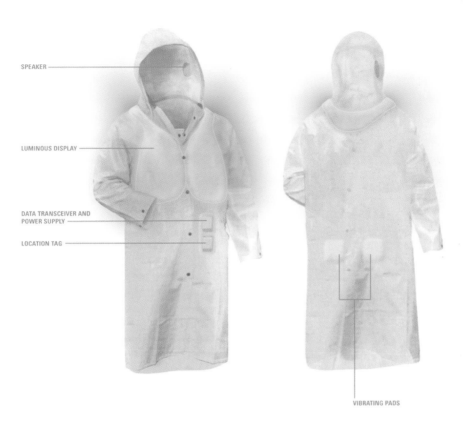

SPEAKER

LUMINOUS DISPLAY

DATA TRANSCEIVER AND
POWER SUPPLY

LOCATION TAG

VIBRATING PADS

Fig. 6: A prosthetic skin in the form of a "braincoat,"
equipped with a sixth sense – a new form of "social
radar" – allowing each visitor to interact speechlessly
with other visitors.

Architecture is intellectually, methodologically and materially connected to other fields in ways never before imaginable. It is becoming a less pure and more composite discipline. Architectural processes are thus constitutionally affected by logics traditionally defined as lying outside the field. With the increasing sophistication of emergent software and emergent materials it is possible to design cities, processes and architecture that together exhibit the qualities and behavior of naturalized systems, thus interrelating object-systems, virtual infrastructures as well as natural ecosystems in a networked whole.

Sulan Kolatan received a Diplom-Ingenieur degree from the Rheinisch-Westfälische Technische Hochschule Aachen, Germany, and a Master of Science in Architecture and Building Design from Columbia University, New York. Since 1990, she has been teaching at Columbia University's Graduate School of Architecture, Planning and Preservation. In 2002/03, she was Acting Depart- ment Chair of Design and Technology at the Technical University Darmstadt, Germany.

William J. Mac Donald studied at the Architectural Association in London, England, and received a Bachelor of Architecture from Syracuse University, before obtaining a Master of Science in Architecture and Urban Design from Columbia University, New York. He has taught at Columbia University's Graduate School of Architecture, Planning and Preservation since 1985, where he was Director of the Post-professional Design Program between 1985 and 1988, and where he is currently Co-Director of the Master of Architecture Core Program. He and Sulan Kolatan are founding principals of KOL/MAC Studio New York (since 1988).

Sulan Kolatan, William J. Mac Donald :

impact of network logic on space and its making

Technology's shift from exclusively visual to immersive-haptic, coupled with its increasing "transparency," has given rise to the ambient environment in which virtuality and physicality are contingent – not contradictory – qualities.

IMPACT OF NETWORK LOGIC
ON SPACE AND ITS MAKING

KOL/MAC's digital design research has recently focused on two operative models: the chimera and co-citation mapping. A combination of these two models informs KOL/MAC's computational design methods based on network performance between heterogeneous systems. Currently, KOL/ MAC is employing these methods withthe addition of artificial intelligence to its dynamic software. Networks are represented as interrelated crowds of "intelligent agents" while heterogeneity is scripted as decision-making capacity in agents. This nonreductive approach allows the management of complexity in the design process, specifically through the "nature-ing" of agents and the "nurture-ing" of relations. The scalable organizational patterns and performances are then transformed into final designs ranging from building membranes and mass-customized furniture to institutional and high rise projects.

AquaNet(work)

Architecture is intellectually, methodologically and materially connected to other fields in ways never before imaginable. It is becoming a less pure and more composite discipline. Architectural processes are thus constitutionally affected by logics traditionally defined as lying outside the field.

The shift from standard to non-standard approaches signifies above all a fundamental change in understanding and managing complexity, both in theory and practice. While the former approach uses a reductive logic with regard to systems and their constituent elements, the latter recognizes that the emergent-adaptive behavior of complex systems is more than the sum of its parts, and thus has to be examined as a whole. The complexity discourse encompasses network behavior of which we still know relatively little. It is becoming increasingly evident, nonetheless, that the hub-and-spoke metaphor

for connectivity is of limited use in understanding the kinds of connectivities that
play a role in complex systems. In some
fields, such as hypertext theory, this short-
coming has already been addressed. While
early hypertextual diagrams relied heavily
on the hub-and-spoke metaphor, more
recently an alternative called "aquanets"
is being explored. These are three dimen-
sionally intersecting surfaces with resulting regions that are of more than one
surface. Here, connection is constitutional,
not a link. And the emphasis is on connection as an operative mode.

Networked-ness in Eco-logic

Recent fields of study have emerged such
as Urban and Industrial Ecology. In both
cases a non-standard paradigm is at work
that is markedly different from the city
and industry paradigms of the 19th and
20th centuries. Prompted by pathologies
caused by both cities and industries conceived within the latter paradigm, these
new fields are founded on the notion of
increasing urban and industrial viability
by employing the logic of ecosystems and
natural lifecycles.

Fig. 1: (top) The Grand Egyptian Museum of Archeology
(Competition 2002–03): Aerial overview of the museum's plateau with the pyramids' precinct in the background

Fig. 2: (bottom) Elevation view at one of the multiple
entrances to the museum via the Administation Center
and Visitor Cluster

Crucial as it is, the implication of an ecological paradigm goes far beyond the narrow question of problem-solving, however. This is not a return to earthier, simpler ways. Nor is it about balance. It is, in a very fundamental way, about the question What is natural? While nothing is purely natural any more, in that everything is affected by the presence of the man-made to some degree, *everything* is in the process of becoming more *naturalized*.

The ecological paradigm defines the workings of this naturalized world as "massive systematic transformations of materials" with "networks of actors doing the producing and consuming – or disposal – of materials and associated energy"[1]. Much of what makes ecosystems perform in the ways they do – what gives them emergence, as it were – is a function of the networked-ness of its "actors."

Architecture is systemically already linked to city and industry. On a macroscale - a chimerical logic binds architecture into cultural, commercial and industrial ecology. It considers architecture in terms of product systems and related processes. Viewed in this way architecture is but one system organically interconnected with many others, such as artificial object-systems and infrastructures as well as natural ecosystems. With the increasing sophistication of emergent software and emergent materials it is possible to design cities, processes and architecture that together exhibit the qualities and behavior of naturalized systems.

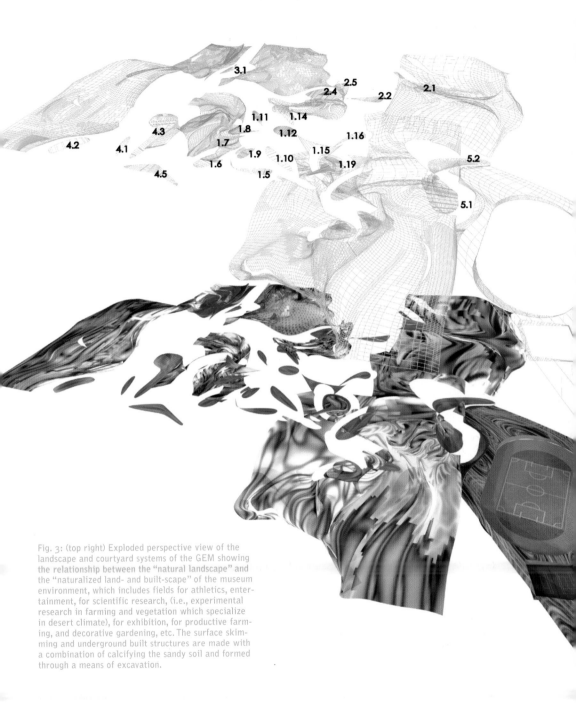

Fig. 3: (top right) Exploded perspective view of the landscape and courtyard systems of the GEM showing the relationship between the "natural landscape" and the "naturalized land- and built-scape" of the museum environment, which includes fields for athletics, entertainment, for scientific research, (i.e., experimental research in farming and vegetation which specialize in desert climate), for exhibition, for productive farming, and decorative gardening, etc. The surface skimming and underground built structures are made with a combination of calcifying the sandy soil and formed through a means of excavation.

Fig. 4: (left) Interior view showing the perforated intersection of the multiple tori-segment shells. The museum exhibits range from actual artifact to haptic digital 3D holographic images (at reduced or actual size) to "live site" projections of real time television broadcasts of portions of the collection on view throughout the world.

Naturalized Network as Meta-Museum

The competition for the Grand Egyptian Museum of Archeology (GEM) in Cairo/ Giza in 2002–03 offered an opportunity to design an architecture of naturalized networks that interconnect with others, such as exhibition object-systems, virtual infrastructures and natural ecosystems. (It is interesting to note that the latter constitutes the only "life" link to the past since many of the plant species survive to this day.)

The GEM is derived through indexing a field of multiply scaled tori-segment configurations with the museums hypertextual relationships of content, topic and space. The GEM campus is comprised of the museum and its adjunct programs of research, business and leisure. Due to the geographic dissipation of its content, the dislocation of archeological sites beyond the boundaries of the museum and the desire to "presence the past," the problem of the archeological museum by definition requires the construction of complex spatiotemporal relations of a physical-virtual kind.

Another crucial function of networkedness is the potential for adaptation. Archeology is a work-in-progress. Ongoing excavations and discoveries due to new technologies such as the virtual unwrapping of

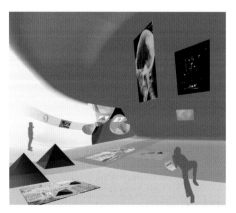

mummies as witnessed recently in the CAT-scanning of Tutankhamen, for example, suggest the notion of a "rewritable museum." The GEM design addresses these conditions through two different but intersecting network strategies:

1) Naturalized Sub-Network: inside2inside2outside

The design intent based on the competition brief was to generate spatial boundaries for thematic categories while simultaneously conflating them through the production of regional aquanets. What distinguishes these trans-spatial regions from other spaces in the museum is that they always belong to more than one territory at a time. While the museum is configured as a series of discrete thematically identified spaces aquanet-formations between them create categorical hybrids that are not without identities but possess manifold identities and affiliations. Inside/ out transition are constructed similarly with fixed definitions of threshold giving way to trans-spatiality with ambivalent, iterated or embedded conditions of threshold.

2) Naturalized Sub-Network: media2space2object

The conception of the Meta-Museum as an adaptive macronetwork of media-, space- and object-systems differs significantly from strategies of layering. Systemic layering fails to register networked operations in compound systems by falsely assuming that systems operate the same way in isolation as they do in aggregation. In contradistinction, the design approach used here is to view connectivity as con-

Fig. 5: GEM – Interior view showing the spatial continuity between the interior and exterior exhibits. The co-citation of material afforded the opportunity to continually cite interior with in the exterior and vice versa. The visitor then oscillates between interior and exterior to view related material.

stitutional, not as mere linkage. Constitutional connectivity in the GEM is based on a de-differentiation of the physical/virtual categories. It is expressed through an ambient environment in which virtuality and physicality are contingent – not contradictory – qualities. Thus enabling the museum-goer to be at once here and there, now and then, alone and among, technology's shift from exclusively visual to immersive-haptic coupled with its increasing "transparency" (the degree to which it recedes from consciousness) has given rise to the ambient environment. The GEM design employs strategies of media2space2object-system connectivity at once complicit with and critical of this techno-cultural dynamic by creating continuous transparencies while instigating fissures.

Fig. 6: GEM – The interior view of one of the spatial clusters showing some of the interactive displays. The visitors' navigation of the museum is through a variety of "museum tour loops." These loops allow for varying degrees of visitation. These gradated visitations range from browsing temporary and "highlight" exhibit loops, chronological exhibits loops, thematic exhibit loops, to customized exhibition loops for research purposes. The use of GPRS and RFID technology assist in affording this particularization of museum use.

References

[1] Iddo K. Wernick and Jesse H. Ausubel, "Industrial Ecology: Some Direction for Research," Foreword, May 1997 – Prepublication Draft, http://phe.rocke-feller.edu/ie_agenda/.

Our reliance upon internal information networks and distant communication to share and exchange project files has become the norm in architectural practice. IT networking of the distributed architectural office facilitates the dynamic workflow between collaborators. As a result of the inception of design and communication technologies, perhaps the greatest challenge to conventional models of architectural practice is the fundamental redefinition of the contingencies and scope of what actually constitutes practice in the age of digital design, manufacturing and communication.

Tom Verebes is a founding member of ocean D, practicing as a design network, with Robert Elfer and Kevin Cespedes in Boston and Wade Stevens in New York and Tom Verebes in London. He has taught as Course Master in the Design Research Lab (DRL) at the Architectural Association in London since 1997, engaging in advanced post-graduate collaborative research projects. OCEAN UK and OCEAN US are the commercial backbone of the expertise of the network, founded in London in 1995.

Tom verebes :

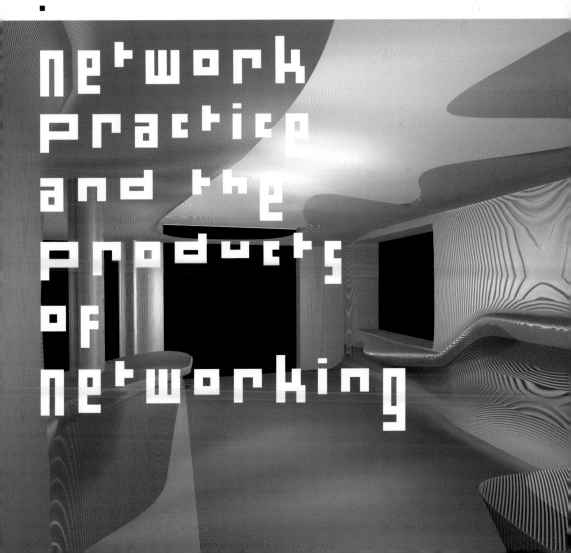

network practice and the products of networking

The use of time-based and code-based software as generative design tools is undermining conventional architectural design methodologies.

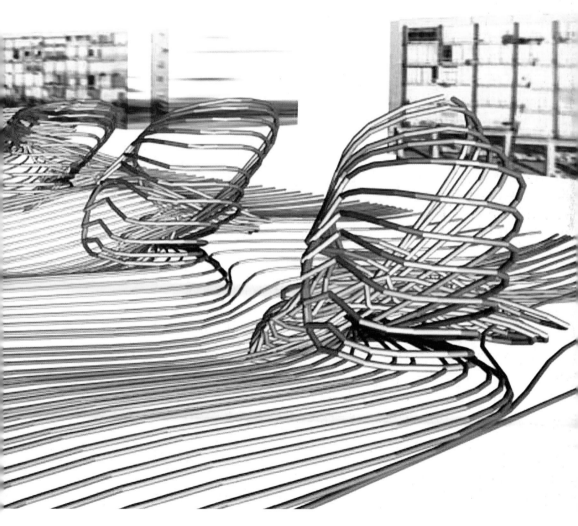

NETWORK PRACTICE AND THE PRODUCTS OF NETWORKING

Introduction

Professional architectural practice faces increasingly constrained design parameters as a result of deterministic planning policies, building codes, and the overly litigational context of the construction and manufacturing industries. Given these apparent inadequacies in the pervasive model of practice, the discipline of architecture is doomed to ever more impotence as a cultural activity, unless it is imbibed with innovative design, production and manufacturing techniques, as well as with a wholesale reformation of the ways in which architecture is practiced. Clients, architects and other building industry professionals must either open their eyes to the cultural and economic value of experimentation or face extinction, only to be replaced by the mediocre professional managers, technicians, cost control specialists and bureaucrats. There are three emerging conditions providing architectural practice with the resistance to avoid this dismal fate, the continued appropriation of contemporary digital design and production techniques, aiming to radically transform the architectural product; the increased connectivity brought about by communication technologies and information workflow systems in the networked office; and lastly, reformulated collaborative models, revised commissioning structures and grass-roots design-build projects with groups of multiple constituents.

Architecture under Three Emerging Conditions

As early as the late 1970s, the largest scale commercial practices recognized the potential of computer-aided design to further standardize the manufacturing and construction industries. Architectural education and practice was subsequently transformed from the early 1990s when students across the world became increasingly immersed in rapidly evolving digital design technologies. This latter digital revolution has shifted the emphasis from efficiency of costs, minimized legal risk, and the latent acceptance of the stipulations of regulatory bodies, to more experimental modes of conceiving, generating and manufacturing an architectural product.

Contemporary architecture has already (mis)-appropriated Hollywood animation software such as Alias Wavefront's Maya, Discreet's 3DStudio Max, gaming industry software, and other code-based scripts and algorithms. Young entrants to the profession are benefiting from the affordability of advances in computer hardware speed, storage and extended and specialized functionalities. Although graduates of the AADRL and other advanced digital research programs and institutions face many career options with their broad skills, the profession risks losing this vast new knowledge resource to the animation, film, Web design, multimedia and gaming industries, where three-dimensional skills are lacking. The enduring self-conception of architecture as a multidisciplinary field can only persist if every mode of architectural practice embraces these new synergies with the software industry. New file-to-factory procedures are facilitating the transfer of complex digital design information to computer-driven material production and manufacturing, setting new standards that overcome the repetitive modalities of modernism. A new internationalism is emerging from the convergence of shared design platforms and formats available in languages all around the world, coupled with the global distribution of young graduates unknowingly challenging the profession to change or die out. The use of time-based and code-based software as generative design tools is undermining conventional architectural design methodologies. With each new software upgrade, new techniques flow to the digirati, assuring this technical revolution in architecture has momentum. Each successive ocean D project gradually evolves a set of design procedures via MAXScript, a scripting interface and language in 3D-Studio MAX. The progressive adjustments of the digital code of each script respond specifically to the varying contingencies presented by each new project. The capacity of scripted design is to describe and constrain multiple potential configurations of point line, surface and volume, articulating diverse and variable imminent formations as opposed to an absolute imposition of form. Given this nonlinear mode of production, an intrinsic link is forged between the digital abstraction to the numerically controlled material artifact. With the possibility of adjusting input parameters, either locally or globally, there emerges a more

serial, evolutionary mode of prototyping an architectural product formed by higher orders of information.

The coding of parametric space has two design implications. Firstly, contemporary design is increasingly concerned with active materials and intelligent structures. Inverse and Forward Kinematics opens the possibility of modeling and simulating the adaptive and anticipatory performance of kinetic structures and architectural systems.

In addition to the synergies of architecture and robotics, interactive and dynamic mediated interfaces are permeating architectural and urban environments, via the networking of scanning, sensing processing and actuating systems, augmenting architectural experience beyond the occupation of space configured by inert materials. The emerging discipline of interface design subsumes smaller scale interactive environments and aims for increased shorter-term customisation to more indi-

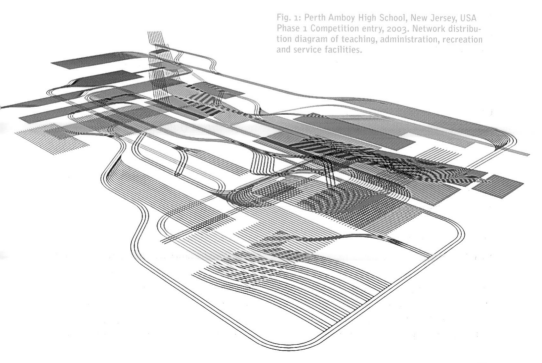

Fig. 1: Perth Amboy High School, New Jersey, USA Phase 1 Competition entry, 2003. Network distribution diagram of teaching, administration, recreation and service facilities.

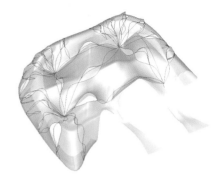

Fig. 2: Interior organization of fixed programs (bath-rooms, admin and kitchen facilities) and flexible seasonal bunkbed arrangement

Fig. 3: Structural spline model, indicating reinforcing in surface and geometry of openings

viduated specifications. The charging of material surfaces with embedded technologies aims to saturate the visible and visceral field of micro-environments with dynamic information graphics, color, lighting, translucency, reflectivity, material porosity and sound. Effectively, these ambient interfaces are already immersed across design scales from urbanism to product design, are controlled remotely and dynamically, and are collapsing the disciplines of architectural and furniture design, environmental branding and interface design.

Our reliance upon internal information networks and distant communication to share and exchange project files has become the norm in architectural practice. From the networking and distribution of collaborators, consultants, clients, manufacturers, suppliers, contractors and sites, the distribution of information flow operates on many scales, from the networked independent office to a broader geography of the distributed design team. IT networking of the distributed architectural office facilitates the dynamic workflow between collaborators. Distributed communication technologies have championed the arrival of compounding global connectivity. Ten years ago we all gradually became linked initially to 14.4 and 28.8 Kb external modems, later, bypassing 50 Kb dial-up connections and ISDN, to

ASDL broadband and wireless technology. By 2004 this seems an outmoded topic concerning innovations in practice. Using real-time digital archives such as servers, ftp sites, newsgroups, messenger mail groups etc., an open-source mode of collaboration within a limited network of project collaborators is set up.

As a result of the inception of design and communication technologies, perhaps the greatest challenge to conventional models of architectural practice is the fundamental redefinition of the contingencies and scope of what actually constitutes practice. Several alternative models of practice have emerged, each with a divergent political implication. The appeal of adjacent design disciplines such as industrial, automotive, product, furniture design, and naval architecture are the shorter timescales of concept to prototype, the empowered commissioning structure and the network of relations necessary to produce and market a design product. Not only must experimental architecture excel technically, but equally in the business management of its team and the marketing of its product.

The design research model pursued is analogous to experimentation in other dynamic creative industries, where each successive and parallel project carries forth an ongoing set of research agendas,

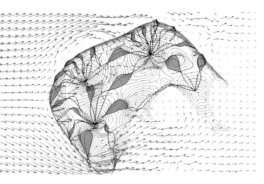

Fig. 4: Prevailing-winds simulation of the microclimate formed by the concave topography at the south-west oriented entrance

tested against the constructive constraints and presented as opportunities with each new project. Community-based design-built models take a more grass-roots approach, working in direct action with local demographic constituencies.

The network model of the distributed office has long promised to revolutionize practice, with the potential to manage vast geographical distributions of clients and commissioning bodies, design teams and project sites being more tangible than ever. Distributed collaborative organizations such as OCEAN, UFO, Servo, and possibly hundreds of others in the 1990s, announced themselves as networked practices. Ocean D operates as a project-based design research network with projects that vary in both their briefs and anticipated products, implying sometimes great differences in the scale, site, program, materials, media and manufacturing processes. Operating as a network practice has not been easier than consolidating efforts in only one market; while the potential for success in augmented, the results of the efforts of smaller distributed offices are slower to emerge.

Aside from the 1990s upstarts, Ben Van Berkel and Caroline Bos rebranded their prolific office as UN Studio in 1997, a transdiciplinary network of designers and consultants with high-profile cultural and

infrastructural projects. OMA introduced the AMO network alongside the increasingly large-scale projects in OMA. AMO was initially charged with specializing on research and development in advanced materials, digital media and other forms of discursive research within a project-based context. Even SOM has re-organized itself as a network of independent and interdependent offices, rather than a head-office-to-branch-office organization.

Amidst this apparent will to be autonomous yet inter-dependent, the novelty is that small organizations persist in promoting a business model that is counter-logical to the understanding that a market is based locally. Other more individuated practices still relying on the identity of a singular star, or limited set of sedentary partners, are also ever more transforming into networks as a result of the distribution of clients and sites. Smaller site-based teams are set up to join with other locally based consultants. The increasing prevalence of digital communication technology has an inherent contradiction, which forces architectural practice to grow smaller, distributed offices to operate on a highly local, shorterterm project-oriented basis.

This geographical dispersal occurs in relation to information turned into ubiquitous digital bits. The spatiality of design networks and workflow systems is uncannily producing a kind of architecture that is organized and performs as a network. This aggregate distribution of practice has emerged alongside the shifts from a territorial surface spatial paradigm to a more component-based organizational logic. Advances in digital design technology and the establishment of information infrastructures are poised to automate the persistent pursuit of innovation.

213

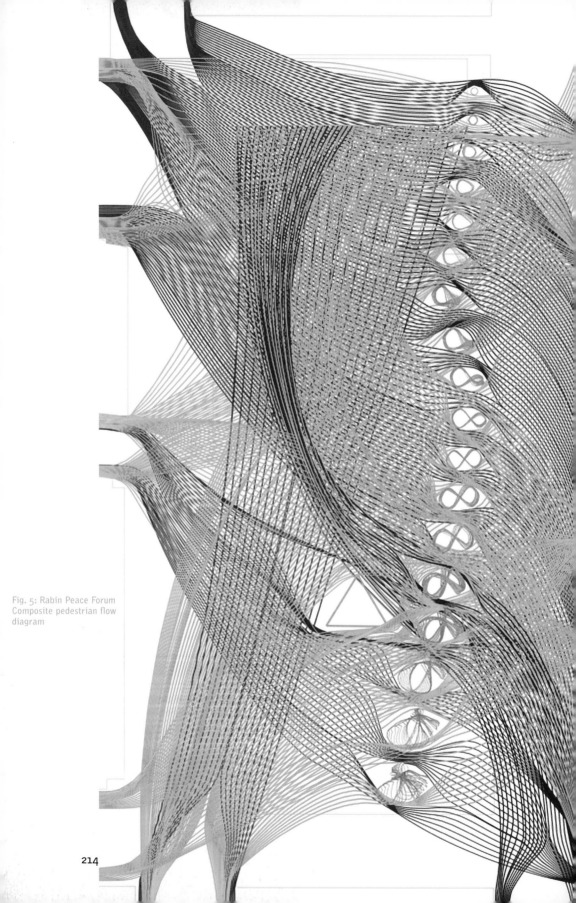

Fig. 5: Rabin Peace Forum
Composite pedestrian flow
diagram

214

Rabin Peace Forum
Tel Aviv, Israel
Competition Entry, 2001

A modulated series of 18 looped object configurations are distributed along an open line, originating from the geographical point of Yitzak Rabin's assassination. The objects grow and change in incremental gradients as a serial event field, both within each object as well as across the range of 18 objects. A homogenous parallel field is interrupted by the 18 insertions, causing an iterative transitional field of 18 events. Each "position" is an "event." The objects increase in magnitude/size, each with a position of its centroid at a continuous and uniform oblique datum level that relates to the +/-3.50 level of the upper terrace. The modulation between each position and the preceding/subsequent position will cause a topographical flow of convex and concave podia, evolving from the surface of the square. An irrigation topography interacts and responds as a geometric iteration of the range of objects, acting as a mechanism of local re-orientation of pedestrian movement, between each object. The upper terrace of the Municipality Building (City Hall) is linked with the +/-0.00 level, reconfiguring the stairway with an integrated terracing topography. The scheme deploys a distribution of water pools, aquatic and desert planting, seating, information and material surfaces within the topographies of the directional field, as an open space for 300,000 people to gather.

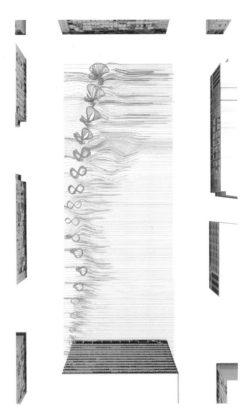

Fig. 6: Rabin Peace Forum – Plan indicating series of objects and irrigation organization

Fig. 7: Detail view of one of the eighteen urban objects installed in Rabin Square, indicating landscaping and urban furniture, formed in relation to the splinal superstructure

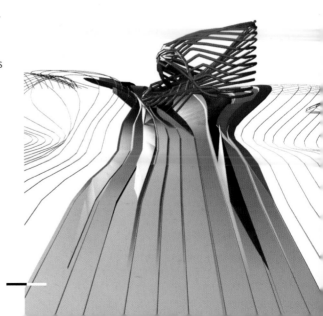

Credits

Felix Robbins, Tom Verebes, George Liaropoulos-Legendre, Cynthia Morales, Sarah Quinn, Wade Stevens, Robert Elfer, Kevin Cespedes

The Mountain Hut
Second Prize Competition Entry, 2003

The Mountain Hut is a small-scale, pre-fabricated, demountable and re-assemblable pavilion which amplifies the vast landscapes of two extreme topographical contexts – Palisades Glacial Park in northern California and adjacent to the Machu Picchu Inca ruins in Peru.

The intelligence of the sustainable roof, wall and floor surface is designed in relation to enviromental performance criteria, harnessing energy (sunlight), water, and natural ventilation. Generated via particle dynamics in MAYA, simulating gravity acting on mobile particles, the orienta-tion of vector fields flow towards four distributed nodes for both structural loading and rain-water collection. An EPDM-Photovoltaic fabric captures solar energy using a thin-film photovoltaic material embedded in the roofing membrane, made from ferrocement composites and Curv, a heat-formed material with capacities to form complex 3D tension-compression topological surfaces. The roof is perforated with two systems of openings, the "zipper" and the "eyelid," organized along a radial network of micro-articulations in the membrane. Located within each of the "eyelids," photo- and heat-sensitive gels act as optical shutters that passively react to heat or direct sunlight by changing phase states of color and opacity values to provide shade and insulate the interior. The "zippers" are large skylight and ventilation openings that are manually operable for passive ventilation, with an outer rubber gasket and an inner zipper mechanism.

Built as a tourist and leisure facility, the Hut distributes information, shopping, restaurant, and between 20 and 80 stackable sleeping units, continually re-organized to seasonally fluctuating demand.

Fig. 8: The Montain Hut – A small-scale, prefabricated, demountable and re-assemblable pavilion

Fig. 9: The Montain Hut in the topographical
context of the Machu Picchu Inca ruins in Peru

Credits

ocean D:
London: Tom Verebes, Boyan Tvzetkov, Abraham Gordn,
Jasmina Jugovic
Boston: Robert Elfer, Kevin Cespedes, Chris Mulvey,
Jonathan Kan, Eric Hanson
New York: Wade Stevens

b Consultants:
Tom Barker, Andrew Siddall, Tim Sutcliffe, Simone
Constanta
BP: Derek Riley
BTG: George Vincent

The prototyping stage of work has been generously
supported by British Petrolium (BP) and Curv.

ocean D and Tom Barker of b Consultants are
currently collaborating on manufacturing a series
of 1:1-scaled material prototypes of the Hut.

As humans we must learn to relate to the dynamics of super-fast real-time computational processes. We must build the computational tools for Collaborative Design and Engineering in order to meet the rich expectations created by looking at the world from one or two levels up. The ultimate goal of Protospace 2.0 is to improve the speed and quality of the design process based on parallel processing of the knowledge of all disciplines involved from the very first stages of the design.

Kas Oosterhuis is the principal of ONL (Oosterhuis_ Lénárd), a multidisciplinary practice in Rotterdam, and Professor of Architecture at TU Delft, head of the Hyper-body Research Group. He is the co-founder of the Attila Foundation (1994), which pursues the electronic fusion of art and architecture. He delivers lectures around the world and publishes his works internationally. His recent writings include Hyperbodies – Towards an E-motive Architecture (2003), Architecture Goes Wild (2002), Programmable Architecture (2002).

kas oosterhuis:

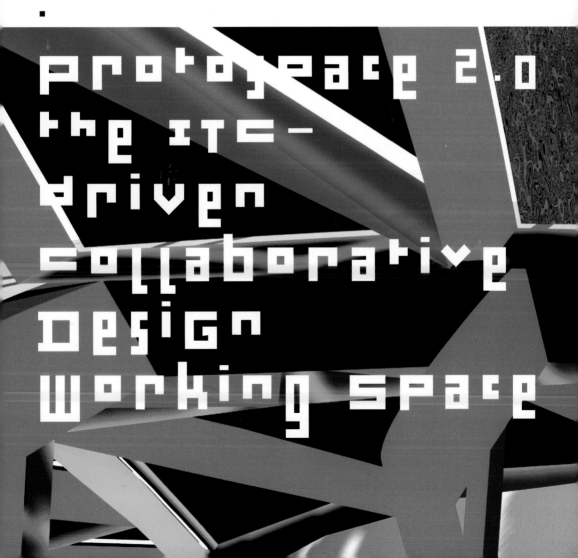

protospace 2.0 the ICT-driven collaborative design working space

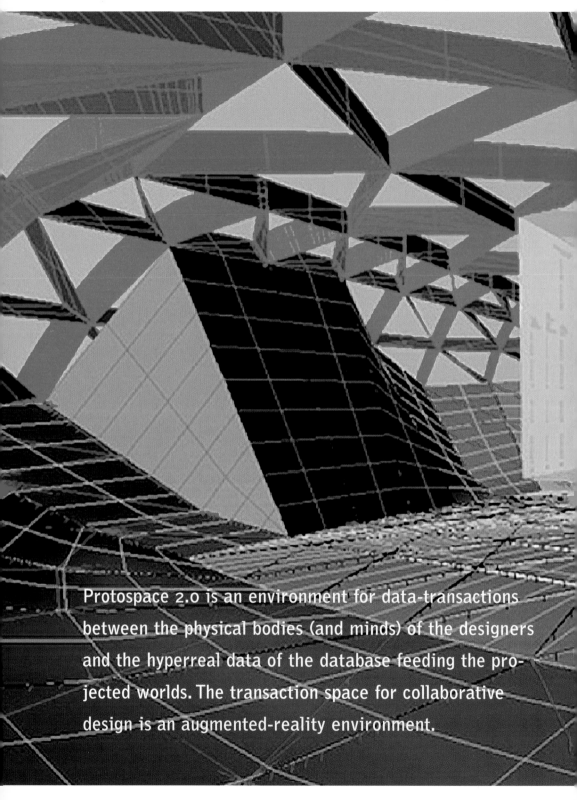

Protospace 2.0 is an environment for data-transactions between the physical bodies (and minds) of the designers and the hyperreal data of the database feeding the projected worlds. The transaction space for collaborative design is an augmented-reality environment.

PROTOSPACE 2.0 _THE ITC-DRIVEN COLLABORATIVE DESIGN WORKING SPACE

Prehistory: The WEB

The spaceship WEB of North-Holland entered the world stage at the Floriade flower show in 2002 (Fig. 1). When the Floriade closed its gates the WEB was disassembled and rested in pieces at the wharf of Meijers Staalbouw. In the meantime the Board of the Delft University of Technology purchased the WEB and has been discussing its future landing at the Mekelweg in front of the Faculty of Architecture. The WEB is destined to become a multifaculty server that will host a truely interactive Group Design Room called Protospace™ for multidisciplinary research and education. The faculties of Civil Engineering (CiTG), Aerospace (L&R), Management (TBM), Electrotechnique (ITS) and Industrial Design (IO) have shown genuine interest in joining the WEB_Protospace™ initiative. Also the CUR, TNO-Bouw and the TI (Telematica Institute) have all proved eager to take part in the Protospace™ program.

Protospace™ [1]

Physically, the group design room in the interior of the WEB is a 360° projection screen around a playing field. The Protospace™ playground is filled with an array of sensors and tracking devices to establish a fine-grained high-resolution and above all emotional communication between the players (experts and stakeholders) and the design worlds in progress. The communication is processed in a game program, which is naturally played in real time. The design task can be a building, a detail of a building, a neighborhood of a city, a bridge, a large infrastructural planning task. It can also be a graphic environment to give shape to

Fig. 1: The Web of North Holland at the Floriade 2002 World Exhibition

an interactive decision procedure. Protospace™ supports and stimulates collaborative design and engineering in real time.

After one year of experiments Protospace™ will invite commercial third parties and nonexperts to join the design game. After all Protospace™ is meant to become an instrument to involve experts, public and clients in one and the same complex but fluid design game. In due time Protospace™ might prove itself to be instrumental for direct democracy.

Protospace is a Vehicle for Research, Education and Commercial Activities

Protospace™ as a server on the campus of the Delft University of Technology (DUT) can be used for variety of purposes:

A Research
- multi-player interactive design laboratorium
- rapid virtual prototyping (protospacing)
- group design/decision room

B Education
- workshops to connect reality to virtual reality
- digital workshops

- lectures (with data projection)
- informal Weblounge (meeting place for students with expert staff)

C Commercial purposes
- pilot projects with building partners – project developers, contractors, advisors
- pilot projects with cities for direct democracy
- highly specific research (larger companies)

The capacity of Protospace™ as a public space for lectures is 100–200 people. The capacity as a playing field for interactive research is (depending on the type of research), 10–20 people.

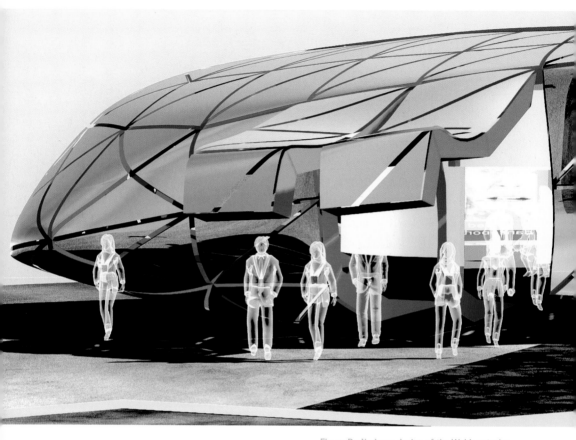

Specifications Protospace™

Fig. 2: Preliminary design of the Web's exterior
at the Floriade 2002 World Exhibition

Protospace™ is the name of the ICT-driven collaborative design working space to be installed at the Delft University of Technology, Faculty of Architecture. Protospace™ is an environemnt for data-transactions between the physical bodies (and minds) of the designers and the hyperreal data of the database feeding the projected worlds [2]. The transaction space for collaborative design is an augmented-reality environment.

Through sensors and actuators the senses of the designers are connected to the hyperreal (hyperreal since we know all constituting data) prototype. The active view on the prototype is projected on a 360° panoramic screen around the playing field.

Active worlds are hyperreal environments running in real time. The active world is conntinuously (re)calculating itself in real time. It exists. It represents a semi-autonomous identity developing a character in an evolutionary way.

Examples of active worlds to be played:

¬ constructive detail
¬ room
¬ building
¬ neighborhood
¬ traffic system
¬ bridge
¬ city structure
¬ content network
¬ immersive 3D browser

Collaborative Design Game

The active worlds are built according to a game structure. A game is a rule-based complex adaptive system that runs in real time. The rules of the game are subject to design. The role of designer changes from designing the shape to designing the rules of the design game. The architects' minds will start to absorb the thought process of the programmer's mind. They will start to think in proce-dures rather than fixed superficial ideas. They will think in constructing the rules of the game, building scripts and proce-dures rather than building just a static 3D model. The procedures develop in the collaborative design process and are visu-alized so that one can see shape, geome-try and material, and experience the per-formance of the structure.

The collaborative design game is played by all players simultanuously. Eventually the structure of the design game will co-evolve while playing the game.

The Space Is the Interface

The people inside the projection room communicate with the active world around them. The basic condition of Protospace™ is that the players can move freely around. They are not chained by a bundle of ca-bles to a computer. They trigger events in the active world in a variety of ways. An event basically represents an instruc-tion or a parameter in the game program, which is running at that moment. The interaction space replaces the keyboard, the mouse and the joystick. The space itself is the interface.

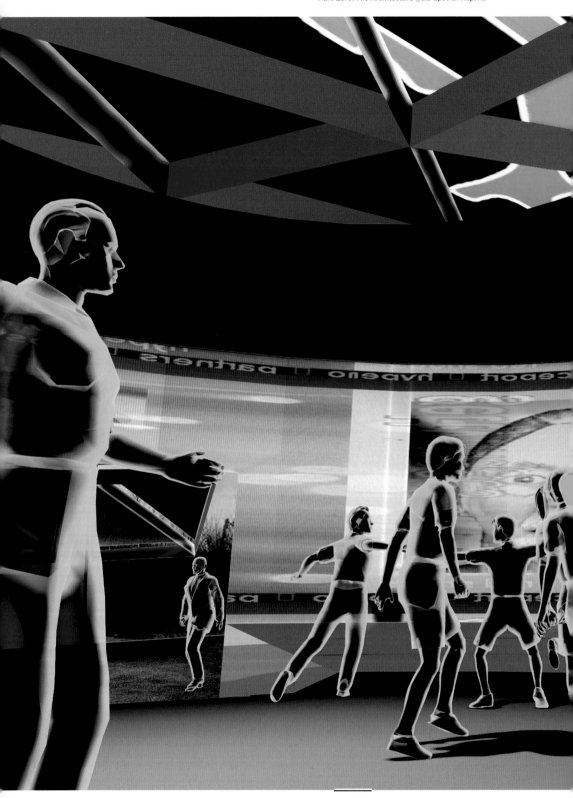

Active worlds are hyperreal environments running in real time. They are built according to a game structure. A game is a rule-based complex adaptive system that runs in real time. The rules of the game are subject to design. The role of designer changes from designing the shape to designing the rules of the design game.

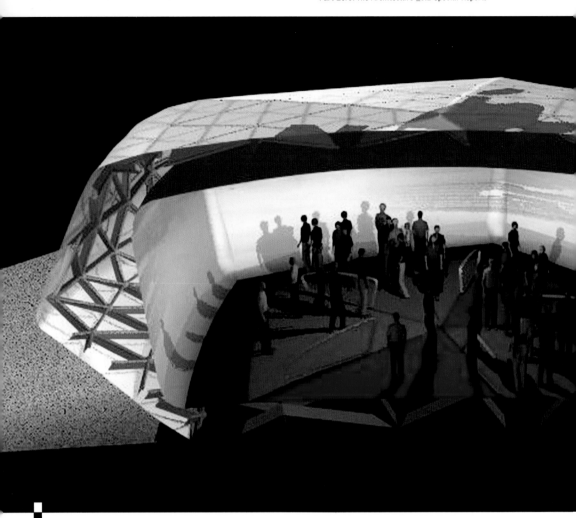

In the year 2003–2004 students and the Hyperbody Research Group (HRG) staff [3] will perform a variety of experiments in collaboration with the professional interface designer Bert Bongers (Bontron). We will install various things, including PIR sensors (recording movement), photo cells, tapeswitch (continuous), accelerator devices and/or gyroscopes, transponders, proximity sensors (continuous), infrared or radiowave pressure sensors, infrared sensors. Numerical information could be transmitted using the numpad of cellphones. Virtual sliders projected on the screens could be moved by bodily gestures of the designers.

What the Sensors Do

To connect the user to the active world a variety of senses and sensors are used. The active world processes and actuates the given input. It reacts to the users and eventually acts according to a process running from within the active world. To be tested tasks of specific sensors and input devices:
¬ Pressure sensors in the floor tiles allow for weight-specific input (if you press hard it connects to different values than pressing them slightly). The pressure sensors are dedicated to navigation by individuals and groups.

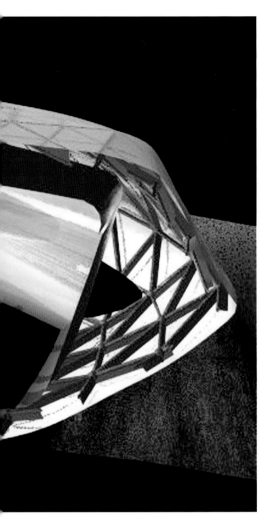

Fig. 3-4: (left, right) Preliminary design of the Web's interactive interior at the Floriade 2002 World Exhibition

¬ Infrared sensors from above define sensitive areas in the playing field. The infrared sensors are dedicated to changing the general atmosphere of the project (day, night, warm, cold, wet, dry, red, blue).
¬ Touch sensors in the projection field. The touch sensors are used for specific choices made by the stakeholders in their own active worlds. They can be seen as settings of the project, as modes.
¬ Voice recognition for the player's captain. Voice recognition is used for one-step operations like switching from one view to the other, open files, hide layers, zoom in – out.

¬ Numpad of cellphone. The numpad of the cellphone wil be used for numeric input of paramaters chaging the properties of the elements in the active world. The numpad is also used for rating what the users see and experience.
¬ Bitmap tracking. Camera's hang from top register patterns of groups of people. If all people tend to be attracted by a particular area in the game and they move towards this place, the camera registers that and adjusts the active world accordingly.
¬ Virtual sliders built in the game structure.
¬ 3D wireless mouse (Gyration) lets the operator move freely in space and click and drag in the active world.

Views of the Active World

Each player constructs his/her own view of the active world. A view is a specific way of representing the data from the database. Constructing specific views facilitate the expert usage by the different disciplines involved in the collaborative design process. The different views are compulsatory to be able to communicate. There is no dominant view.

Possible views on the database:
¬ The view of the **producer** (provider of the money). The producer controls the budget, makes sure that the goals fit within the budget, or pushes the project to create a budget. The producer's knowledge about the project exploitation, inflation, interest rates is controlled in real time in the collaborative design game.
¬ The view of the **director** (project manager). The director formulates the scenario of the game. The director develops the conceptual structure of the project by planning, stimulating, guiding, sorting out, cutting, making choices, changing the course of the workflow. The director controls the planning, the balance between the performance and costs among the constituting elements of the project. The director must see to it that the project works as an integrated effort from beginning to end.
¬ The view of the **installator** (installation designer). Installations are like nerve and lymph systems of the project. The installation designer constructs the flow of gases, liquids, and more solid bodies like people and goods.
¬ The view of the **constructor** (construction designer). The construction designer wants to see how forces are transmitted through the project. Forces like gravity, wind forces, changing loads. The construction designer wants to find a proper form for a chosen performance. It can be optimizing the constructive mesh and members, it can also be the quest for creating maximum tension or volatile programmable members. Sometimes the collaborative design group may decide to resist forces, or they may want to go with the flow.
¬ The view of the **stylist** (shape designer). Giving shape to every possible visible and tangible element in the active world.

This may concern a graphic representation as chosen by the director or a 3D shape of a constructive member.
¬ The view of the **informer** (information designer). This is a relatively new but important form of expertise in the field of time-based architecture. When electrified, architecture is also broadcasting. The way the building handles the information flow through its wires and the way it is communicated through the electronic skins must be devised by the information designer.
¬ The view of the **user**. The client is the future user of the built structure and is involved in the development of the project's identity. User and producer could be the same stake. The user participates in the choices made during the collaborative design process. The user becomes a co-designer.
¬ The view of the **public**. The passenger randomly passing by the project will have a vote in the process as well, according to a process called direct democracy. They may rate the project under development, and have influence on the outcome. The vote of the public matters.
¬ The view of the **referee** (process manager). The referee informs the stakeholders about the bandwidth of their stake. The referee controls the validation and rating of the input from the different stakeholders. The role of the referee is to communicate the validity of the choices made. The referee explains the effect of choices and rules being played, and judges in case of reasonable doubt.

Swarm of Stakeholders

The collaborative team as a whole decides in which direction the project develops. There is no top-down controlling absolute leader in this process. There are managers and designers, experts and public, but none of them has full control. The traditional view of the architect on top of the pyramid is no longer a valid position. All team players are member of the project swarm. There is no longer a position, which can be properly described as the architect generalist (or generalissimo). The team of stakeholders behaves as a swarm of intelligence raising the developing project database. The shape of the active swarm of experts is continuously synchronized with the scope and the extent of the developing project. While the traditional architect has been a combination of all disciplines embodied in one person, in the collaborative design process one specific expert chooses to embody one discipline. One stakeholder may represent and play two or more stakes. Theoretically it is possible that the collaborative design process is simulated by a single person (playing multiple roles).

Parametric Design

The collaborative design process is based on a dynamic parametric 3D model. All elements are defined in the form of the simplest formula possible. All relations between elements are described in its most compact form, leaving space for a maximum of future adjustments. The more compact the description, the higher the information index of that description. A set of descriptions, relations and behaviors shapes the symbolic and physical genetic code of the project. Behind everything that is represented on the projection screens there is a set of formulas running the active world.

Database

The modifications as proposed by the players of the collaborative design game are submitted to the project database in real time. The running script of the project processes the new data, and comes up with a modification. The refreshed

project is the actual state. The actual state is developing according to a versioning system able to retrieve previous configurations. The development of the project is administered in a history. The project may also resist the proposed modification, defending itself according to the rules already set in action.

Intelligent seduction of the project may convince the running scripts from the defensive state of mind, and prepare the project to open up for advantageous transformations. In the 2003–2004 bachelors project we started experimenting with similar exchanges of data in real time between the 3D model of the designer and of the construction engineer. The mechanical engineering sector of the Building Technology Department directed by Professor Jan Rots and assisted by Gerrie Hobbelman cooperated with the bachelors of our Hyperbody Research Group (HRG) to experiment with the data-exchange.

Evolution of the Game

The project develops a self-conscious view of itself. We allow the project to develop a personality of its own. In other words, it is not only the stakeholders, who develop the project. The project is a self-executing set of rules as well. We want the project to be seen as a running process, and the input by the stakeholders to be viewed as proposals for modifications of that process. In the end none of the stake-holders own the project (not even the client); the project is owned by itself, and has acquired certain rights to be, to be evolved, to be used and to be torn down with respect.

Collaborative Design

How do the stakeholders collaborate in real time? Imagine the following scene. The game leader opens a file, the active

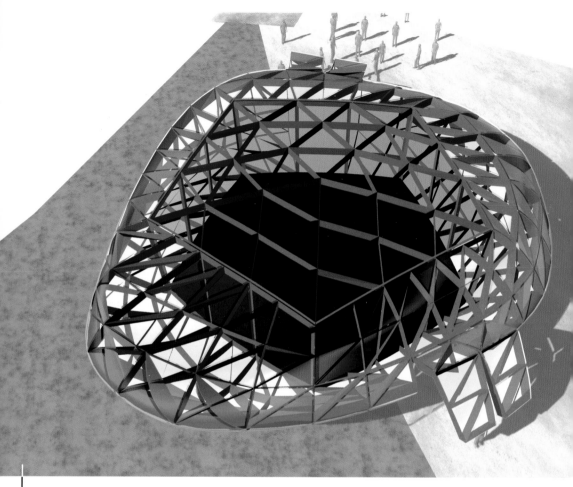

Fig. 5: Steel construction of the Web of North Holland

world. Each file has a specific set of rules on how to propose changes in the file. However, a detailed Protospace™ protocol will be developed on how to play by the rules. The referee explains to the players how to play the game. Each stakeholder chooses a view on the file. One player may choose different roles at the same time. The players come into the action according to the rules of the game when it is their turn to propose a change.

When playing the role of a specific stakeholder, only that particular view on the database is displayed. While delivering the input through sensors and numpads

the players are free to walk around and chat in the group design room. The group design room is an open design studio, a social transaction space. The other players watch the active player and respond immediately as in a normal conversation.

Hardware Protospace™

¬ 4 beamers
¬ 5 computers
¬ curved projection screen
¬ Sensors
¬ position / pattern tracking
  input devices

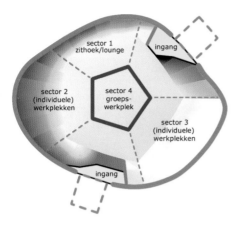

Fig. 6: Planned space lay-out of the Protospace in the Web

Software Protospace™

¬ Virtools Multi-player (active DUT license)
¬ Virtools VR pack
¬ Virtools 2.5 licence for 10 users
¬ Virtools VR on 2 screens with stereo view
¬ Green Dino VR software
¬ Multichannel development kit Green Dino
¬ ProEngineer Wildfire (active DUT license)

Protospace™ at the Faculty of Architecture

Protospace™ has been installed at the Faculty of Architecture of the Delft University of Technology on the mezzanine level above hand drawing. There is a mental link between hand drawing and the interactive way of designing in real time in Protospace™. Also we prefer direct physical action to construct our worlds. Instead of pencil and paper we use bits and bytes. The location of Protospace™ seems close enough for a future synergy between rapid prototyping and rapid protospacing. I already have proposed for consideration renaming the Media Department the Rapid Prototyping Lab.

Embedding Protospace™ in a Broader Spectrum of the Faculty of Architecture

After the evaluation of the first demos the Hyperbody Research Group aims to establish a structural cooperation between the departments of Architecture, Prototyping (Media), Building Technology (including TO&I) and Real Estate & Management. The HRG is interested in research by doing. Each step to be taken must lead to a concrete working prototype within one semester.

Protospace™ Foundation

To develop and exploit the collaborative design studio Protospace™ further in order to be able to implement the concept in the WEB, a foundation is to be established: the Protospace Foundation. The goals of the Protospace Foundation are:
¬ installment of the collaborative design space Protospace™ as a server of the DUT in front of the Faculty of Architecture
¬ installment of the collaborative design space Protospace™ in the WEB
¬ installment of augmented reality in Protospace™ using sensorial and actuating devices
¬ further development of interactive games for collaborative design
¬ further development of the Protospace™ protocol for data exchange
¬ project-based cooperation with other faculties of the DUT
¬ research on swarm theory
¬ development of working virtual prototypes to support and play the game of collaborative design
¬ development of working physical prototypes (hands-on research, testing ground for pro-active architecture)
¬ applications for financial support from EC, national state (NL) and business partners (founding partners, program finance, project finance)

¬ involve institutions and companies concerned with planning and design for rapid implementation and testing of concrete prototypes
¬ commercial exploitation of Protospace™
¬ synchronized collaboration with other disciplines: art, media, technique, politics.

Description of an Examplary Case Implemented in Protospace™

The parametric detail is built in the form of a spreadsheet. In the spreadsheet the dynamic relations between all faces are monitored. There will be no difference between column, floor and wall. There is no difference between fixed and mobile parts of the whole construct. Such differences are treated as parametric values in the complex set of realtions and formulas. The detail is a complex adaptive system, adapting to the input of the different stakeholders. The detail is a complex geometry described by a surface consisting of a number of vertices. Each vertex has its own characteristics (parametric values for the vertex handles). Use the strength of mathematical formulas to describe the complex behavior of groups of vertices. The number of vertices, the displacements of the vertices, the characters (labelled, flagged, tagged) of the vertices are subject to change. The parametric relations deal in real time with quantitative data.

Game Structure of Construction Detail

The changes of the vertices and hence of the surfaces are proposed by an authorized stakeholder. The stylist may propose a change to make it look better. The construction engineer may propose a change to make sure that it takes the loads. The way to communicate the changes is a built-in feature in the game structure of the detail. The game structure is a series of "what if" operations. One stakeholder

proposes, "What if I changed the size of this part of the detail into that size?" The parametric construct would position this proposition within or outside the bandwith of possibilities. The game structure allows that stakeholder to be authorized to propose that question or not. The stylist stakeholder may propose, "What if I changed the rectangular shape here into a rounded shape?" The game structure would propose an interpretation of these data and make it retrievable for other views on the data. The construction engineer will be able to quickly scan if that rounded shape still performs the

tasks of load transfer properly. The geometrician might highlight the fact that there is a loss of structural integrity, and that the rounded shape must change its position or thickness. Or the stylist might get a message informing him/her to change the material properties to be able to perform better.

This complex process of interaction and transactions is organized in the game structure, which basically is a dynamic 3D flowchart working in real time. The game structure deals with qualitative operations, with emotive values.

References

[1] Protospace™ is an initiative of Professor Ir Kas Oosterhuis at the Delft University of Technology, Faculty of Architecture.

[2] "Hyperbodies – Towards an E-motive Architecture," book in the series IT Revolution in Architecture, edited by Professor Antonino Saggio, Birkhäuser Basel, 2003.

[3] Current staff of the Hyperbody Research Group: Professor Ir Kas Oosterhuis (general director and tutor MsC), Ir Hans Hubers (universitarian tutor BsC and MsC), Ir Menno Rubbens (tutor MsC), student-assistents (tutors BsC) Misja van Veen, Chris Kievid, Christian Friedrich, Michael Bittermann, Sven Blokker, Remko Siemerink, Nimish Biloria (PhD candidate).

Fig. 7: Preliminary design of the Web's interactive interior at the Floriade 2002 World Exhibition

Protospace is an open design studio, a social transaction space.

Virtual architectural environments as augmentations of physical space offer the opportunity for unique spatial experiences and challenge our definition and understanding of what constitutes "real" experience and "actual" space. The evolution of these fluid architectures will be interesting to follow as architects become less concerned with differentiating between physicality and virtuality, and increasingly explore beyond the conventional boundaries of spatial, formal and aesthetic concerns to redefine what actually constitutes space, architecture and event.

Hani Rashid is the co-founding Principal, with Lise Anne Couture, of Asymptote, an award-winning architecture, art and design practice based in NYC. In 1990 he assisted in the development of Columbia University's Advanced Architecture Design program and in 1995 co-developed the Digital Design studio program. Presently he is a Professor at the ETH Zürich, and has held teaching posts at the Royal Danish Academy in Copenhagen, the Southern California Institute of Architecture, UCLA, the University of Lund and the Graduate School of Design at Harvard University. In 2004, Asymptote were the exhibition architects for Metamorph, the 9th International Architecture Exhibition in Venice.

hani rashid :

entering an age of fluidity

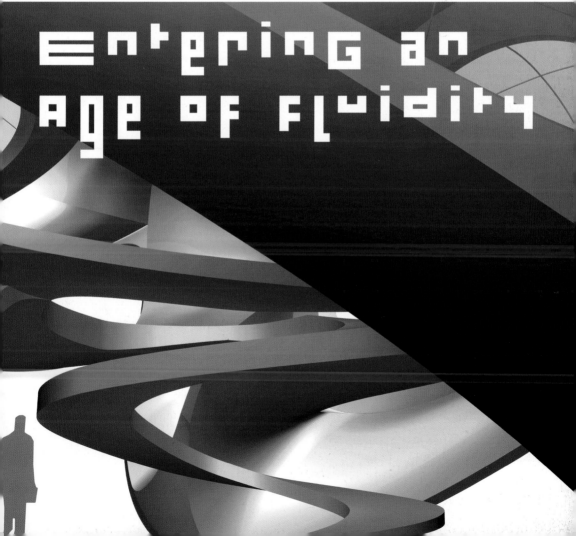

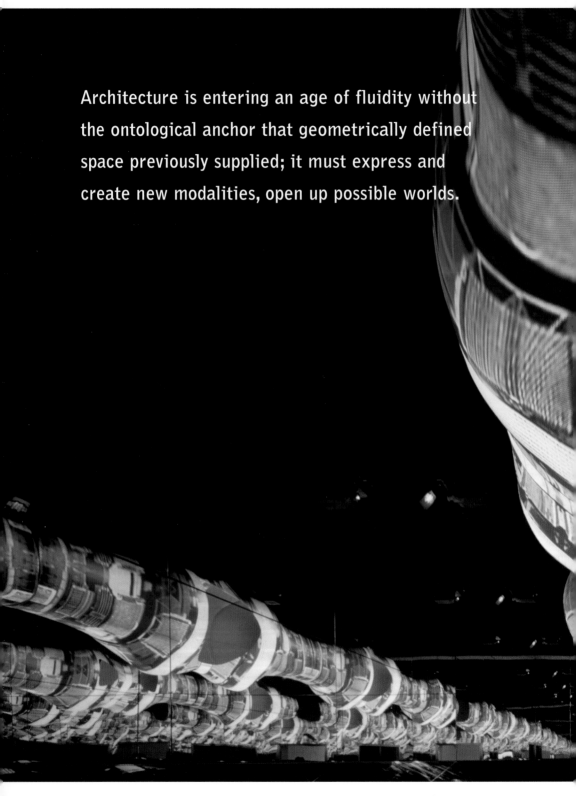

Architecture is entering an age of fluidity without the ontological anchor that geometrically defined space previously supplied; it must express and create new modalities, open up possible worlds.

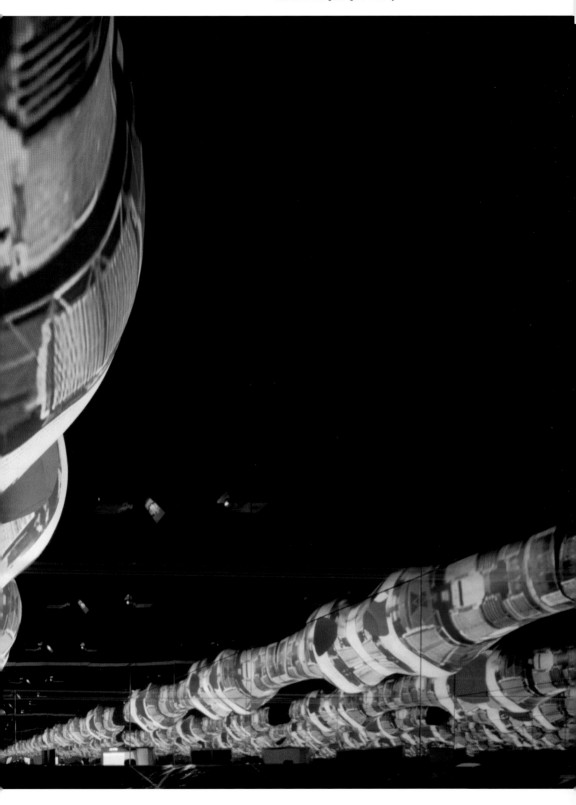

ENTERING AN AGE OF FLUIDITY

Today architecture must organize itself into different configurations, simultanously hybrid spatialities nourished by technology and media. Architecture is entering an age of fluidity without the ontological anchor that geometrically defined space previously supplied; it must express and create new modalities, open up possible worlds. What we are in general experiencing is a continually mutating spatiality.

As we navigate through information- and network-based space, we become increasingly aware of new possibilities within spatial perception and augmentation as the environments we devise and traverse become technologically infused with our ever more powerful arsenal of digital tools and means. It is precisely because of this continually "acquired" expertise that spatiality – and therefore, by extension, architecture – is in a state of radical change.

Fig. 1: Mscapes (detail), Documenta XI, 2002

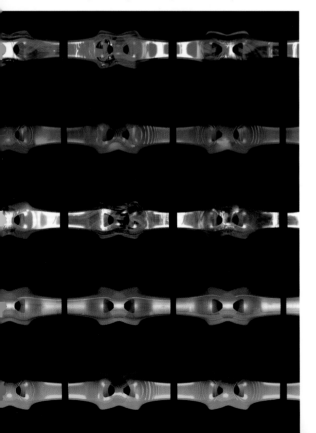

As computing has become absolutely pervasive, having found its way into every aspect of the discipline of architecture, the promise of increased efficiencies and control over the procedural proliferates. As we conceptualize, envision, represent and produce architecture, we turn more and more towards the digital in all its guises. For increasing numbers of architects, the computer is in fact becoming such an important and indispensable tool that today works are emerging that can only be enacted using algorithmically based digital tools. Even among more traditional practices, it is the digital in one form or another that is put to the task of analyzing formal strategies, spatial flows, time-based spatial conditions, programmatic efficiencies and essentially any aspect capable of being "visualized" graphically or numerically. The digital tools at our disposal are affording us new ways of translating the purely conceptual into plastic actualization. The technology that is now available, such as laser cutting tools or multiaxis milling machines capable of cutting any shape in any material, and 3D printers, was not long ago seen only in science fiction. As sacrilegious as this may seem to many architects today, the once omnipotent hand-drawn sketch or hand-crafted model is increasingly being supplanted by processes that can move ideas immediately into digitally animated sketches, stereo lithographed models, "printed" prototypes and digitally fabricated components on a one-to-one scale.

For a new generation of architects it is the seamlessness of process that holds promise, where the computer is not only a conceptual and design tool but also the means to make building manifest. This double occupancy elicits a new understanding of architecture in a state of simultaneous virtuality and augmented reality. Virtual architectural environments

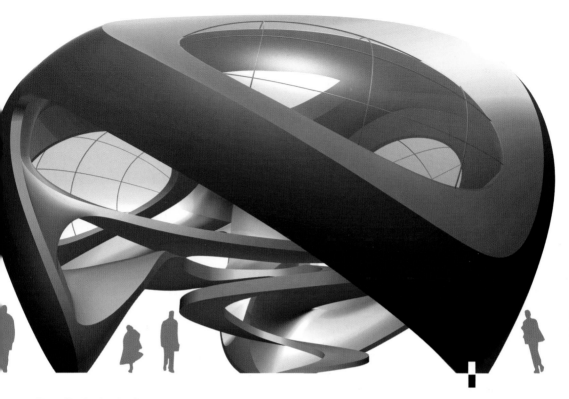

Fig. 2: Flux Pavilion Involucri, 2002–03

as augmentations of physical space offer the opportunity for unique spatial experiences and challenge our definition and understanding of what constitutes "real" experience and "actual" space. The evolution of these fluid architectures will be interesting to follow as architects become less concerned with differentiating between physicality and virtuality, and increasingly explore beyond the conventional boundaries of spatial, formal and aesthetic concerns to redefine what actually constitutes space, architecture and event.

With the aid of computing we are beginning to find ourselves maneuvering in what one might call an evolved architecture. This architecture inflected and influenced by the infinite and provocative possibilities that digital technological tools are providing, beyond the simple promise of greater efficiencies and production capabilities, is becoming at once familiar and strange. Coupling these new processes and methodologies with history, theory, conceptual thinking, experimentation and engineering is radically changing not only the way we envision and think about spatiality but also the means by which we occupy and inhabit such territory. In one form or another it is within the grasp of architects and artists today to discover and evoke a digitally induced spatial delirium, where a merging of simulation and effect with physical reality creates the possibility for a sublime morphing from thought to actualization to experience. This eventually begs the penetrating question, What actually constitutes architectural experience and presence – architecture or media?

241

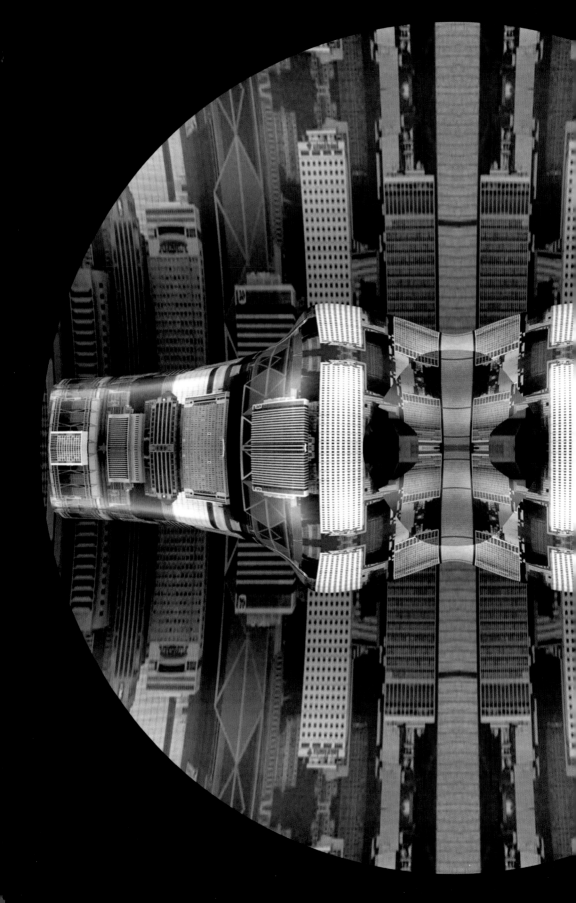

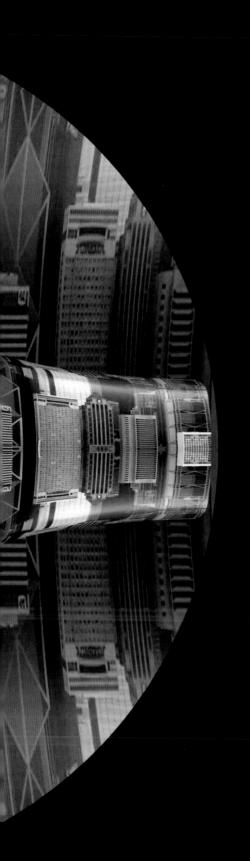

FluxSpace 3 Mscaps
Installation at Documenta XI in Kassel, 2002

Flux 3.0-Mscape City is a large-scale digitally augmented physical environment structured on the hyperurbanism of cities like New York, Hong Kong and Tokyo and made apparent through digital abstraction of building forms and soundscapes.

The project was first installed in the "Binding-Brauerei" exhibition space at Documenta XI, which opened on June 8, 2002 in Kassel and later reinstalled at the NAI in Rotterdam as part of the Asymptote survey exhibition: The Asymptote Experience.

The skyline of each city was abstracted into an animated image map and projected onto a large suspended form. This abstracted automobile body functions as a receiver or absorber of information as it moves through the space of the city, i.e., creating motion scapes (mscapes). The notational systems that result from the abstraction of the skylines can be interpreted as diagrams that "replay" the city as a sonic poem or soundtrack. While the texture maps reveal an apparent repetitiveness and similarity between one urban entity and another, the soundtracks allow for cultural inflections to be discerned.

Credits

Architects
Asymptote: Hani Rashid + Lise Anne Couture

Assistants
John Cleater, Noboru Ota

Fig. 3: Mscapes, Documenta XI, 2002 –
Digitally augmented physical environment

WritingSpace
1996 International Paper Biennale Düren, Germany

Dematerialization begs two questions, What is the net residual effect and what, if anything, is left in place of the original material artifact? The installation Writing-Space by Asymptote sought to capture the essence of paper itself as data through a process of digital recording and virtual output, thereby transforming the material reality of paper itself into a spatial phenomenon rather than a tectonic one.

The installation originated with the video-taping and subsequent digitizing of paper in the process of being physically manipulated, cut, folded, scored, crumpled and so on. The resulting video was then projected onto a 5x10 m folded and contorted scrim surface suspended and stretched between two walls of the large gallery space. The recorded and digitized sound of the paper filled the room while the image of the residue virtual paper was captured on the surface of the scrim and filled the space behind. The folds, creases and surfaces of the virtual paper were transformed into voids and solids, a liquid space constructed of sound and light. Using video projection units, a folded scrim backdrop and digitized sound, the installation represented paper under various states of manipulation and in various tectonic conditions as an immersive multimedia installation.

Credits

Architects
Asymptote: Hani Rashid + Lise Anne Couture,

Assistants
Oliver Mack, Henning Meyer, Oliver Neumann, Takeshi Okada

Awarded second prize at the 6th International Biennale der Papierkunst.

Fig. 4: The installation WritingSpace for the International Paper Biennale Düren, 1996

What actually constitutes architectural experience
and presence – architecture or media?

Fluxspace 2.0 Pavilion
2000 Venice Biennale, Italy

This large-scale, freestanding installation in the gardens sought to engage an audience, including but not limited to visitors to the Biennale by providing a simultaneous real spatial experience for both an actual and virtual audience. The outdoor installations measured 30 m in length and rose two stories in height, so it was visible throughout the historic grounds of the Biennale. The form and structure, a combination of steel frame and pneumatic envelope, created a tangible oscillation between the physical exterior and the fluid, continuously reconfigured state of its interior. The work housed two 180° Web cameras set within two circular rotating mirrors in the Fluxspace interior. As a visitor approached the structure and entered it beneath an air-filled shell, he or she experienced an interior world under perpetual transformation. Through the quasi-transparency of the rotating one-way mirrors one could see the interior space in a constant state of change and reassembly. The visitor was forced

into an ambiguous relationship with the architecture, somewhere between its real condition and its augmented state. This experience of the interior flux was enhanced by Internet images broadcast at 30 second intervals throughout the five-month duration of the exhibition. The camera catured and cataloged some 1.6 million variations on the space's interior. Both Biennale contributions sought to bring technology into the fold, not only as a tool of production and representation but as a means of engagement via interactivity and connections to global networks.

Fig. 5: Fluxspace 2.0 Pavilion for the 2000 Venice Biennale

Credits

Architects
Hani Rashid and Lise Anne Couture,
John Cleater, Noboru Ota, Florian Pfeifer

Structural Engineers
Buro Happold, New York

Steel Fabrication
Metallwerkstätte Walter Schulz GmbH

Pneumatic Structure
Michael Schultes, Vienna

Fluxspace 2.0 was generously supported by The Bohen Foundation. Fluxspace 2.0 is in the collection of the Solomon R. Guggenheim Museum, New York.

two voices _1 and 0

More and more of what determines architecture today is invisible. The codes of the computer, of financing, and building and safety matter much more in shaping the spaces we find ourselves moving through everyday than traditional aesthetics or building practices. Moreover, we spend more and more time in virtual environments or places determined by image production rather than space making. The question is what the architect can do in such a situation. The answer is that she or he can create simple, flexible structures in which these codes are manipulated to create dense, varied and clear experiences. Architecture becomes a question of interiorizing and designing the crossroads, not the building

Aaron Betsky is the Director of the Netherlands Architecture Institute in Rotterdam. Before that, he was the Curator of Architecture, Design and Digital Projects of the San Francisco Museum of Modern Art from 1995 to 2001. He has taught and lectured extensively, writes for many publications, and has published several books on architecture and design, most recently False Flat (2004), Architecture Must Burn (2000), Landscrapers: Building with the Land (2002).

aaron betsky

:

from box to intersection — architecture at the crossroads

FROM BOX TO INTERSECTION _ ARCHITECTURE AT THE CROSSROADS

Introduction

Walk through Times Square, Shibuya or Potsdamer Platz, drive towards any airport anywhere in the world, visit any suburban shopping mall, or live in any multiple-unit dwelling structure and the insignificance of mere building becomes clear just by looking around you. More and more, buildings are nodes in networks, intersections of multiple flows, and unstable accumulations of variegated material. This is not altogether a new phenomenon. One could argue that the common view of buildings as stable objects that are static and durable is only a question of perspective. Seen from the traditions of architecture as a discipline and a profession, buildings can be understood as particular constructions of a certain type and with a character appropriate to their function. They can be analyzed in terms of form, function and beauty. Seen from the viewpoint of regulations and financial regulations, they can be seen as recessive objects that are the results of investment decisions, or as the fixed accumulation of capital shaped by safety codes, zoning regulations and other building rules. Seen from the perspective of users, buildings are fixed objects filled out with repetitive spaces and structural grids that organize how one lives, works, or recreates in such a manner that daily routines and places become recognizable.

A Sprawling Reality

The building where our office is was designed to last, to look like an office building, not to fall down or otherwise harm us, to work as efficiently as possible, and to be there when we return to work tomorrow. And yet we experience all that work only in distraction as we move through a sprawling reality of which architecture is

only a small part with which its makers try, at best, to produce some semblance of order.

What is more, architecture seems to matter less and less when seen from the perspective of users. More and more of us spend more and more of our time in a virtual place that exists independently of buildings. It has its own rules and manner of appearance, but those are derived more from the disciplines of graphic design and the logic of a technology that has no physical presence than from the tradition that taught us how to create storage and access places for knowledge. For WiFi, walls are impediments or irrelevant, not place-givers.

In that chaos architects stick to what they know. That is the commonplace set of definitions of buildings that has allowed architecture to develop an elaborate set of rules by which it can validate its own practice. Architects know how to design buildings that meet codes and regulations, that look right, that function with a reasonable amount of efficiency, and that don't fall down unless subjected to extraordinary stresses. Yet architects are always trying to do something else, something more or less. They abstract buildings so that they become unrecognizable. They cover them in decoration or strange materials. They create spaces that can be used and interpreted in a number of ways. They question all the regulations according to which they are supposed to build, making structures that are more expensive than they need to be, that don't always function very smoothly and that above all else assert the primacy and singularity of the building itself. For this is what architects want to do: Prove in built form that they have produced something that is not just the result of all the conditions, restrictions, regulations, expectations and traditions in which they build, but that remains even after all those factors have been analyzed and answered. This is their building. It looks unlike whatever has come before, is a more refined version of what has come before, or changes our idea of what has come before. It invents space out of nowhere, uses new materials, or somehow is just and fundamentally other. That nobody beyond his or her own community notices is just a matter of perspective.

The arguments for this behavior are varied and range from the ability to invent or develop a signature within a tradition (a style, whether neo-classical or modernist, or a recognizable way of making "a Gehry" or "a Koolhaas"), to the notion that architecture must liberate us from the formal and physical restrictions in which we live. Whatever the justifications might be, they propose an architecture that finds its core in the making of an autonomous object that by its very nature must be, in at least one of its aspects, outside our daily experience. It must be something more, something else, something weird, new or alternative. By producing such a structure, the architect justifies her or his existence.

Certainly it is necessary for architects, like any actor in the social sphere, to develop a critical stance towards the task she or he is given. From the perspective of a critical architecture (or one made by people who at least try to be aware of what they are doing, why, and in what context), they must resist the fast flows of capital that leech meaning out of every object around us. They must resist the demand for isolation and security that tears apart the social web connecting us. They must refuse to waste natural resources, land and space. They must not make buildings whose size, appearance, or placement has a negative effect on the site where they appear. In all these ways,

they must do no harm. They must also aspire to contribute to making a world that is more beautiful, however they interpret that charge. But in all these ways they continually come up against the fact their very desire to make the world better creates fissions, problems and waste. The best definition of architecture, as opposed to "just" building, may be, if the roof leaks, it must be architecture. That is because exactly what architects do to move beyond the built affirmation of social, economic and physical status quo creates problems.

So perhaps what is needed is a change of perspective. If architecture is not the making of buildings but the establishment of nodes, intersections and flexible accretions of material that change as needed, it can perhaps avoid the contradiction of its wasteful and difficult desire to do better and thus become other. If architecture, in other words, can see itself as moments of intensification in larger structures, not all of which come out of the traditions of architecture, it might be able to do better. Perhaps architecture needs to look at how spaces and forms cohere and open up, how they catch meaning and material in their structures and allow them to develop, and how they produce both images that can last only as long as they are effective and forms that endure.

From Domestic Interior to New Architecture

I have long argued that the interior, and especially the domestic interior, might be understood as such an intersection of forces and the source for a new approach to architecture. In particular, the domestic interior exhibits design as a participatory process that changes and accumulates over time as the inhabitants collect objects and images. The interior becomes an intersection of such fragments of a continuum in time and space, ranging from antique furniture or knickknacks to family photographs to modern couches or lamps. The rules governing the arrangement of these objects are less the result of rigid preconceptions, and more part and parcel of the activities of everyday life: Design becomes a way of ritualizing and fixing social patterns and systems of use. The interior is, paradoxically, an open system that can accept objects and images from the outside and make sense out of them by the way they are integrated through use and arrangement. The interior is the realm of the *bricoleur* and thus of the magician who transforms everyday objects, fragments of the past or new appearances into significant and precious icons of daily life, all merely by arranging the way in which they are placed and used.

This *bricolage* is well understood by those artists who seek to use their particular craft to make us aware of how we make sense of the world through the work of collecting, representing, looking and arranging. More and more art today takes on the quality of being an accumulation of already formed material in a manner that mimics and comments on the ways in which these objects are used in daily life. In so doing, art finds the *unheimlich* (the uncanny) in the home. Unlike architecture, which must in the end remain static, useful and efficient, art can do so purely as critique; and when it chooses to do so by using familiar artifacts or by concentrating on basic phenomena of perception, it can achieve exactly the liberating effect to which some modern architecture wishes to effect. It builds the "other" self-consciously, and that becomes its point, its particular perspective.

The intersection between art, architecture and everyday life occurs when certain images, objects and spaces that are part of our daily routine achieve, through a combination of repeated use, particular form, cultural contingency and marketing, the status of icons. These shapes draw into themselves some of the magical powers of transformation that the act of collecting, daily use and promotion produce. By this mechanism a pair of blue jeans or an otherwise normal office building can take on the quality of being instantly recognizable, part of a wider and rationalized culture of production and consumption, and yet a completely individual or an extension of one person's body. Expressive structures such as the Bilbao Guggenheim and the Sydney Opera House achieved this, but more often it is undesigned buildings or fragments that become iconic, i.e., the public squares mentioned above, public monuments, certain parks, or shapes such as the Flatiron Building that are defined by unusual circumstances. This is to a certain extent the result of their forms, which have become abstracted, tied to usage patterns and either fragmented or smoothed, as if worn down by use, but also so open to different interpretations that they can call up a number of different meanings to each viewer.

The interior, the art of making strange and the icon all offer lessons for the making of an open architecture that exists at the intersection of social forces. The ad hoc, strangely familiar, iconic, collage-based and personalized forms and organizations that could be adapted from these different fields might change the perspective on a critical architecture that until now has developed only from the history of the discipline.

What makes such integration possible is the dissolution of boundaries between maker, material and user, between different design and artmaking disciplines, and between, on a fundamental level, the subject of design and its object. This process is occurring because of new computer and communications technologies.

Architecture as Data Bricolage

In the computer, there are essentially just zeros and ones and the combination thereof is a dynamic and open-ended system governed by rules that are the same for the making of text, image, object, or any other product. From the perspective of the computer, what we imagine is loose data, what we make is accumulated or stored data, and what we are designing is data in flux. It is all just information, but that information is either latent or visible, presented or just floating in the ether. Technologies catch and harness that information. The question of design is how to make sense of such data in an open-ended manner, i.e., in a manner that allows for the fullness of information to become adoptable and adaptable, visible and manipulable by the user.

Thus, the computer and its attendant technologies acts first of all as a great gatherer, a box into which nearly endless amounts of information can be crammed. All the codes to which a building must answer, but also data on geography and geology, climate and other physical conditions, can be stored in relation to the particulars of the site and program. In addition, it is theoretically possible to add all information about the possible impact the building could have in every aspect of those physical conditions, and to play the codes as a kind of chess game, aligning potential outcomes with endless permutations of spatial sequences, scales, arrangements and materials. This is what Rotterdam-based firms like MVRDV and KCAP have done, but one can also see similar experiments in Barcelona and other cities around the world.

What is important in this respect is that both site and program, and perhaps many other aspects that are usually "given" to the designer, can be set, within the program the designer chooses, as variables. Thus different site usages or different sites altogether, different programs, and different characters can be proposed within a fluid process in which the information the client or authorities (though rarely the users) add can become part of an open process. The building, in other words, becomes a direct translation of the social, economic, political and physical processes, articulated in relation to each other only in the final building. Architecture becomes a way of realizing the network.

Some would say that the act of architecture has to proceed beyond this level of negotiated collage, interpretation and assembly. They would argue that the very abstraction of these relationships at the level of data means that wholly new objects, images and spaces can emerge out of familiar situations and deep, complexly related realities. The danger is that the resultant forms, in skipping over the process of negotiated realization, seem as alien and abstract to us as the programs that produce them, thus entombing their new-found liberty within monumental forms that are as self-referential and outside of daily experience as any in the history of architecture. This is the danger of those who would produce "blobs" or "machined architecture."

There is another possibility for such realization, and that is to allow there to be no final realization, no final form and no final image, but to let the building exist as the almost chance intersection of different programmatic elements on a site. What coherence there is comes exactly from the relationships established between elements, not from the overall form the building might achieve. It is in fact possible that the building has no form of its own but can exist as an urban agglomeration, or underground, or in existing buildings. The building can, as in the McCormick Center in Chicago, by OMA, or in some of the proposals by Field Operations, be a critical realization of sprawl.

Architecture as Enabling Infrastructure

There are precedents for this kind of intersectional architecture, especially if we look at architecture from the perspective that is becoming more and more prevalent, namely that of infrastructure. Just as the government is reducing itself more and more to the function of maintaining or enabling infrastructure at every level, producing a few iconic images floating above the roads, armies and bureaucracies of regulation that are its true reality, so architecture is becoming more and more the provision of a minimal and highly efficient structure in which a plethora of activities can take place. The architect can then sign the added value of that intersection, which is also the value of the architecture, through certain expressive forms or a highly worked (but almost always highly tenuous) skin.

The history of such forms can be found in the mobility infrastructure that has provided far larger and far more expressive forms than traditional architecture has: train stations, highway interchanges and the spaces such as rest stops that service them, and airports. All of these structures exhibit architecture as the provision of a large volume, as open as possible, in which many forms and functions intersect. Equally flexible in their uses, though not in their forms, are the large shopping malls that must accommodate changing retail components and increasingly are also the sites for many community activities, as well as diverse

forms of mass entertainment. In many large Asian cities, these two traditions come together in sprawling hybrid commuter nodes and shopping districts, in which the independence of buildings is lost in the continually morphing and spreading sequence of retail, commuter and recreational strutures.

Starting in the 1980s, in schools such as the Architectural Association in London and the Institute for Architecture and Urban Studies in New York, architects began theorizing such structures, basing themselves at least partially on the theories of the members of Team X, Archigram, Superstudio and the Metabolists. They thought of their architecture as an analogous city whose formal elements were a kind of infrastructure of streets or construction through which space flowed freely. The act of design would be to create attractors and intense intersections that would order and organize these activities in an open-ended manner.

Reduced to the level of a building, these nodal network schemes became 3D grids in which any number of activities could co-exist, and in which the careful progression through spaces or their composition into facade, plan and section gave way to loose clumpings or agglomerations tied together by stairs, escalators, lifts, service cores, directional systems and all the rest of what had previously been the building's buried infrastructure. Certain architects, such as Rem Koolhaas, went further, eliding floors, walls and ceilings, balancing forms in seemingly unstable piles, and purposefully bulging out of any kind of straight composition. In a kind of latent desire to create form, they made coherence exactly out of flow, elision and incoherence.

These boxes of delight, which can contain everything and nothing, are in a sense also the critical and open-ended equivalents of that other form of building that more and more dominates our urban environment, namely, the storage box. Whether at the small scale of U-Store buildings or, more commonly, in the explosive growth of distribution buildings at every scale, these places of temporary accumulation have become the most evident result of changes in computer and communications technology.

I call the critical riffs on these structures Pandora's Boxes, because they contain all our sins, desires and fears, locked into the infrastructure the architect has created and just waiting to escape in order to rend what is left of social, economic and physical cohesion in our society. For this is what architecture as the making of such infrastructural boxes finally does achieve: It brings disparate parts and functions, pieces and people, structures and relations together at one open intersection where they establish, if even for fleeting moments, a sense of coherence. It might be this act of gathering, this weaving together the strands of a networked society into a crossroads, that might save architecture.

To do so, architecture may have to look towards the logic of the virtual world, rather than towards its utopian wanderings into grand structures. The floating world of the computer that, like a magical mechanism of bricolage, can bring together disparate forms and images without worrying about their provenance is disciplined by the aesthetics of logic and communication, which is to say, graphic design. Graphics are thus becoming a more and more important part of what makes architecture.

This does not mean that architecture is becoming superficial, but that it understands itself more and more as a cloak thrown over the unstable intersection of human beings, goods and information. On the other hand, if we move our perspective from that of Western civilization, in which the crossroads is the place of commerce and order, and look at the traditions of Western Africa, which has so informed and shaped American culture, we might remember that in that crossroads one meets the devil. It is up to architects whether they sell their soul and open Pandora's box, or create the kind of design that, in providing a strange and magical coherence among our disparate desires and fears, keeps us on the high road towards the utopian future of which architecture still dreams.

Designers must not merely take note of the new technology but also seek out its creative potential. Rather than automatically adjusting to current practice, they should adjust current practice where necessary to the new ideas. In this way architecture is able to conquer a new field of activity in a digital era. It can produce environments we have as yet barely encountered. It can create experiences we have never had before. It can also organize itself in a way that challenges professional certitudes and makes the existing role play look hopelessly old-fashioned.

Ole Bouman is a writer, curator and designer based in Amsterdam. He is editor of Archis magazine and www.archis.org. His major projects are: The Invisible in Architecture (1994), RealSpace in QuickTime (1996), Manifesta (2000), and Archis RSVP events (2004).

OLE Bouman:

Building Terminal — for an architecture without objectness

BUILDING TERMINAL _
FOR AN ARCHITECTURE WITHOUT
OBJECTNESS

Introduction

Many people think that the new media are
pushing architecture into the role of help-
less victim. It can only stand by and watch
how millions of people are spending more
and more of their valuable time in digital
surroundings; they no longer need architecture as the backdrop to the important
moments of their lives. On top of this,
the role of permanent carrier of cultural
meaning has lapsed. The mother of the
arts is becoming a marginal phenomenon.
Others take a more optimistic view of
things. As far as they are concerned, the
only interesting architecture is computer-
generated architecture. In this essay I will
explore the fertile area between these two
extremes.

Three Attitudes to the New Media

The key question for the coming years is
whether architecture will succeed in developing other strategies besides the ratio-
nalization of existing practice. What other
options are there apart from cost-cutting
and streamlining? Equally important is
the question of whether potential new
strategies will in fact constitute genuine
alternatives within the practice of building. Will creative innovation at the conceptual level really get a look-in? In any
event, for this to happen designers must
not merely take note of the new technology but also seek out its creative potential.
Rather than automatically adjusting to
current practice, they should adjust current practice where necessary to the new
ideas. In this way architecture is able to
conquer a new field of activity in a digital
era. It can produce environments we have
as yet barely encountered. It can create
experiences we have never had before. It

can also organize itself in a way that challenges professional certitudes and makes
the existing role play look hopelessly old-
fashioned.

Before going into the nature of the new
environments and experiences, we must
first pause to consider the artistic menta-
lity necessary for their creation. In order
to be able to intervene actively in the
development of the new media an architect must be adequately equipped mentally. A key element of this question of men-
tality is the relationship with technology
itself. In architecture, as in other areas,
it is possible to distinguish three broad
attitudes to the new media. The first is
the negative attitude where people stub-
bornly stick to the old familiar way of
working and simply ignore the cultural
significance of the new media. At best,
since the computer has become indispensable for drawing, they will employ someone to take care of this side of the business. The whiz kid as alibi for not making
any substantive changes. The architecture
continues to look the same as ever.

The second attitude is that of an un-
abashed surrender to the hype in which
the new media are lauded with quasi-
religious fervor as architecture's saviors.
The design identity of these architects is
synonymous with their use of the computer. In the final analysis, they are asked
only by virtue of their reputation as a
computer apostle, a preacher of the digital gospel. However versatile their designs,
it is above all their use of the computer
that attracts attention. For those who
adopt this attitude it is then only a small
step to restrict themselves voluntarily to
this stance. Eventually, they can talk of
nothing else. At which point a true community of faith is born.

Finally there is the pragmatic attitude in
which the two domains are seen side by

side, as two parallel worlds. Such prag-
matists have no difficulty accepting the
existence of virtual reality, of digital networks, and they are also prepared to use
the computer for the design of architecture. At the same time, however, they stick
to the production of a physical, analog
world, appropriate to the functions we
have always known and adapted to the
physical movements we have always made.
Even if the entire office is computerized,
the benefits of the new technology are
barely if at all conceptualized and as such
taken into account in the designs. Media
remain what they are: means. Nothing
more.

Hybrid Environments

There is, however, a fourth attitude possible. Something that has so far received
much less attention is the possibility of
allowing the physical and virtual domains
to merge, of integrating them. By refusing
to let oneself be reduced to either a worn-
out dinosaur or a stressed-out cybernaut,
a whole range of innovative possibilities
capable of injecting architecture with
enormous vitality comes into view. It is a
matter of crossing the analog and digital
worlds, of hybrid environments that can
no longer be classified as one thing or
the other. The behavior of such worlds is
similarly hybrid, consisting partly of biological and physical reactions, partly of
cybernetic acts appropriate to a cyborgian
existence. The environmental quality of
such a hybrid world can never again be
reduced to the typical architectural parameters that have stood us in good stead
for centuries. All previous architectural
definitions, from Vitruvius to Peter Eisen-
man, run up against their limits here.

Beauty and functionality and solidity, tectonic and cladding, program and meaning,
all these old concepts acquire a new con-
notation. The task is to chart the architec-

tural potential of a digital world, not in
spite of, not instead of, not even alongside, but in the physical world. This I will
do by exploring the concept of architecture conceived as terminal. As such it is
still a building, an object. But it is also
a computer, an interface. As a nodal point
in a wider communication network.

What if architecture were to become no
more than a prop for a display or projection screen? If the separation between
its two main functions, shelter and symbol, were to become definitive and the
sheltering function were to divest itself
of any iconographic ambition and with-
draw behind the exterior? What would
remain of architecture as we know it if
spatial expression were to become a mere
adjunct and all designing capacity and
visual intelligence were to be put into
directing the surface? Would architecture
survive if the entire tectonic tradition
of construction and making connections
were to vanish as a source of design inspiration in favor of the visual story for
architecture when any of its buildings
can be animated and transformed by projections and electronic displays? What is
left of architecture if our architectural
"sign" language is no longer etched in
stone?

In the past, architecture also needed sunlight in order to be seen. As soon as dark-
ness fell it lost its shape and substance.
Its meaning vanished, cloaked in shadows.
Even when it became fashionable to spot-
light monumental buildings, it was above
all the building as volume, as object, that
was emphasized. Out of the nocturnal
gloom there suddenly rises up a majestic
object, a representative of the realm of
things, that must try to last until dawn –
until the invention of neon light. Nearly
everyone has memories of the flashing
lights of Times Square, Shinjuko, Picca-
dilly Circus or Place Pigalle. These places

provided the defining images of the metropolis at night. Simple light-switching circuits strung along the upper edge of urban elevations created a deliriously metropolitan atmosphere that owed virtually nothing to the materiality of the architecture. The absolute acme of such urban animation (partly because of countless famous film scenes) is the Strip at Las Vegas. The ultimate funfair. But neon signs are only part of its story nowadays. Entire virtual edifices are contrived by means of lighting effects. Gigantic Jumbotron and Napcom displays dominate the scene. The best the visual display industry has to offer is on show here. And it is growing all the time. Ever larger LCD and magma screens. Ever finer resolution, ever sharper pictures. And although a surface of around 2x3 m quickly runs into millions of dollars in production and management costs, the price of hardware looks set to fall. Facades and walls could be brought to life by designers and provided with a new, dynamic iconography. Now that a good deal of public life is conducted indoors, in shopping malls or car parks, the game can continue by day. No longer must the use of light in architecture wait for nightfall.

A New Role for Architecture

At first glance, it would seem that these developments need not really affect architecture. They could remain an addition, a revitalization. But of course there is something far more fundamental going on here. It concerns a new role for architecture in a pervasive visual culture where the mass media have less and less need of the enclosure of the box (TV, cinema). The audio-visual media continue to find new outlets in the city. For the static nature of architecture, bound up as it is with concepts like foundations, durability, inertia and tradition, this has serious implications. Mobilization, which has long had

society in its grip, is now impinging upon the material environment. When stationary objects are visually animated they lose their objectness, their fixity. However sturdy their construction may still be, they appear to be moving. It looks as if we have here the next step in the rich history of parallax manipulation.

Where the baroque played the game of convex and concave and investigated the *trompe l'œil*, where neo-classicism discovered the mirror, where 19th-century engineering made a hero of the freestanding structure, where modernism turned the free facade and the free ground plan into ideology, we are now on the threshold of a new development in the psychological game of spatial design. For this new spatial effect the physical space is no longer strictly necessary, although duplication has its attractions. The great leap consists of uncoupling spatial perception and architectural structure. Now that really is "lite" architecture. In addition to striving after ever lighter structures, transparent and translucent walls and gravity-defying, curvilinear forms, architecture can now, via film, become truly immaterial. Contours fade, forms become fluid. The relationship between human beings and architecture is no longer polar or dialectical, but "immersive." You can quite literally be swallowed up in it... Who will be the first architect to win the Oscar or Golden Palm for best director?

Building as Terminal

I offer you the following scenario. Suppose that architects were to incorporate video walls and projections in their initial sketch designs. Suppose that in their negotiations with the client, investment by the likes of Fuji, Coca-Cola or Lucky Strike, by Sharp, Zeiss Ikon or Polaroid, by Silicon Graphics or Alias WaveFront, could be calculated in their budgets from the start. It might then be possible to use the image-carriers thus procured for noncommercial, experience-heightening effects. Apart from one-dimensional messages from the multinationals, urban facade displays could at given moments become total theater, with the architect as director, as creative brain. This is the urbanism of the future. In addition to the advertisements, conscious and unconscious sensations are evoked. A mixture of film loops and abstract images affords artistically profound experiences. The consciousness industry, to resurrect that old concept, will help energize the public domain.

And as if that were not enough, we are also continuing to develop interactive paint, contorted facade surfaces and curved windows, to use sandblasted or LCD-programmed glass, with zinc and aluminum cladding. One can imagine a whole range of architectural interventions aimed at intensifying this projection game. And who will invent the double-curved display screen? Frank Gehry's Bilbao fantasia will be child's play in comparison with the building that really (re)acts as a terminal.

The actual revolution of the spatial experience lies in the bodiless transmission of signs. When signs could for the first time travel without a body, be it via electromagnetic waves or cable etc., the foundation for bodiless spatial experience was laid. Telematic machines, ranging from trains to planes, and the telematic media, from television to the Internet, have ultimately dismissed the discourse of location and forced the discourse of dislocation to be the foundation of our society. What we urgently need now is a new dynamic concept of space that is characterized by immateriality and nonlocality. Architecture as spatial design has to adapt to this new "condition humaine."

Peter Weibel was appointed professor of visual media art at the University of Applied Arts, Vienna in 1984. He was head of the digital arts laboratory of the Media Department of NY University from 1984–1989, and founded the Institute of New Media at the Academy of Fine Arts, Frankfurt/M in 1989. From 1986–1995, he was artistic consultant and later artistic director of the Ars Electronica in Linz, and from 1993–1999 curator at the Neue Galerie am Landesmuseum Joanneum, Graz. He commissioned the Austrian pavilions at the Venice Biennial from 1993–1999. Since 1999, he has been Chair and CEO of the ZKM | Center for Art and Media Karlsruhe.

peter weibel:

architecture — from location to nonlocation, from presence to absence

ARCHITECTURE _FROM LOCATION TO NONLOCATION, FROM PRESENCE TO ABSENCE

Introduction

During the 20th century not only distances and scales have changed under the influence of telematic media and machines, but even more so the relation to the location itself: hic et nunc, here and now, here and there have become variable quantities. Location and space as the basic media of architecture are being questioned (refer to Deconstruction). Nonlocation, dislocation, dematerialisation are new radical architectural categories. Individual decision procedures that position the architect as a building artist in the proximity of a traditional understanding of art, based on sculpture and painting, are also being replaced by new planning methods that are based on the complex system theories of the media and machines. Therefore computer-based algorithms can replace data of individual signatures as proved by deconstructivism and primarily by its successor, the metamorphic or biomorphic school of architecture (blob-architecture).

This approach exceeds by far the recent understanding of experimental architecture and acts beyond material experiment, alternative buildings and model architecture. In this sense unconventionalities alone are not experimental. The new definition of experimental architecture experiments with architecture's semantics. Only by applying new parameters to well-known architectural rules does a new, almost "experimental" definition of experimental architecture emerge.

With the following we are going to concentrate on the relation of location and space as a variable: place-displacement / site-parasite.

About the Discourse of Dislocation [1]

In traditional architecture everything has its place. A flat, a room or a desk is tidy when everything is in its place; a citizen without a residence has no place; having no place is forbidden. Not least, functionalism and its connected theory of short distances refer to places: City Hall on Main Square, the dining room next to the kitchen, the night stand by the bed. Even each detail has its allocated place and the nail has been hit on the head, at the right time at the right place. Building means to organize where something belongs [2].

Location is everywhere, and where there is no location it is immediately produced through orientation and through memory. Architecture can also heighten an amorphous nonlocation to a place: adoration of the location is expressed in the metaphor of the *genius loci*; each location is ingenious; buildings are allegories for these imaginations of location.

The idea of a location is the unity of body and space while in the Greek theater it is the unity of time and place, as well as the unity of space, time and architecture for Sigfried Giedion. These ideas of the location use the body-oriented spatial experience, the technique of localization through the body. When a person crossed a room, changed the location step by step or moved from one place to another, this happened with the help of his body or with the help of another organic body such as a horse. Over the centuries the experience became phylogenically ingrained in man's mind that changing location, dislocation, was only possible through one's own physical body. This is how phylogenically the paradigm of body-focused spatial experience developed, which has dominated civilization for millenia. With the exception of ships it has hardly been two centuries, since the beginning of the

266

industrial revolution, that dislocation has occurred with the help of machines such as trains, cars, or planes. The machine-made change of location happens much faster than the physical, in fact so fast that for the historically physical experience of space the distances between points of places seem to vanish and we therefore metaphorically speak of the vanishing of space. But even with the machine-focused spatial experience we are still dealing with physical objects, with comprehensible artificial moving apparatuses whose criteria are still comparable to our natural-moving apparatuses.

The traditional techniques of displacment: The floating away in mysticism, the displacement in shamanism, the nonlocation in nirvana – they all served to free the body from its location. Since the 19th century new techniques to escape the prison of space have been invented. The body is freed from the prison of location through media and machines (1830, the train; 1969, the landing on the Moon). The beginning of a new spatial experience can be related back to the scanning principle, discovered around 1840, which was used for the first telegraphic trials (picture transmission over distances) which contained the idea of transforming a spatial dimension (drawing on a surface) into a linear sequence of points in time. The telemachines (1840, telegraphy; 1906, radio; and 1927, television) released the messages (signs) from the messenger (body). Sign messages can travel without a body. The separation of message and messenger introduces the discourse of nonlocation. Until this historic moment each (immaterial) message needed a (physical) messenger who transmitted, transported, or displaced it from one place to another. Before the industrial revolution these messengers were primarily bodies (soldiers, horses, pigeons) and during the industrial revolution primarily

moving machines. In the postindustrial phase these are the communication media. The actual revolution of the spatial experience lies in the bodiless transmission of signs. When signs could for the first time travel without a body, be it via electromagnetic waves or cable etc, the foundation for bodiless spatial experience was laid. After the physical transport machines such as train, car and plane, it is primarily the telematic transport media such as telephone, television and internet that introduce the discourse of dislocation. Dislocation (of space) and disembodiment (of the body) create bodiless spatial experience.

During the industrial revolution the machine-focused spatial experience took the place of the physically focused experience of space, followed by the sign-focused symbolic spatial experience during the postindustrial revolution. Without this sign-focused spatial experience, from the screen for the pilot to the map of the hiker, the entire body of modern civilization would break down. Nonlocation as a metaphor of sign-focused spatial experience rather than the machine and body focus is therefore the origin of dislocation.

The new spatial understanding beyond physicality cuts the ground from under architecture, which has so far been defined as spatial art and, as we have shown, has always been tied to the body-oriented spatial experience. When the architecture group Coop Himme(l)bau states that architecture begins beyond space or architecture begins where space ends, they mean exactly that: contemporary architecture begins beyond the historical physically experienced space. Daniel Libeskind too denies the historical term of location or space in architecture as already suggested in his book title *Kein Ort an seiner Stelle* (No Place in its Place) [3]. Telematic machines, ranging from trains to planes, and telematic media, from fax to television, have ultimately dismissed the discourse of location and forced the discourse of dislocation to be the foundation of our society. This discourse of dislocation also can not be ignored by architecture. Architecture as spatial design has to adapt to the new spatial understanding. The telematic media ultimately force a new dynamic concept of space onto architecture. This concept of space is characterized by immateriality and nonlocality. So if historic space can no longer serve as a foundation for architecture the only way out can only be to claim the criteria derived from the varieties of nonlocality such as mobility, flexibility, dynamics, viability etc. Ideally architecture would have to free itself from a condition of two- and three-dimensionality and, like the telefax, transform into a nonlinear sequence of configurations, into a spatial-temporal system that is. Through telematic media space has become a linear sequence of points in time, a string of signs. Therefore spatial art has become a temporal art and the two-dimensional flat picture has become a form of time. Hence rather than the site (topos or the three-dimensional room) the nonsite, nonlocality (*atopos*), heterotopy and utopia play a much bigger role than before. A shifting of accent from location to nonlocation, from presence to absence has taken place.

This shifting of accent unfolds the conceptual range of location (*topos*). Apart from the classical function of location, nonlocation [4] and nonlocality (*atopos*) play a bigger role in contemporary architecture, primarily heterotopia in the sense of Foucault, utopia and atopia in the location itself (such as prison or hospitals), most of all heterotopias and dystopia in the sense of Helmut Wilke [5]. While atopias are characterized by contingencies and dystopias by symbolic dismissals, heterotopias offer the diverse structured forms of disorder of today's complex society.

The idea of a heterarchitecture as "hybrid mixed reality" tries to fulfil exactly this new experience and design an architecture which creates a new order between contingency, disorder and dismissal. It is understood that this architecture can be neither standard nor a deconstructive architecture but only a nonstandard architecture [6]. The classical architecture disappears into the heterarchitecture.

About the Language of Absence

In the telematic era where signs travel without a body and where this immaterial sign traffic keeps the world economically and culturally together, the significances, symbols and signs, which are the nonpresent, the nonphysical, hence the language of absence, play a larger role than ever compared with physical presence. The order of the modules becomes the order of the signs. More than ever architecture has to adapt sign or text character in order to be able to react to the primacy of the significances that have developed through the freedom of (the bodiless traveling) signs, caused by the telematic revolution, as well as through the shifting of location, the dislocation through the telematic media. Present architecture builds on the dematerialized, disembodied space, on the space of signs and significances.

Through the principle of scanning and its relevant technologies, messages without a body have become possible. Messenger and message, body and sign have been separated. The bodiless codes have also led to a separation of body and location. The historical equation of body and location disintegrated, nonphysicality led to nonlocality. The telematic media, the spatial experience through telematic media have once and for all introduced the nonphysical nonlocality. The location, the physical, physically experienced location, is not lost to architecture as a medium, but is joined by the nonlocation space of telematic machines and media, which overforms and deforms the classical spatial experience. Media experience and spatial experience create hybrid forms of a bodiless and body-orientated experience of being. The individual experiences itself in one location and at the same time in several other locations. It experiences itself decentralized and eccentric. The eccentricity becomes obvious in the blurring of the borders between exteriority and interiority. What is inside and outside, in the body and outside of it becomes a mixed experience of a mixed reality.

This discourse of dislocation has naturally its roots in the history of architecture itself. Architects have always stormed against the physical limits of space and time, against the prison of bricks and stones, against gravity and mass. What today's electronic media and glass facades offer as opportunities to exceed the limits of walls had been tried in former times with the available contemporary means: perspective illusion painting simulated rooms beyond the architect's possibilities. Looking back it can be said that within the discussion between architecture and mural painting in churches and palaces, this radical differentiation between presence and absence had already taken place. As an architect Palladio produced local architecture with presence. Through the painting of Veronese this was extended by the dimension of a nonlocal architecture of absence: with illusion painting (virtual architectures and landscapes) the painter exceeds the physical and the physical limitations.

The influence of perspective painting on architecture was enormous in the Baroque era. The perspective through painting encouraged bringing the previously neglected side sections and rear facades also into the view of the architecture. Apart from these traditional approaches of nonlocality, which architecture owes to painting, there are also moments of dislocation in the history of architecture which it owes to machines. The idea of underground architecture and the Baroque mural painting have the problem of the visual in common, however, in contrasting positions that are on the one side a negation of the visual and an apotheosis of the visual on the other. The *trompe l'œil* technique of mural painting in the Baroque and the Rococo eras created rooms that didn't really exist and in this sense weren't really visible or which visualized the invisible that could not been seen in reality. The virtuosos of illusion painting in churches and palaces were the first architects of cyberspace, the virtual space [7]. The underground architecture was invisible architecture anyway.

Illusion painting has therefore – slightly and unnoticed – already disturbed the classical equation between reality and visibility. Within the classical understanding of reality until 1840 the rule said, what is real is visible, what is unreal is painted. The visual and the present form a unit. What cannot be seen is the absent and the unreal. Illusion painting has made the nonpresent partly visible. The classical equation therefore states that what is present is visible and the absent is invisible. What the subject sees is the present. The nonpresent is not visible. The painter, however, could already paint the nonpresent. This was not the main task of painting, which in most cases insisted on the realistic depiction of the present, but as heresy illusion painting could break this rule. It is however the central task of the media as a language of the absent to make visible what is actually not present. In his book *Civilization and its Discontents* (1930) Freud has defined writing as the language of absence and stated that technology as the language of absence would continue this task of writing. Therefore the task of technology and subsequently of the technical image and sound media is to make present what is spatially and temporally absent or past. The telematic media have set new emphases in the dialectic of presence and absence, thereby leading from the architecture of presence to the architecture of absence. The dialectics of presence and absence has always included the dialectics of the visible and the invisible. The telematic and technical media in their annihilation of the historical equation between location and nonlocation as presence and absence have also introduced a new equation between location and visibility and therefore between presence and visibility. The discourse of dislocation has shattered the old equation. The classical equation – the present is visible and the absent is invisible – is no longer valid. The new equation, introduced by the telematic media says, even the absent can be made visually present. Instead of the static definition of visibility there is now a dynamic discourse of the visual; rather than clear borders between visible and invisible, between presence and absence there are variable zones of visibility. Technical viewing has destroyed the classical ontology and thereby the classical concepts of the visual.

Architecture as a building art must react to the changes through the visual dislocation and the loss of the anthropomorphic viewing. The disembodiment in the realms of the mechanistic visual has provoked a new language of space. The media that are parallel to real space set up an electronically immaterial data space – particularly noticeable in the worldwide data net, recognizable in cyberspace – don't operate with the historically constant concepts and realities of space but rather operate with the signs of space. The separation of messenger and message, of body and sign is

followed by the separation of space and sign. The signs of space float freely; they dislocate from the real physical location. The discourse of classical architecture was built on location, space, body, matter, mass, gravity and so forth. The techno-discourse of dislocation has dissolved the historical differentiations and borders. The discourse of nonclassical architecture is based on nonlocation, immaterial signs, dynamic systems, floating data and so forth. The discourse therefore not only concerns the physical location but also the separation of the sign-reality from sensual reality and the separation of the visual from space or presence. In the era of the primacy of technologically supported and integrated viewing, the language of architecture becomes increasingly a pure language of signs and of a new form of technologically supported visibility.

About the Readability of Invisible Space

Modern glass technology made glass facades possible, which make the readability of space become ambivalent. Glass panes, electronically controlled and built from quartz crystals, allow a mobile play of zones of transparency and opaqueness. Such glass panes repeat the discourse of dislocation within the discourse of visibility and invisibility. With the help of variable zones of visibility that are systemically controlled, a variable dislocation of the visual unfolds, ranging from transparent to opaque areas. The same areas can both be transparent and opaque. The visual state is not definitively defined and not static; it is mobile, flexible, transitory and dynamic. In this dislocation of the visual the discourse of dislocation, which in a hidden way rules architecture, is visually expressed.

Architectural space does not only approach a space of lines, in the sense of Deleuze [8], but modern architectural space is more to be understood as a space of "mapping" and "re-mapping." The physical and the electronic spaces merge by projecting themselves within each other and mixed up. The visually present is mapped onto the absent, which is thereby made visible. With illusion painting it was exactly the other way round: The visually absent was mapped as a painting onto the architecturally present. In contemporary architecture that reacts to telematic changes, reality becomes a wire model, which architecture, by functioning as a variable texture (rather than in the old skin, membrane, facade function), makes temporarily visible. Architecture controls the zones of visibility. Reality becomes a range of absence and presence. Like a moving pointer architecture regulates visibility even in previously invisible zones, making spaces readable and unreadable [9]. You only see people and objects if architecture as the control systems wants you to. Architecture itself can become absent and invisible. Invisible architecture can become visible through users. Architecture maps virtuality and reality intertwined. In the universe of variable zones the subject can understand medial architecture like selecting television channels. The user of contemporary architecture zaps through the visual zones of architecture and controls the visibility and invisibility of the architecture himself and thereby the degree of its virtual or real character. In contemporary architecture reality itself becomes a window. It is no longer about watching reality through a window, but reality is the window.

Conclusion

Architecture becomes the meat for a wireframe model of reality. This theory of the mapping of different electronic, physical or social spaces within each other as a new "location" of architecture is based on the concept of virtual and real-life space. In order to be able to readjust or remap the space of virtual or real life according to the user's requirements, not only are new high performance computers, as they appear in quantum computing on the horizon, necessary but it also requires the ubiquitous presence of computers in order to enable the architecture of absence.

"Ubiquitous Computing," "DNA-Computing" and other next-generation computing systems are building the necessary prerequisite for an "Architecture of the Multiverse." The nonlocal architecture requires a "ubiquitous computing" in order to set up its presence and its location anytime and anywhere.

References

[1] Peter Weibel & Manfred Wolff-Plottegg, Seminar for Experimental Architecture and Algorithm Design, lecture at Innsbruck University, May 30, 1996. In 1996 Wolff-Plottegg showed me the manuscript for a publication in a book, a collection of essays that I called "Architektur Algorithmen (Architecture Algorithms)." We jointly wrote a preface to this book on which this essay is based.

[2] See also Mark Wigley. "Architecture has always been a central cultural institution valued above all for its provision of stability and order." In: Philip Johnson and Mark Wigley: "Deconstructivist Architecture," The Museum of Modern Art, New York, 1988, p. 10.

[3] Daniel Libeskind, "Kein Ort an seiner Stelle," Verlag der Kunst, Dresden/Basel 1995, p. 172.

[4] Marc Augé, In the Metro, University of Minnesota Press 2002.

[5] Helmut Wilke, Atopia, Frankfurt 2001; Helmut Wilke, Dystopia, Frankfurt 2002; Helmut Wilke, Heterotopia, Frankfurt 2003.

[6] "Architecture non-standard," ed. Edition Centre Pompidou Paris, 2003, exhibition 10.12.03– 1.3.04.

[7] "Architecture in Cyberspace. Architectural Design," Academy Group, London 1995. See also Peter Weibel (ed), "The Media Pavilion. Art and Architecture in the Age of Cyberspace." Austria, Biennale di Venezia, Vienna 1995.

[8] See also: Gilles Deleuze, "Le Pli," 1988.

[9] "To make the Invisible visible," Christine Boyer calls "the progressive aspect of technology." In: Christine Boyer, "Cybercity. Visual Perception in The Age of Electronic Communication." Princeton Architectural Press 1996, p. 50.

Cover Image and p. 11 and p. 265: "From HardWare to SoftForm" courtesy of Winka Dubbeldam, Archi-Tectonics

p. 1–2: illustration "I am many", courtesy of Julie Rousset / xplicit bln

p. 15: illustration courtesy of Jean-Pierre Cagnat / La Recherche

p. 45: all images courtesy of University of Amsterdam and Holger Marten

p. 46: all images courtesy of Slovak Academy of Sciences, Institute of Informatics, and Holger Marten

pp. 55–57: photos courtesy TecO, University of Karlsruhe

pp. 65–75: graphics courtesy of Daley, Cirac, Zoller (p. 70: with permission of Rainer Blatt, p. 73: with permission of Daniel Loss)

p. 83: (top) photo courtesy MIT Special Collections, (bottom) photo courtesy William J. Mitchell

pp. 85–86: photos courtesy William J. Mitchell

p. 91: image courtesy of ONL [Oosterhuis_Lénárd]

p. 92: Smart Dust, courtesy of Kristopher Pister et all / ONL [Oosterhuis_Lénárd]

p. 93: Nano-scale Foglets shaking hands, courtesy of John Storrs Hall (Utility Fog) / ONL [Oosterhuis_Lénárd]

p. 94: Flocking Behavior, courtesy of Craig Reynolds (Bolds 1987) / ONL [Oosterhuis_Lénárd]

p. 95: illustration courtesy of Stephen Wolfram (A New Kind of Science 2002) / ONL [Oosterhuis_Lénárd]

p. 97. illustration courtesy of ONL [Oosterhuis_Lénárd]

pp. 98–101: photos/images courtesy of ONL [Oosterhuis_Lénárd]

p. 102: (top) illustration courtesy of American Scientist (March 2003) / ONL [Oosterhuis_Lénárd], (bottom) courtesy of ONL [Oosterhuis_Lénárd]

pp. 103–115: images/photos courtesy of ONL [Oosterhuis_Lénárd]

pp. 119–131: images/photos courtesy of W. Strauss and M. Fleischmann

pp. 133–135: photos © Kurt Henseler

pp. 136–137: renderings courtesy of Cybernarium GmbH

pp. 138–139: photos © Kurt Henseler

pp. 140–143: images/photos courtesy of Cybernarium GmbH

pp. 145–151: photos courtesy of iCinema / ZKM

p. 159: (bottom) photo © Elliott Kaufman

p. 160: photo © Elliott Kaufman

pp. 153–161: images/photos courtesy of Archi-Tectonics

pp. 163–173: images courtesy of ORTLOS architects

pp. 175–177: images courtesy of veech.media.architecture

p. 179: photo courtesy of veech.media.architecture (© ORF Ali Schafler)

pp. 180–181: images courtesy of veech.media.architecture (© ORF)

pp. 182–183: images courtesy of veech.media.architecture

pp. 185–195: photos/images courtesy of Diller Scofidio + Renfro

pp. 197–205: images courtesy of KOL/MAC

pp. 208–217: images courtesy of ocean D

pp. 219–235: photo/images courtesy of ONL [Oosterhuis_Lénárd]

pp. 237–247: images/photos courtesy of Asymptote